# COUNTRY GARDENING: COUNTRY STYLE

# COUNTRY GARDENING: COUNTRY STYLE

*A Natural Approach to Planning and Planting*

## Peter Thompson
*Line illustrations and notes by Josie Owen*

Everything that lives,
lives not for itself,
nor alone.
*William Blake*

DAVID & CHARLES

**British Library Cataloguing in Publication Data**
Thompson, Peter
Country gardening: country style: A natural approach to
planning and planting.
I. Title
635

ISBN 0-7153 9821 0

Typeset by ABM Typographics Ltd
and printed in Hong Kong by Wing King Tong Co. Ltd
for David & Charles plc
Brunel House Newton Abbot Devon

# Contents

## CHAPTER ONE

This book started as an evocation of a countryside lost, but turned into a discovery of a countryside being regained.

Wherever we look we see happenings in villages and the countryside which are changing the face of rural Britain. There are many who feel strongly that these are intrusions which destroy the qualities and character which make the countryside a special place in which to live. But seen in a different light, or from a different aspect, they become innovations full of opportunities.

For the first time ever, money, resources, imagination and initiative are available, not to a small minority of people inhabiting a small minority of houses in a few favoured villages, but throughout Britain. For the first time, the ways that rural areas develop, their appearance and the aesthetic pleasures they have to offer, have become the responsibility of all of us. Those are the challenges and the opportunities to make a new Arkadia which today's revolution in rural life offers us. If we want to, and we take the trouble, we can keep the things that we love and value in villages and the countryside, and graft on new styles and new opportunities to make life more enjoyable and more interesting for all who make their homes there. The country garden is central to this challenge.

It is easy to gaze at an attractive view or walk round an old and beautiful village and succumb to a vision of traditional landscapes, and age-old settlements which have scarcely changed for centuries, but these are retreats to a cloud-cuckoo-land which never existed and never, ever will. It is easy to condemn all changes as destructive, and see them as the outcome of the plans of developers and businessmen, interested only in their profits. It is easy to ignore the real forces behind these changes – which are the hopes of people who dream of living in the countryside, or enjoy it for recreation, and their willingness to pay well for places to live, and places to play.

What we see today is an inevitable part of a renovation serving the needs and aspirations of twentieth-century neo-rustics, whose emergence is changing the pace and face of rural communities throughout Britain.

# Renaissance?

By and large, our present problem is one of attitudes and implements. We are remodelling the Alhambra with a steam shovel, and are proud of our yardage.

*Aldo Leopold*

In the past villages were forced by a providence which was often nothing less than penury, to be inward-looking, self-sufficient and frugal; built of local materials by local craftsmen using traditional skills which gave each place a style of its own. That is over. No longer do they provide homes only for those who make a living from the traditional ways of the countryside, a rare breed today; for those who retire to country cottages with roses round the door, or for weekenders whose second homes, lying unused and empty, destroy the heart of a village. At long last villages are again becoming places where large numbers of people with jobs to do choose to make their homes and bring up their children.

Inevitably there are conflicts and regrets. There are bound to be. This is nothing less than the greatest evolution in village life since Saxon tribes crossed the North Sea to plunder, rape and win the remnants of Roman Britain, rubbing out most of its Celtic inhabitants on the way. The pattern of community life on country farms and settlements which they set up a thousand years ago remained the foundation of rural existence until recent times; and often a memory of their names still lingers in the places where we live.

Today's less violent changes are as far-reaching, and sometimes only a little less resented, even though they are reversing a historic decline in the fortunes and significance of country living, bringing in its place a renaissance of hope and prosperity.

Changing methods of farming during the eighteenth and nineteenth centuries destroyed the communal aspects of farming inherited from the Saxons, but did not disturb the largely self-sufficient nature of village life by which almost all daily needs and a great deal more besides were produced within the community.

The final decline of the interdependant village community began a hundred years ago. Farming and the prosperity of the countryside had always experienced cycles of fortune; but this time the changes were more far-reaching and did not go in spirals that returned eventually to something like what had been before.

Easier, more efficient ways to carry goods on canals and later the railways undermined the self-sufficiency of the countryside. The introduction and eventually all-pervasive spread of mechanised farming changed the role of the villages themselves. The numbers of people who could make a living from the countryside fell to a fraction of what it had been before, and changes in our expectations of the variety and quality of food and other daily necessities made it impossible to provide more than a small part from local resources.

By the early part of the mid-twentieth century, when industrial depression reinforced agricultural decline, most of the villages in Britain no longer fulfilled the purposes they had been built to serve. As populations dwindled and cottages fell empty, local authorities responded by condemning abandoned cottages, often on very slender grounds, and pulled them down to reduce their numbers. The self-sufficient, inter-knit communities based on farming and the land were well and truly dead.

Those days are over. Decaying cottages, barns and even derelict pigsties, are no longer condemned. Local authorities value them as sources of revenue. Estate agents describe them as exceptional opportunities for imaginative development, and they are sold at auction for sums which cause comment and astonishment.

Newcomers have arrived to make their homes in the villages, and travel daily to work in towns – often many miles away, or carry on businesses of one kind or another from their homes. The countryside in which they live is incidental scenery – it has nothing to do with the ways they earn their daily bread – and, for the most part, how it is farmed or used has no effect on their standards of living, and makes little difference to the quality of their lives.

These neo-rustics bring new life and prosperity to villages and rural areas. Not because they depend upon them for the daily necessities of life, which they are more likely to obtain from nearby towns, but because they have brought with them resources and ideas which were never available to the villagers of the past.

They bring opinions on how they like their surroundings to look, which incline them to make changes. They bring ambitions and aspirations and social pretensions, which are not restricted to small communities and local conditions, and have nothing in common with the customs and values of older village communities. They look on the countryside as a place for relaxation and enjoyment, not as the workshop where they earn a living. Above all, they have the money which gives them the power to get what they want.

The sense of being part of a community with a distinctive identity rooted in the past is one of the attractions which draws newcomers to village life. But villages are not exhibits in a museum. The changes which result from building homes for more people, and the ways these changes are made, not least in the gardens which surround the houses, can destroy the very qualities which people seek when they decide to exchange urban existence for country living. Those who make the move, or who live in the country already, naturally expect to have gardens and to follow ways of gardening which match twentieth-century lifestyles, and they take it for granted that they are free to do so in whatever way they please.

We have grown accustomed to planning regulations which restrict the ways we build, convert or use our homes and the buildings around them, and have no difficulty seeing how useful they are when neighbours propose to make socially unacceptable improvements. Similar restrictions are less heavily applied to gardens, and though the Englishman may have surrendered his bungalow, he, and even more probably his wife, retain more freedom in their dungpatch. But recently local authorities, noticing that changes to gardens are as conspicuous to neighbours and passers-by as changes to the house, and can be a great deal more intrusive or light-denying, have become more inclined to direct the ways gardens are planned and are attempting to regulate the plants put in them.

Gardening by direction of local planning departments is not a pretty prospect; particularly when many lack officers with training or special skills to help them make informed decisions. Nevertheless, there are good reasons for remembering that the qualities which make many of our villages beautiful and attractive places to live in stem from a past when their inhabitants depended for life and sustenance on the fields and countryside around them, and that this dependence formed the villages we see today. When developments in villages and the countryside ignore their surroundings, they destroy Arkadia. They smother or alter what is distinctive, eliminating the qualities which appeal to those who turn to the countryside as a place to live and enjoy life. And they impose humdrum, usually undistinguished styles which confer no sense of place or identity.

By a curious, felicitous coincidence, the appetite for country living and demand for things to do and pleasures to enjoy, coincide with a growing awareness of the problems produced by farming policies which lean too heavily towards maximum productivity. It has become fashionable – in many areas it has become essential – to find other ways to make a living from acres which are needed less urgently for agriculture.

Landscaping and gardening are certain to be conspicuous features of almost any new uses for the land. The ways they are done, and the success with which they combine inspiration from existing features of the countryside with the commercial elements necessary for the new venture to thrive,

will decide whether we rediscover the art of creating countryside which is a joy to live in, or allow the dream of Arkadia to fade away before our eyes.

The flowers in our gardens may seem to be our business, and nothing to do with the activities of developers. But our gardens are places where we try out ideas about how we should like our surroundings to look. Developers remain in business by selling dreams which match, flatter and slightly extend the tastes and aspirations of their customers, and they can sell us only what we are prepared to buy. If we lack the imagination, or simply see no need, to find ways for gardens in rural settings to contribute to the sense of place, we shall make each merely another frame in a peep show where Leyland cypress,
pierced concrete blocks,
    *Robinia* 'Frisia',
        asphalt drives with concrete kerbs,
            *Erica* 'Myretoun Ruby',
                brown panels of wooden fencing,
                    lawns with mower stripes,
                        mass-produced wrought iron gates,
                            'Whisky Mac',
                                lions moulded in cement on
                                gate posts,
                                'Nelly Moser',
                                    'Victorian' conservatories,
                                    *Spiraea* 'Gold Flame'
                                    and plastic parodies of
Georgian urns appear and reappear on an endless film loop that runs from Pevensey to Peterhead. We should not complain when developers churn out similarly hackneyed, synthetic offerings.

9

'And so,' said Mr Chester, 'before you came here you had a nursery? That's something I've never been able to understand – how anyone could make a living by selling plants. My wife's the gardener, and she's always in her garden, moving plants from one place to another. But I can't see why people spend money on plants – look around – there's plants everywhere!'

He was right. Mr Chester lives, as he has always lived, amongst the hills of south Shropshire. A brook runs in front of his white-washed stone house, and fields, grazed by sheep and surrounded by rough hedges, separate his wooded valley from the slopes of the Long Mynd: a humpback of heather, rough grasses and sheep-worn turf on the borders of England and Wales.

This is a countryside dominated by plants, but not all are wild – it could be said that scarcely any are truly wild. The woods have been cleared, allowed to regenerate, cleared again and replanted; in many places with conifers. The regular pattern of the field hedges shows that most are not very old; probably nineteenth-century additions to the landscape, when enclosures of the old communal arable fields, ancient heaths and common grazing reached the further corners of England. The meadows have almost all been ploughed, fertilised and reseeded during the past forty years, turning them into featureless grass leys or arable fields. The landscape, and the plants in it, are no more natural than farmed landscapes anywhere else – but in our eyes they appear as unspoilt countryside.

Unspoilt countryside, unspoilt villages, unspoilt views are phrases which are used perhaps unguardedly – sometimes assertively – to make a point. More often than not they are intended to suggest, without actually stating anything of the

# Leaping the Fence

The art of gardening is the history of hope and renewal. It links the past with the future. It is always beginning and without an end.

*Walter Heydecker*

kind, that change – change of any sort – is bound to be for the worse. It is a device that saves thought and argument, and places the speaker firmly, righteously and fashionably amongst the ranks of those whose responsible view of their social obligations recognises the importance of preserving and handing on the heritage of the past to generations yet unborn.

Yet the countryside everywhere has been formed by changes that go on all the time. Within months of arriving in this unspoilt part of Shropshire we had found, lying in the bed of the brook, a neolithic hammer head; also the handstone of a quern used thousands of years ago by forgotten predecessors who farmed here and grew grain in small fields amongst the trees. The name of the township itself recalls a Saxon farmer who also cultivated those fields amongst the trees. Much later the remaining heath and pastureland was overlaid with a grid of quickthorn hedges and regularly planted hedgerow trees during enclosures which made no concessions to the nature of the surrounding countryside. In Victoria's reign alien conifers appeared, and in this century conifer plantations have made their mark amongst the more natural deciduous woodland.

Not so long ago, the ancient track which travellers followed on a muddy course by the brook was replaced by a road halfway up the hillside – a road whose course, and metalled surface must for years have been an ugly scar cut through the trees. The houses in the valley have changed too; clay tiles cover their roofs in the place of the clumsy split stones of earlier times. The middens and decaying outhouses which George Morland might have painted if he had come here two hundred years ago have been replaced by discreetly invisible septic tanks and brick-built stables. These changes, and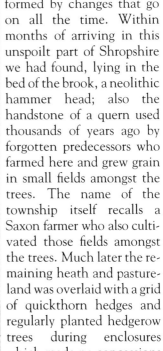

By the example of the garden at Sissinghurst, Vita Sackville West taught us to view plants and their properties as elements in the composition of pictures

a great many more, are not just taken for granted, but are regarded appreciatively as we look around at this 'unspoilt' countryside.

## WEED OR WILD FLOWER?

Our reactions to what we see depend on what we have become accustomed to. The plants which Mr Chester was talking about are different to those which were so familiar to me on my nursery at Godspiece Leaze in Somerset. The ways they grow, their proportions, their massing, interlocking and weaving together, the contrasts and harmonies of their forms, produce impressions unlike those we look for in plants we grow in gardens. To tidy-minded gardeners, plants which occur naturally in the fields and woods around us grow in a disorderly chaos, which would be out of place in a garden.

As in much else, fashion plays its part in gardens. We peep over the fence to see what our neighbours are up to, or we find ourselves wary of following our instincts because of what we imagine they think about what we are doing. We are inclined to believe what we see, hear and are told in books, magazines, radio and television. We may resist doing what we are told but ask ourselves – sometimes we ask others – if it is 'all right' to do

things which seldom or never seem to receive any seal of expressed approval. Few people possess the inclination, imagination or spare energy to create their own styles, and most follow the conventions seen in gardens all around them.

Botanists arrange flowering plants systematically and taxonomically into two great divisions: calling one group the dicotyledons, the other the monocotyledons. Gardeners suspect this academic, irrelevant and confusingly scientific idea, and prefer to divide plants into those that grow in gardens, and those that are wild. They also understand that when any of the latter happen to be found in a garden they are called weeds, and should be pulled up or sprayed with something to kill them. Sometimes, if they are attractive and seem to be doing no harm, they are tolerated – but they are still weeds!

This distinction between the gardened and the wild is applied equally firmly to gardens and anywhere that is not a garden. Instinctively, we set limits to what we do, and boundaries round where we do it, and take defensive refuge in definitions which restrict the plants we use and the ways we use them. We avoid confronting all the opportunities which plants and their cultivation offer by creating precise and artificial conventions to restrict the range of our vision.

Time and again, gardeners appear who see beyond these restrictions. They are the people who, as Horace Walpole wrote in his endlessly quoted comment about William Kent, leap the fence and see that all nature is a garden. But in that famous instance it was not Kent who leapt fences: it was Walpole. It was Walpole whose imagination saw beyond his own gothic suburban garden at Strawberry Hill and recognised that what Kent was doing could be called gardening of any kind. William Kent and others like him, and Mr Chester is one of them, need not jump fences, which they cannot see, to discover that gardens extend beyond the boundaries others erect to separate them from the countryside. Nor do they need persuading that the countryside comes no nearer than the fences which mark its frontier with the garden.

This book is about leaping fences. It is about ways of gardening which allow the countryside to permeate gardens in villages and in towns. It is about the removal of barriers which lead us to label plants as wild or cultivated, and regard most of the creatures which walk or fly or crawl or slide through our gardens as pests. It is about sloughing off conventions which restrict the ways we garden. It is about responding to changes in our villages and the countryside as part of an inevitable, unending process which offers at least as many opportunities as threats of disaster.

Some who read this book will be unaware that fences are there to be leapt. Others will find the surrounding fences so high that the effort of leaping them seems unimaginable. But when Walpole made the leap he found it so easy that he never realised he had done it – he thought that Kent had. Like other fashions or conventions, our opinions about gardening depend upon our prejudices; and prejudices change in an instant when a different point of view is discovered.

## THE STOLEN REVOLUTION

A hundred and twenty years ago William Robinson, a man who enjoyed a stir, started a campaign against Victorian bedding and formal gardening in general. He opened fire with a short book called *The Wild Garden*, followed up by editing and contributing to a more portentous assault in *The English Flower Garden* and maintained the pressure as proprietor and editor of *The Garden*. After discovering that they shared common interests on the subject, he combined forces with Gertrude Jekyll.

Robinson's was a voice crying in the wilderness – and was doubly suspect to all true Englishmen as an Irishman with strange ideas about gardening derived from visits to France – mocking those who employed gardeners to use plants as blatant, labour-devouring displays of brilliantly contrasted colour. He scarcely persuaded the gardening establishment to leap fences, but dragged it through behind him, ruffling its feathers in the process. The revolution he started influences gardens still, but the establishment neither forgot nor forgave, and honours which he did more to earn than many others eluded him in later years.

Gertrude Jekyll arrived like a messiah in Robinson's office and then laboriously, precisely and imaginatively devised the details of the new gardening. This depended on understanding the properties and opportunities of the colours, textures, forms and even sounds of an enormous range of plants, many recently obtained by plant collectors from distant, often very dangerous, parts of the world. Vita Sackville West in a pauline role, by the example of the garden at Sissinghurst and weekly epistles to the rosarians in *The Observer*, conveyed the logic and the ethos of Jekyll's ideas to an entire stratum of gardening society. In doing so, she persuaded this new gardening establishment to view plants and their properties as elements in the composition of pictures: something far removed from Robinson's attempts to impel gardeners to see them as creatures with distinctive and different natures which, once understood, provided the foundation for their successful use in gardens.

Everyone who gardens very soon discovers that this seemingly gentle art is all about exercising control. It is about manipulating, dominating, steering, conducting, guiding or commanding the ways that plants grow and perform, so that somehow or other they combine to make a garden. Some exercise this control by outright domination and command: others, more subtly, manipulate and steer their plants towards the effects they hope to create.

Vogue gardens today, after one hundred years of Jekyllism, exemplify the arts of control by steering and manipulation. They are characteristically highly contrived, with subtle colour theming, and plants carefully combined to create intricate interactions between contrasts and harmonies. The style has now attained a maturity in which practised devotees have discovered how to achieve a chocolate-box appeal which meets with enormous popular appreciation.

This gynocentric style of gardening figures prominently in books with titles like *The Country Garden*, and in glossy magazines devoted to country living; though there is little about it which places it in the country rather than the suburbs or the town. It has, however, assimilated many plants traditionally associated with cottage gardens – to a large extent it has taken over cottage gardens – finding new settings and new uses for them. This, and the impact of Gertrude Jekyll's work on gardens of houses in the countryside, are responsible for its rural flavour.

It remains a complex and difficult style to master. Effects depend on precisely timed coincidences of growth and development whose creation relies on dreams born of experience, but which still remain at the mercy of the weather. It demands skilful, or at least practised, understanding of the visual effects created by placing one plant beside another, and on an almost intuitive approach to control and maintenance based on intervention at critical but often not well-defined points in the garden's growth cycle. It could be said that the style is seldom mastered, since the gardens where it is most successfully applied are very often those where the moving spirit is a woman, and a woman prepared to spend a great deal of her life working in and thinking about her garden.

It is not an easy style for a novice to comprehend and contains few inbuilt guide-lines. Colour is of predominant importance but the subtle combinations of colours are not easy to achieve. Plants are encouraged to grow together, forming masses of foliage and flowers, but careful spacing and judicious intervention are needed to prevent the strong suppressing the weak. Herbaceous plants and shrubs are combined to produce mixed borders in which different elements develop and mature at different rates. A great deal depends on the gardener's understanding of plants, their colours and seasons, rates of growth and likes and dislikes.

All this is a joy to those who are knowledgeable, who enjoy the creative challenge of gardening, and who have learnt the tricks and ploys which experience has shown to contribute to a successful result. It can be dauntingly difficult for those starting out, or those whose involvement in gardening is less than total.

The male interest in such gardens is usually deflected away from the plants, and towards less subtle aspects of control. It is particularly likely to be assigned to mechanical activities like mowing the lawn and clipping hedges, and to aspects of gardening such as growing vegetables and trees – even including collections in an arboretum – where regimentation and visible means of restraint are more likely to be given credit as essential garden virtues.

But the long-established traditions of androcentric gardening in Britain are not confined to these minor roles. The ghosts of innumerable head gardeners can rest easy in the knowledge that the central institutions of British horticulture, including Wisley and the great botanic gardens of Kew and Edinburgh, as well as the vast array of suburban gardens throughout the country, have been scarcely touched by trends undermining the dominance of the male's view of how gardens should be run.

Establishment gardening has now taken the Jekyll garden as its own, occasionally rewarding it by referring to it as 'the English Garden Style', and in doing so has penned it firmly back behind the garden fence. Whatever its origins may have drawn from nature, it now owes very little to the world outside the garden. Like all revolutions, William Robinson's has been stolen. His Pre-Raphaelite inspiration has been smothered, muffled at first by Gertrude Jekyll's books and boots and Impressionist artistry, and then overwhelmed by the response to Sackville West's pen, and Sissinghurst's appeal.

But, at a time when many people have become anxiously aware of the existence and the plight of the natural environment, and have misgivings about the virtues of total control and subordination of all things natural, it is a style of gardening which is beginning to look a little old-fashioned, a little out of step with the times. The artifice behind the disordered orderliness of the combinations of colours and forms; the unnaturally natural use of exotic plants and planting patterns; the calculatedly imprecise shapes of borders, lawns and routes of paths is beginning to show through and

Finding simple ways to link a house with its surroundings, rather than making a splash with the plants, would be more likely to respond to the spirit of the place

can be recognised for what it has become: a way to keep nature out of the garden by only apparently, not actually, inviting her in. When the fence is leapt once again it will not be done by using the Jekyll garden as the spring-board.

## THE CONFORMIST COUNTRYSIDE

Any journey will reveal a hundred examples of the ways that villages are changing. The gardens of houses in the countryside and in villages share these changes, tending to take on the appearance of gardens found in suburbs and towns throughout Britain. The same universal collection of orange, bright yellow or brilliant coral roses; shrubs with golden foliage planted in strident contrast with others which glow crimson in spring and fade to liver in summer; identical conifers with steel-blue or golden foliage provide focal points in gardens from Dover to Wick; endlessly tumbled masses of silver foliage combine with soft mists of purple, mauve and rose; identical collections of annuals in arrays of scarlet, yellow and purple attract attention like wayside guards of honour.

The individuality which once made every village distinct and different is neglected or forgotten when gardens are made and planted, and in its place we see unimaginative, banal planting; inappropriately used plants; and walls, fences, paths and pergolas constructed from mass-produced, ubiquitously available materials.

It is regrettable that opportunities to create gardens which complement the house and location are not taken more often; but there are problems. Vernacular styles of gardening scarcely developed in the past, or they linger on as easily overlooked fragments. They seldom offer the ready-made, recognisable patterns to be found in buildings and architecture. But should we really allow ourselves to be persuaded that the same plants and gardening styles which look so good around a whitewashed, thatched cottage with rounded walls of pounded clay in Devon will be equally attractive set against the tawny iron-stone walls of Northants? Or, that farmhouses in Kent hung with clay tiles in every shade of burnt umber, terracotta, tanned leather and russet match the same styles of gardening and the same groupings of plants as pargetted, pastel-colour-washed plastered walls of cottages in Suffolk?

Posing the question invites an answer in the negative. But opportunities offered by the vernacular styles which make our villages so different one from another are scarcely considered as inspiration for gardenmaking. On television, in books and in the glossy magazines that guide the trendy's lifestyle it seems to be taken for granted that a garden is a garden is a garden. If red-hot pokers, alchemilla and hostas make a brave display in Epsom they will look equally good in Arbroath. The bright faces of French marigolds and the blue powderpuffs of ageratum that look cheerful against the whitewashed wall of a cottage in Camarthen will be just as enjoyable surrounding a red-brick villa in Berkshire.

Current gardening trends, which emphasise plants and the use of strongly contrasting forms and forceful colours do not make the task easier. Alternatives emphasising informality and unobtrusive control would be more likely to let the influence of the countryside make itself felt in a village, and finding simple ways to link a house with its surroundings, rather than making a splash with the plants, would be more likely to respond to the spirit of the place.

The rural atmosphere in villages often owes much to innocence of style, and certainly of artifice, and the answers may not lie in listening attentively to those who garden keenly. Those who present programmes on television or write about gardening in books and magazines, or design gardens for a living, have opinions and a certain facility in their profession which they enjoy indulging. They are tempted to pay too much attention to the garden and not enough to its purpose or its

setting. The results are inappropriate sophistication, and demands on the gardener which appeal only to those who are keen and interested in the sport.

Very often a grove of trees and a patch of meadow would fit the scene better than elaborate planting and an immaculate lawn, and leave more time for other things. Perhaps we should seek advice from those with less knowledge of gardening, but a sensitivity to their surroundings, whose inspiration would come from natural materials and the individuality of building styles and other local differences. They might be more inclined to think of gardens as part of a setting, and less tempted to look for ways to display the gardener's art.

## THE ENDLESS SUBURB

The neo-rustic incursion is largely a movement of people whose previous homes were in towns and suburbs. The Flower People of the sixties, grown prosperous and conventional, are returning to earlier dreams but in the meantime they have discovered ways of gardening which would have seemed stiflingly decorous and orthodox in their youth.

Overwhelmingly, the conventions they have adopted are those that mark them as followers of the 'Suburban Style', for this is the predominant, popular style of gardening. That would not be the impression conveyed by reading or just looking at illustrated books by garden designers and trend-setters, which are more than likely to ignore it altogether, for sophisticated and fashionable gardeners affect to disdain this kind of gardening.

Nevertheless it stems directly from the inspiration described as gardenesque by John Claudius Loudon, early in the nineteenth century. It has a longer pedigree than the Jekyll garden, and has proved flexible and adaptable over the years, retaining its essential qualities while making use of new plants and new lifestyles – particularly the pursuit of leisure and pleasure. It flourishes as a popular and naive form of gardening, attaching great importance to the setting of the individual plant and even of the individual bloom, but paying little or no attention to the pretensions of plantsmen or the niceties of designer gardening.

The surburban style depends on domination and command for control. It is an androcentric style in which gardening is organised as a highly regulated operation. Lawns are not only trim but should be smart, with tidy edges and mower stripes; flower beds are neat, and each plant has a space within which to grow, preferably separated from its neighbours by a *cordon sanitaire* of well-tilled soil; hedges are clipped, and shrubs are too if they threaten to intrude upon their neighbour's space; strongly contrasted mixtures of conifers, and shrubs with coloured foliage, are important and reliable visual elements; and plants with substantial, brightly coloured, individual blooms, like tulips, roses and dahlias, are particularly appreciated. The garden is subdivided into spaces with recognised functions: the lawn, the patio, the vegetable garden, the rose garden, the herbaceous border – today more probably the mixed border – the rock garden, and perhaps the orchard where regularly spaced fruit trees grow amongst long grass.

These gardens make no concessions to low maintenance – they are not intended to. The success or failure of the garden is judged largely by how neat and trim it is. Irregularities are remedied by mowing the lawn, hoeing the flower beds, forking over the vegetable garden, taking shears to hedge or shrubs, spraying the aphids, or removing weeds from the paths. In each case the remedy is clearly indicated by the problem, providing guidelines for success that are clear and easily followed – and do not depend on detailed knowledge of the plants, or the acquisition of arcane gardening skills.

The suburban style, with its inbuilt guide-lines, tells even inexperienced gardeners what they should do, and when they should do it. It is easily and satisfyingly followed by hundreds of thousands of people who enjoy gardening without professing to be particularly knowledgeable or skilful at their craft. The style is learnt in gardens around houses on estates throughout the country, and is ideally adapted to a situation where each garden is an episode, separated from its neighbours by fences and hedges which provide frames and backgrounds for the plants. Each plant is an incident, to be admired and enjoyed as part of a continually unfolding display. The owners of the gardens enjoy the greatest possible opportunities to do whatever they wish within them, with the least need to think about what is going on beyond their boundaries.

Strong guide-lines ensure that, once learnt, this way of gardening is not easily discarded and, when moves are made to houses in more rural situations with larger gardens, it is brought along with the rest of the domestic paraphenalia. It so happens it is a style which conflicts discordantly with its surroundings when transplanted from its suburban cradle. Its guide-lines contain no encouragement to leap fences, or to think about the garden as a part of its setting. Fences and hedges are invariably intended to separate one garden from another, never to link the garden with its surroundings.

Transported to the countryside, suburban forms of gardening convey a mood that is forceful, intrusive and alien, and are amongst the most destructive influences affecting the appearance of our villages today.

## CHAPTER THREE

Down the garden path and beyond the fence lies the countryside: the source of the floating seeds of dandelions and thistles, the home of harmful insects and garden-threatening birds, a place of scrub, tangled vegetation, and great fields of cereals or grass, where cattle, sheep and horses live, and sometimes break through fences into the garden. In short an unruly, crude, primitive domain to all who struggle to keep their gardens trim and beautiful.

This home of the un-official rose seems a place of unregulated growth, where precious fragile things would have no chance against the weeds of the wildwood, the roadside verges, or the rough con-fusion of old meadows. But look more closely, because in just such places plants as fragile as the pasque flower and the moonwort can sur-vive – not for a year or two, but for decades or centuries in the same spot.

Think for a moment of the plants that grow in woods and meadows and roadside verges. In each place they will be different and will not be weeds with that word's suggestion of aggression and rampant growth, but wild flowers, growing in communities subject to all kinds of checks and controls. Some of these controls are blatant, others so subtle they are almost indiscernible, and they define precisely which plants grow where, what their companions are, and what part each play in its community.

## CHOOSE YOUR WEEDS

Think of the weeds, which are the wild flowers, that grow in gardens. Their destruction becomes a battle with an irrepressible enemy, but anyone troubled by groundsel, chickweed, purple dead nettle, shepherd's purse, fat hen, annual meadow grass or sow thistles, can choose to be rid of these

# Patterns of the Countryside

This is an art
Which does mend Nature: change it rather;
but the art itself is Nature.

*William Shakespeare*

weeds within a month or two, and never be bothered by them again. Turn the vegetable patch or the flower beds where they grow into lawns and they will disappear.

It will be a short respite. Within a year or two a different group of wild flowers – plantains, yarrow, cocksfoot, hop trefoils, white clover, Yorkshire fog, daisies, eyebright and hawkweeds – which were never seen before will in-filtrate the lawn. Zealous gardeners will return to battle against these new weeds with sprays of chemi-cals whose nature and effects on their children and animals are a mystery to them.

Abandon chemical war-fare and make another change. Replace the grass with trees and shrubs above a carpet of perennial plants. As the new regime settles in the grassland weeds dis-appear but a new cast moves in. Foxgloves, willowherbs, bugle, stinging nettles, ground elder and brambles amongst them, and later on celandine, herb bennet, red campion, goosegrass and stitchwort.

Gardeners may feel beset by weeds, but they exist only at their behest. At any time, they have an option to choose their weeds, and in doing so discover that they don't appear haphazardly or by casual chance, but each exists in alliance with a limited number of other plants. Only a few species will be able to cope with the conditions in that particular place, hold their own against encroachment and competition from other members of the community, and find niches where they can survive and, vitally important, reproduce successfully.

Gardeners will also discover that the plants they grow, and the ways they grow them, decide which weeds will plague them – not the weeds which happen to be there already. When flower beds are made into lawns annual weeds, which may have plagued generations of gardeners, disappear. They are for-gotten but not gone. Their seeds lie in the ground, and they will reappear very quickly even years and years later if anyone digs up the lawn and again uses the place to grow flowers.

Busybodies peering over garden fences chant 'one year's seeding makes seven years weeding', and they have a point – though seven years is a modest estimate for the soil-borne life of many weed seeds. But what they mean is that dutiful, attentive gardeners like themselves, who destroy every weed before it seeds, will attain nirvana where no weeds grow. That is nonsense! In most soils the numbers of weed seeds are so enormous and their ability to survive so great that few, if any, gardens attain that state of grace where weed seeds are no more. It makes little difference whether every weed is conscientiously destroyed, or left to seed itself. That formidable, vulnerable and eccen-

tric lady, Ellen Wilmott, commanded a hundred gardeners who maintained Warley Place in a state of weedless splendour; within a year or two of her death it had reverted to a wilderness.

But life can be made difficult for weeds. They are vulnerable as one generation gives way to another, when seedlings must find places to grow. Thousands or tens of thousands of seeds may be produced for every plant that finds a place where it can survive, and anything that can be done to deny weeds these lodgements pays dividends.

As a stopgap, herbicides can be used. These chemicals are poisons – less poisonous to wildlife perhaps than pesticides and fungicides but life-denying nonetheless, and only to be used with sense and sensibility. Pre-emergence killers like simazine and atrazine massacre seedlings as they leave the security of their seeds, and have trans-formed the problem of keeping paths weed-free.

| METHOD | ADVANTAGES/DISADVANTAGES |
|---|---|
| Hand weeding | Very neat and tidy; self-sown seedlings are easily seen and saved. Perennial weeds can be dug out when found. But extremely time-consuming, and must be repeated at frequent intervals. Hand weeding will tell you a great deal about what is going on in your garden, and can be a satisfying and instructive way to spend an afternoon, but never pay anyone else to do it for you! |
| Hoeing | A rapid and very effective way to destroy annual weeds. But not much more than a waste of time when dealing with most perennials. It prepares a seed bed which provides ideal conditions for the germination of yet more weed seeds, thereby perpetuating the problem ad infinitum. |
| Herbicides | Can be very effective against almost any weed when well chosen. Pre-emergence weedkillers can be used to prevent the reappearance of weed seedlings. But need careful, well-informed selection to work safely and well, and must be used specifically and accurately. Liable to confer a feeling of power leading to a ruthless, scorched-earth style of gardening. |
| Mulches | Help to conserve moisture, as well as smother weeds, and improve soil texture, fertility and other conditions which favour plant growth. But suitable materials may be hard to find, or expensive to buy in sufficient quantity. Some must be replaced annually, and most from time to time. |
| Plant alliances (ground-cover) | Provide long-term solutions to problems with weeds; very little maintenance needed. But take time to become established and interim measures must be used meanwhile. Success depends on skilful matching of plants to the situation, and either the possession of a fortune or the green fingers to propagate the plants that will be wanted. |

They can also be used, more daringly and with occasional mishaps, but very effectively, amongst trees and shrubs and many perennials.

Or mulches can be used – almost any kind of mulch to cover bare soil, and we shall return to them later. But the best results come from copying the patterns of the countryside, and allowing the plants themselves to form more or less self-maintaining alliances which provide inhospitable conditions for outsiders.

## KEEPING WEEDS UNDER CONTROL

Ways to control weeds are summarised opposite. Some are more time-consuming than others. They appear in an order which corresponds to the time they take to do, the most demanding appearing first.

## NATURAL PLANT ALLIANCES

Wild plants grow in communities, made up of different plants with a common aptitude for the conditions present in the places where they settle. Once established, these communities form re-

*Time forms part of the recipe for creating the fairly stable, overall matrix of foliage, stems and roots within which the plants exist as an alliance that resists intrusion by interlopers*

markably stable alliances, occupying virtually every available niche where plants can grow and very resistant to intrusion by newcomers. They comprise probably only a few score plants, seldom as many as two hundred different kinds out of the fifteen hundred or so species to be found in Britain.

The vegetation of the countryside reveals these alliances. Sometimes their effects are stunning – acres of bluebells, stitchwort, red campion and birdseye beneath the translucent leaves of beech trees in May; a dry bank with ox-eye daisies, birdsfoot trefoil and chicory; or white stems of birch trees on acid sands, with bell heather, ling and bracken. Sometimes they are subdued or sombre – the leaden greens of oakwoods in summer; acres of scrub with thorn bushes, rough grasses, willowherb, nettles and thistles on half-abandoned land; or drab moorland in winter with heather stretching to the horizon.

The casual, tumbled growth and flowering and going to seed of grasses and wild flowers provide patterns to which all of us respond; although some find them untidy, and would reject them as models for their gardens. Woodland, and the kinds of trees in it, not only leads to ideas for gardens, but also shows how easily foreign conifers steal the scene from native broad-leaves, and warns against their over-enthusiastic use in gardens. Rough meadows filled with ant-hills and wild flowers, and overgrown hedges, have become uncommon where high farming has replaced them by arable prairies with barely discernible, shaved-down hedges. These offer little inspiration to the garden designer, but suggest the need for gardens where shelter and seclusion relieve their pervasive openness. River valleys with alders and pollarded willows; moorland, orchards or the patterns produced by scattered farmhouses and small fields; each is distinctively different, and each suggests particular forms of gardening and the use of particular plants.

## Creating Plant Communities

Plants in the fields and woods around us form their alliances in stages – one set merging with, then giving way to, another. Time forms part of the recipe for creating the fairly stable, overall matrix of foliage, stems and roots, within which the plants exist as an alliance that resists intrusion by interlopers.

Space is another part of the recipe. These structured communities occupy space in three dimensions, best thought of as a series of layers each dependent on and interacting with the others. Later the parts played by these layers will become self-evident, but for now it is enough to identify them as follows.

### TREES

These provide the shelter within which many plant communities form. In gardens, as in the wild, they are likely to do better by growing much closer together during their youth than they will be when mature. Young trees do better in the company of their peers and, as time goes by, can be thinned out to provide space for those left to develop, or managed in some way, such as coppicing, which repeatedly resets the clock that times their development and progression towards maturity.

### SHRUBS AND CLIMBERS

These occupy the middle and upper layers of the space beneath the tree canopy. Many will be small at first and can be planted thickly to allow for removal and thinning as the community develops. This must be done so as to retain the key shrubs which will eventually grow on to make specimens, or clumps, at the expense of the fillers, which occupy space initially and are removed progressively during the first ten years or so.

### PERENNIAL PLANTS

These provide the close-knit ground-cover which is mainly responsible for resisting the intrusion of seedling weeds. It is essential that as complete a cover as possible is formed as soon as possible. This can be done by planting thickly, using key plants backed by fillers, as with the shrubs. The fillers, or matrix formers, should be plants that are easy to grow and propagate, and naturally adapted to making a living by finding the spaces amongst other plants. Some can even be annuals and biennials – particularly if they are able to self-seed in later years. Alternatively mulches of various kinds can be used *pro tem* to suppress weeds while the key plants develop.

### BULBOUS PLANTS

It is helpful to think of these as a separate layer growing up through the other plants, adding to the variety but, more crucially, occupying space in winter and early spring when perennial plants may not be much in evidence.

Woodlands, dominated by broad-leaved deciduous trees, are natural examples of the development of all four layers. Once mature they form very persistent and stable communities, and it should come as no surprise to find that in gardens too some of the most successful, easiest to set up, and least demanding forms of planting are those which are similarly complete.

What is surprising is the widespread conviction that shrubs, planted by themselves in a border, are labour-saving; that turning flower beds into lawns is labour-saving; that the hoe is an effective way to control weeds; that it is necessary to dig, or at least fork over, flower beds to look after them properly; and that the shaded parts of gardens are the problem parts. Every one of those convictions is misbegotten and pays no attention to what we can see all around us every time we go for a walk in the country.

## THE CHANGING SEASONS

The patterns formed by hills and valleys, and the vegetation which clothes them, are the most noticeable features of any view, but almost as important is the season of the year. Amongst the great expectations of life and of gardening in the countryside, are the changes we look forward to as one season gives way to another.

Perhaps these changes are more muted in towns, but, for whatever reason, it has become fashionable to introduce monotony into gardens. The differences between the seasons are subdued by banking on plants which remain unvaryingly eye-catching for as long as possible – known jargonwise as having a long season of interest.

After toying with golden privet and *Lonicera nitida* for hedges, the Leyland cypress Castlewellan Gold is now used in any and every circumstance to enwrap a garden in bright, textured foliage. Lawns with grass trimmed repeatedly to a uniform length form the garden's heart. Patios with timber decking or concrete paving slabs, backed by screens of pierced concrete, create links between house and lawn that remain as unvaried as possible throughout the year. The bright contrasts and powerful forms of conifers underplanted with heathers feature strongly in borders, and shrubs and trees are preferred with colourful foliage that remains bright for months on end. The backbone of every garden, sometimes complying to a rule of thumb proportion of the planting, depends on evergreens and ever-silvers which hardly change from summer to winter. Climate and chance are reduced to minimal elements in the making of the garden, and androcentric approaches directed towards minute control of every detail predominate.

The trend suggests an inclination to do without gardening at all; to avoid the trouble of coping with living plants and their likes and dislikes, and their tendencies to grow too big or drop dead. An inclination that would be better served by enclosing the space around the house beneath an air-conditioned transparent dome, where artificial lighting ensured year-long sunshine. None but plastic plants would be needed, hired out by garden centres and replaceable at whim to suit any occasion. Lawns would be perpetually immaculate and wormcast-free, made of washable artificial fibres with built-in mower stripes – comfortably padded and kept luxuriantly warm by heating cables beneath their surface. Rapture would be completed by recordings of birdsong, or the muted notes of children at play somewhere suitably distant. For some reason this never seems to be done, though why it should not be is a mystery.

Instead a halfway stage is attempted. This hardly avoids the problems and shortcomings of exposure to sun, rain, snow and mud, which make most gardens uninhabitable for half the days of the year, and relegates to second place the pleasures of looking forward to the first crocuses, the fragrance of *Lilium regale* on a warm summer's evening, the flaming foliage of *Vitis coignetiae* in autumn, or the glow of dogwood stems erupting through a covering of snow in winter.

Attempts to garden as though seasons were non-existent are doubly limiting. They provide little encouragement to plant imaginatively to make the most of particular seasons and, less obviously, they reduce awareness of how plants respond to the seasons, and discourage efforts to take these needs into account as we garden.

Many of our garden plants come from places where the climate restricts growth to particular seasons. Our oceanic climate, often referred to as fickle but in fact merely unpredictable, is such that there is no regular season of the year when plants cannot grow at all. Now that most of the plants we buy are grown in containers we are being persuaded that – provided the weather on the day does not happen to be so dry or so freezing that the plant's life would obviously be at risk – we can indulge ourselves by planting whenever it is convenient.

The planting season used to start as the leaves fell in October, and well-organised gardeners made sure everything was in place by the time they sat down to lunch on Christmas Day – most of us let things slide until time ran out in March. Now plants in containers are mostly bought from garden centres between the first weekend in March that is warm and sunny enough to tempt us out, and the day in June when thoughts of the cost of impending holidays puts a block on all other spending.

This change has nothing to do with the way that plants behave, or with new opportunities to grow them better because they are bought in containers. It has a great deal to do with the greater appeal of gardening or visiting garden centres in springtime

Woodlands, dominated by broad-leaved deciduous trees, are natural examples of the development of all four layers. It should be no surprise that in gardens some of the most successful, easiest to set up, and least demanding forms of planting are those that are similarly complete

rather than during the winter. But, whatever salesmen may tell us, plants in containers are only a little less dependent on the seasons than those with bare roots. They react to the seasons in the same ways, and go through the same cycles of growth and development.

### THE ANNUAL CYCLE OF ROOT GROWTH

The shoots of most plants are plainly visible and the ways they behave are familiar. We cannot see what the roots are up to, but these too have cycles of growth, renewal and decline. They too go through their equivalent of leaf fall, when much of the root system is lost, and grow vigorously at other times to support the growth of the tops.

Trees and shrubs – including conifers – as well as perennial plants, have an annual cycle of root growth which starts during late summer. Never demur when generous friends offer gifts from their gardens of heleniums, hostas, hemerocallis, geraniums, pulmonarias and other perennials in July or August. Say 'thank you' and dig them up. Below ground they will be producing strong new roots that grow out into the soil to anchor the plants securely through the winter. These are also storage organs – like elongated tubers – which, filled with starch, become the life-support of young shoots in the spring. Then a network of fine feeding roots spreads from them through the upper layers of the soil, foraging for water and nutrients to support the rapidly developing plants.

The lesson to be learnt from this pattern is that the best time to introduce plants in containers to the garden is the late summer or early autumn; at the start, rather than towards the end, of the processes which lead to a successful get-away in the spring.

Trees provide the shelter within which many plant communities form. Woodland, and the kinds of trees in it, leads to ideas for gardens

This restored farmhouse in Devon sits in gentle, rounded hills clothed in small deciduous woodlands. Soft colours and soft textures change through the year. Deciduous trees do not look the same throughout the winter: the colours of buds change noticeably from week to week – even day to day.

The new garden here looks like a badly iced cake; prissy little blobs and splodges of annuals, alpines and conifers look out over new stone walls which, though sturdily built, take no account of local building details. Once the conifers are established this garden will look very sombre and will vary little from season to season. Changes of colour will be achieved by using bright annuals – more gentle annual and perennial plants would be overpowered by the conifers. With so little response to the seasons and the surroundings, why not just stay inside?

In this version of the garden the boundary hedge echoes those of the field. It is made of hawthorn, holly and blackthorn. A common hawthorn tree marks the front gate and gives spring blossom, autumn berries and a dense, twiggy winter texture. Plants vary according to their position in the garden. The corner bed by the gate is cool and shady and contains plants which would not like the warm, sunny beds against the south- and west-facing walls. These sheltered spots are filled with plants which enjoy sunbathing, including many herbs with fragrant foliage. A clipped box chicken greets visitors and cheers them up even on the dullest February day

Gardeners are wary of planting in July or August before the leaves are off trees and shrubs, or perennial plants have died down, but it is not only container-grown plants that benefit. Even in dry weather, and even with plants like conifers which are sensitive to drought, the risks from moving a plant in late summer are very small – the active renewal of the roots sees to that. Also, this is a season of heavy dews which refresh the foliage each night and supplement any watering that has to be done. The foliage on the plants is mature enough to tolerate short periods of adversity much better than the tender, immature shoots of spring.

## READING THE SOIL

Popular garden plants are heathers and silver birches. Both are often planted with conifers – partly because this has become a stereotype for ground-cover, but also with the notion of introducing a little 'nature' to gardens where suburban order seems oppressive.

Few would argue that the heaths, moors and mountains where these plants grow together are amongst the wildest and most seemingly natural to be found anywhere. But heathers and birches, with or without pine trees, are not part of the scene where houses and villages are set in pastoral or arable countryside, and there they look no more natural than a rockery or a herbaceous border.

The needles of heathers are small but can be very colourful – particularly in winter. A peculiarity of conifers is their inclination to produce dwarf forms with strikingly precise silhouettes and chromatic foliage. The combination makes a brave and dramatic *tour de force*, but does not fit easily into the framework of a garden in the country, or have any affinity with the countryside around.

Ling and all our native heathers are confined to acid soils and fail to thrive where chalk, or the limestones which are the foundation of so many attractive villages, have formed the landscape. The nature of the soil has a very great influence on the vegetation it supports, and hence on the patterns of the countryside: and it must be taken into account when plants are chosen for gardens.

Gardeners are divided into the 'haves' and the 'have nots'. The former live on acid soils and their gardens are filled with rhododendrons and azaleas, summer-flowering heathers, kalmias, fothergillas, lithospermums and lilies. For them, a move from acid Berkshire to Mendip limestone is a gardening bereavement which leads to perpetual mourning for lost azaleas. The 'have nots' discovered long ago that soils derived from limestones have more varied and interesting floras than acid sands and peats, and revel in gardens filled with lavenders and sages, mulleins, columbines, box hedges, sea hollies, scabious and a host of aromatic, fragrant-leaved plants – many of which are herbs of one kind or another.

In new gardens, or old ones where changes are intended, it is important to know whether you are a 'have' or a 'have not'. One way is to become a chemist and buy a kit to test the pH of the soil, another is to look at what grows naturally and in neighbouring gardens.

### INDICATOR PLANTS FOR ACID/ALKALINE SOILS

Plants which grow wild on acid (pH less than 7.0) and alkaline (pH more than 7.0) soils are listed below. The plants included are mostly conspicuous, widely distributed and not difficult to identify. The presence of one or two of these species in a particular place may not mean very much; but a number found growing together can usually be taken as a reliable indication of the nature of the soil.

| *Plants Likely to be Found Growing on Acid, Lime-free Soils* | | | |
| --- | --- | --- | --- |
| Bell-heather | Bilberry | Bracken | Broom |
| Blinks | Brown Bent-grass | Bulbous Rush | Common Bent |
| Corn Marigold | Cowberry | Cudweed | Foxglove |
| Greater Woodrush | Hard Fern | Heath Bedstraw | Heath Rush |
| Lady Fern | Ling | Rhododendron | Sheep's Sorrel |
| Silver Birch | Soft Rush | Corn Spurrey | Common Tormentil |
| Wavy Hair-grass | Wood Cudweed | Wood Groundsel | Wood Sage |

| Plants Likely to be Found Growing on Base-rich, Alkaline Soils | | | |
|---|---|---|---|
| (very often with high levels of lime) | | | |
| Box | Blue Flea-bane | Blue Gromwell | Buckthorn |
| Bugloss | Carline Thistle | Chicory | Clustered Bellflower |
| Common Privet | Corn Camomile | Cowslip | Dark Mullein |
| Deadly Nightshade | Dog's Mercury | Dogwood | Dropwort |
| Early Purple Orchid | Enchanter's Nightshade | Felwort | Field Maple |
| Fragrant Orchid | Garlic Mustard | Gladdon Iris | Greater Butterfly Orchid |
| Greater Knapweed | Gromwell | Ground Ivy | Hairy Rock-cress |
| Hard Rush | Hoary Plantain | Kidney-vetch | Jacob's Ladder |
| Juniper | Lily-of-the-Valley | Lords and Ladies | Marjoram |
| Meadow Buttercup | Musk Thistle | Old Man's Beard | Oxlip |
| Pyramidal Orchid | Red Campion | Ribwort Plantain | Salad Burnet |
| Self-heal | Shining Cranesbill | Small Scabious | Small Teasel |
| Spindle-tree | Spurge Laurel | Squinancywort | Sweetbriar |
| Sweet Violet | Sweet Woodruff | Twayblade | Wall Pepper |
| Wayfaring Tree | White Beam | Wild Basil | Wild Carrot |
| Wild Parsnip | Wild Strawberry | Woolly Thistle | Yellow-wort |
| Yew | | | |

## LOOKING AFTER THE SOIL

Stables once stood where garages do today, horses pulled carriages and there were no cars. Horse manure, not carbon monoxide and lead from the exhausts of petrol engines, was the result. But horse manure had more substance, more obvious nuisance value, and could not be left to blow away. It had to be got rid of, and the easiest way to do that was to pay a strong lad to double-trench the garden, and bury it as he did so. The tradition grew up that digging deep and burying muck is the foundation of a good garden, and we live with that tradition still. But horse manure is rarer than it was; large lads who must work for tiny wages or starve are rarer still, and anyone who wants their garden double-trenched need look no further than the mirror to see who will do it.

Those gardens that once were double-trenched and dunged can still be found. Their soils are black, soft, friable and easy to work. They look, and sometimes still are, fertile. More often their dark soils hold only a memory of fertility – the humus which once bound the soil particles together and held water like a sponge has oxidised and gone; the black is the burnt-out carbon from nineteenth-century straw; the nutrients have been leached away and not replaced. For deep digging is a way of gardening which depends for success on the repeated applications of tons of compost, or muck, and a great deal of muscle power. There are other ways that will save a remarkable amount of backache, and make just as beautiful a garden.

Once again the patterns are in the countryside around us. Plants develop in cycles of growth and decay. They use sunlight, water and carbon dioxide to put together the carbohydrates which are the building blocks of the cellulose from which their bodies are constructed, and provide the energy that enables them to function. As leaves and roots die, flowers fall or trees collapse, this cellulose is broken down to produce the humus which holds clay particles in the soil together to make a loam, or packs between grains of sand to make starved, parched soils more fertile and water retentive. Eventually these remains disintegrate through exposure to sunlight and oxygen and break down into carbon dioxide and water, bringing the cycle back to where it started.

Gardeners may fancy that they invented compost; but nature did that aeons ago, and never needed bins to make it in but did it on the spot. Where growth is thick and lush the annual contribution of decaying plant remains is very significant – equivalent at least to crops of green manure, well grown and carefully dug in.

Gardeners are divided into the 'haves' and the 'have nots'. The former live on acid soils and their gardens are filled with rhododendrons and azaleas

The 'have nots' discovered long ago that soils derived from limestones have a more varied and interesting flora than acid sands and peats, and revel in gardens filled with lavenders, sages, and a host of aromatic, fragrant-leaved plants

This natural dressing mixes with the soil more gradually and with less disturbance than by digging. Some comes from decaying roots. This quickly becomes a part of the lower layers of the soil, forming channels in clay and other retentive soils through which water drains. Above ground, the remains of plants are eaten by slugs, worms, innumerable small insects, and tiny nameless members of the soil fauna, and eventually broken down by bacteria and fungi. Some are carried by worms deep into the soil, but most stay near the surface. There the remains gradually turn into humus that is not mixed haphazardly and indiscriminately with the relatively enormous bulk of the top soil, as when a spade is used, but concentrated where it can work most economically and effectively.

The soil at Godspiece was a silty clay loam, endlessly fertile but exceedingly heavy: not sticky-heavy as clay would be, but densely opposed to the thrust of a spade. Traditionally it had always been meadows; once ploughed it packed down too obstinately to cultivate unless fed lavishly with humus.

Nearby was a stable where half a dozen resident horses were constantly in production, on the edge of a village sensitive to too authentic a country atmosphere. Effective waste disposal was essential and arrangements were made with the owner to collect the fresh horse manure each week. Time

was pressing and it was spread straight onto the ground – not stacked to rot down. To start with it was piled on ground lying fallow before being planted; then, as the garden took shape it was pushed in under shrubs and between herbaceous plants to make a deep steamy mulch. This caused plenty of misgivings – especially in warm sultry weather when plants were growing fast and the air became thick with ammonia. But the leaves never scorched or suffered ill-effects, and after a year or two the change in the texture of the soil was dramatic. A hand could be pushed into the soil, where previously it had been hard work to force in a spade. Weeds, which would have been so firmly fixed that they snapped off at soil level when pulled, could be tweaked out without difficulty.

The stable litter had decomposed where it lay. Some was drawn deep into the soil by worms, but most mixed gradually with the upper layers to form a humus-rich top dressing. It was never dug or cultivated, and plants were simply slipped into holes where they were wanted. Many other materials can be used in the same way, but whatever is chosen the temptation to adopt high gardening styles should be resisted. Just spread it on the surface, or work it in amongst the plants, to be absorbed economically, naturally and effectively.

### SOME MATERIALS THAT CAN BE USED AS MULCHES

Mulches have two major effects; providing humus, and covering the soil surface with a weed-excluding, water-retaining blanket. Some do one better than the other. The materials that can be used range from plant remains through minerals to plastics. Even old carpets make an excellent mulch, if the thought of littering the garden with them is not too unappetising.

| MATERIAL | ADVANTAGES | DISADVANTAGES |
| --- | --- | --- |
| Garden compost | Costs little to make. Improves soil fertility and water-holding capacity. Can look attractive. | Labour intensive to make and spread. Carries weed seeds. Likely to be in limited supply. |
| Lawn mowings | Provides an efficient means of disposal. Adds some nutrients, and humus. Helps water conservation. | Must be spread very thinly, but can be applied repeatedly. Best used where they will not be conspicuous. |
| Horse manure (wood or straw) | Widely if not abundantly available. Contributes to soil fertility and water-holding capacity; excellent weed suppressant. | May not be visually acceptable. Can be awkward to transport and handle without a trailer or similar bulk-carrier. |

| MATERIAL | ADVANTAGES | DISADVANTAGES |
| --- | --- | --- |
| *Cow manure* | Often available in quantity. Usually well-rotted and not unpleasant to handle. Likely to be the most economical bulk source of humus. | Very variable in quality, and not always inoffensive. Supply may depend on being able to make arrangements for collection. Likely to carry weed seeds. |
| *Straw* | Readily available, and easy to transport and handle. Suppresses weeds well and good for water conservation. | May not be visually acceptable. Rots down very slowly, and may need added nitrogen to counter deficiency while it rots. |
| *Wood shavings* | Clean and easy to handle, can be bought to order in any quantity. Attractive appearance. Long-lasting effects. Very good weed suppressor. | Local supply may depend on being able to make arrangements for collection. Likely to be more or less expensive. Additional nitrogen may be necessary. |
| *Bark* | As for wood shavings, but widely available in bags. | Price likely to be on the high side, unless bought in bulk. |
| *Peat* | Pleasant to handle. Available everywhere. Looks very attractive. | Short-lived effect and high cost make this an uneconomic choice. |
| *Mushroom compost* | Low-cost bulk material that is pleasant to handle, looks attractive, and is widely available. | Short-lived effect. Repeated use will lead to build-up of lime and copper. Most useful for short-term cosmetic effects. |
| *Grit* | Economical when bought in bulk. Very effective long-term action on heavy clay soils. Reasonably effective weed suppressant. | Heavy to handle. Appearance may not be appropriate in some situations. Not suitable for light soils. |
| *Gravel* | Highly effective long-term treatment for problem areas. Can make an attractive garden feature needing very little maintenance. | Not acceptable in some situations, producing a major change in appearance and atmosphere. |
| *Polythene sheet* (black) | Cheap, flexible material, ideal for short-term use. Excellent as a weed suppressor and for water conservation. | Unattractive appearance with a tendency to become tatty. Does nothing to improve the fertility or humus content of the soil. Impedes absorption of rainwater by soil. |
| *Polypropylene sheet* (woven, black) | As for poly sheet. Can also be used as a more or less permanent membrane beneath a surface layer of bark or wood shavings, to make a minimal-maintenance flower bed. | Extra cost makes this a less economic, but more practical choice than poly sheet. Unattractive, and when exposed deteriorates in sunlight. Adds nothing to the soil. |

## GARDENING WITH WILDLIFE

Gardeners inherit long-established inclinations to take a dim view of uninvited animals and plants. They are suspicious of mischief afoot, and extend a welcome only to a very few creatures for which they happen to have a soft spot.

Minor misdemeanours lead to summary verdicts of guilty. An inclination to tear yellow crocus flowers to pieces and dust-bathe in seed beds condemns the poor old sparrow as 'the avian rat'. It lives for most of the year on weed seeds and spilt grain, and for part of the year on harmful insects. It maintains impeccable, and surprising, constancy in matrimony, but all to no avail.

Gardens are battlefields where success is measured by the number of corpses, and the absence of insects, small animals and all plants which are not under total control. There is an air of a place besieged – preserved from destruction by vigilant resistance to threats and attacks from pests and diseases. But on country walks it is unusual to find wild flowers being devastated by pests and, except on arable land and disturbed ground, most of the plants we call weeds will be conspicuous by their absence. Sometimes the shoots of plants will be found covered with greenfly, or caterpillars detected devouring leaves in a hedgerow or in a bed of stinging nettles. But a return visit a week or two later will not encounter millions more greenfly crawling over every plant in the neighbourhood, and the caterpillars will be gone – moved off to pupate – if they have been lucky enough to escape becoming the victims of ichneumon flies. Left to themselves most of the pests we fear are either eaten by predators soon after they start to increase, or are transient and move on before they inflict serious damage.

Yet gardeners feel so threatened by pests that they are willing to try out the most drastic measures, and the most dangerous poisons, to eradicate them. A regular job I performed on my father's nursery, soon after leaving school, was to progress backwards down a long greenhouse filled with tomatoes scattering spoonfuls of powder on the dampened floor. This produced cyanide gas which was very bad for the whitefly, and temporarily discouraged their attempts to multiply; it would have been extremely bad for me, rapidly and effectively, if I had lingered any longer than necessary at my task or thoughtlessly used the spoon to stir my tea.

These deadly poisons are now illegal or strictly controlled. We use a totally different band of organic chemicals whose poisonous properties, we are told, are more specific and less indiscriminately dangerous than the poisons of the past. Often, it would seem, they are hardly poisonous at all – although the worldwide effects of some of these chemicals during the past fifty years have been more insidious and far more devastating than any we have ever used before.

Today the effects of these chemicals, coupled with changes in agricultural practices which have wiped out much of the shelter and many of the resources on which wild creatures depend, have become disturbingly obvious. We are no less troubled by pests than we ever were, but the incidental wildlife of the countryside is less abundant than it was a few decades ago, and gardens are being suggested as places where such animals might find sanctuary.

These suggestions offend most gardeners' basic instincts. They conflict with the belief that the freedom to spray is the only way to preserve a garden from the phenomenal capacity of one aphid to produce more, and more, and more, and more; that pellets of bran and metaldehyde are the thin blue line that defends our plants from slugs and snails. In short, the feeling prevails that we garden successfully only so long as we hold the line against nature, and to let her into our gardens on any other terms would be disastrous.

Perhaps that would be so if we kept on gardening as we do now; growing the same range of plants, in the same ways and with the same expectations. But we could take more trouble to look for plants that are less susceptible to infestation or infection. We could pay more attention to the balances and counterbalances between prey and predators that preserve the plants beyond our gardens.

Gardens in the countryside are exposed to the insistent presence of wildlife, suggesting the need to look for ways to garden which respect its presence, and make it a part of the attractions of the garden. This can work only if we avoid destructive forays against species which our opinions label undesirable. By no means all the wild creatures and plants we shall encounter are innocuous, appealing

It is not necessary to be involved on a grand scale to carry the responsibilities of recognising the genius of a place

or pretty; but there are very few – probably none – about which we know so much that we can predict all the consequences of taking action against them. Our gardens can be friendly to wildlife only when we recognise our limited ability to intervene constructively, and avoid blundering, spasmodic attempts to destroy pests and weeds by chemical warfare with results we cannot predict or measure.

## MOVING INTO THE COUNTRY

To a planner the countryside is landscape: a series of patterns created by the topography and the colours, textures, and variations in scale of the vegetation, overlaid by man-made geometric features such as walls, hedges, the shapes of fields and woods and the forms of buildings. These landscapes are the setting for gardens in the countryside and offer endless scope for imagination in the ways we relate our gardens to them.

It is not necessary to be involved on a grand scale – as a Capability Brown or a Humphry Repton laying out great estates, or a Sylvia Crowe providing a setting for a power station – to carry the responsibilities of recognising the genius of a place. The smallest garden can contribute sympathetically to its surroundings, or its setting can be ignored and the garden made a place apart.

By definition, custom and inclination gardens are places which are enclosed. They are places where order and intention take the place of the apparent chaos of the wilderness, and provide somewhere pleasant and secure to sit or play, chat or work. An acre of the wildwood, or a meadow or two, can never be a garden; and when patterns from the countryside are borrowed they need to be reworked to meet our expectations of what a garden should be. The most effective and flexible ways to do this depend on our sensitivity to patterns and arrangements which state that a place is as it is by design or intention, and reassure us that it is both safe and special. Somehow, somewhere the way the garden is designed and planted must get this message across.

It can be done blatantly, by boundaries unmistakably defined with fences or closely clipped hedges; with well-kept lawns, and borders massed with large and colourful and obviously highly bred flowers. It can be done as a brilliant self-sufficient display, an episode complete in itself that ignores everything around it.

Or it can be done very subtly, using symmetry and asymmetry to draw attention to the more ordered arrangements that separate a garden from the haphazard patterns of the countryside. This approach enables patterns to be created within the garden which reflect or relate to features over the fence, so that the garden's setting becomes a part of its overall design.

The activities of its inhabitants have changed every part of Britain and these modifications have left such a mark that even the wildest most unspoilt-looking parts of the countryside owe only a little more to nature than the gardens we create within them. We are taught from infancy to call the countryside natural, and this has become a deeply embedded response to what we see. Nevertheless, forestry, agriculture, landscaping and gardening are all expressions of mankind's compulsion to control his surroundings, and each plays a part in manipulating the landscape in which we live.

There have been times when fashion decreed that gardens be regarded as the antithesis of the so-called natural forms of the countryside. It would be easy to find many today who take this view, and many of them are amongst the neo-rustics moving out to make homes in the countryside. Such a view makes it very hard to think of a garden as anything other than an extreme contrast to its surroundings, and inevitably leads to styles of gardening that emphasise the differences between garden plants and wild flowers.

One of the aims of this book is to find ways of recognising points of similarity between gardens and the man-made countryside, in a search for patterns in one that can be used to inspire ideas in the other.

Conservative traditions are strong in the countryside, and the folklore of its unchanging nature so pervasive that country styles are synonymous with those that are backward-looking and reactionary. Now that country living is undergoing its most sensational transformation for more than a thousand years, that view is out of step with events and the needs of the moment. This is a time to use the creative energies and the financial resources being poured into our villages on new approaches, and to develop new styles of gardening that make an original contribution to the quality of the neo-rustic revolution.

## CHAPTER FOUR

Little Jack Horner, when he wasn't sitting in corners on the look-out for plums, lived in a village called Mells, not far from Bath. This pleasant place is still a secluded country village, where small groups of cottages cluster in irregular terraces along winding alleys. Meadows and streams, trees and orchards spread right into its middle, making spaces amongst the cottages and between the larger houses within their walled gardens, and the whole place reflects the feeling of the countryside which surrounds it.

Some years ago a resident of Mells wrote to the editor of the *Somerset Standard*. The writer was upset by the appearance of his rural retreat; it was becoming untidy, and the state of the kerbs and verges left much to be desired. Kerbstones, he felt, were conspicuously absent leading to an ill-defined, often muddy, margin between road and bank, and the verges, left unmown and untrimmed, became ragged and unkempt when moondaisies, Queen Anne's lace and dandelions erupted amongst long grass.

The writer was playing a bit-part in a long-running performance. In the eighteenth century Humphry Repton moved to a comfortable little cottage in a village in Essex, and a well-known pair of drawings – one showing the village as it was, the other after he had made some changes – tell us how he dealt with the problems of rural life. A nice tripod of roses was put up to hide hams hanging outside the butcher's shop on the other side of the road, and small flower beds were cut into the lawn to make a splash of colour in the summer. In a bolder gesture, that owes much to the spirit of the time when enclosures of all kinds were a sign of progress, he added the village green to his domain, excluding with a neat clipped hedge and a few shrubs the ducks which had enjoyed the run of it.

# Country Settings

Many places that would be beautiful if left alone are spoiled by doing away with some simple natural feature in order to put in its place some hackneyed form of gardening.

*Gertrude Jekyll*

One of the locals, a disreputable-looking old fellow, lacking a right arm and with an eye-patch, can be seen squinting into the garden over the fence in the 'before' picture. He was moved on and disappears from the 'after' scene but a respectable woman with a little girl in a long, clean dress continue their walk past the pub as though nothing has changed. Taste and sensibility had prevailed over the ruder ways of the countryside, and we can only imagine what those bred and born in Harestreet had to say about such improvements.

Gentrification continues to this day, and at an enormously increased rate. When Repton moved to Harestreet he was down on his luck, and the move was forced on him by his financial situation; the changes he made had to be modest. Neo-rustics today bring resources which they can use most powerfully to transform their surroundings.

And transform them they do! The villages' past has made them what they are today. They were formed when resources were short and local materials provided the most economical way to build, and local craftsmen with a limited repertoire of building skills were the only people to do it. It is easy to draw the conclusion that the villages' atmosphere, integrity and character can only be preserved by recognising this, and to insist on using traditional materials and methods to meet present needs.

That is easy to say, but local materials have become hard to find and expensive to buy. In their place we have mass-produced brand-names, made familiar by advertising and promotion wherever we look. The skills of builders and designers are tuned to these new materials. Even if that were not so, should we really let ourselves be persuaded that going back to the past is the most creative way to find what we want in villages today?

If we look out of the window of a house in a village to neighbouring houses across the garden; to the old marketplace, church and pub, or the fields around, and think about the reasons for the houses being built and laid out as they are, and for the gardens between them looking as they do, how many of us end up much wiser? We see a hotchpotch of brick and stone and timber; gardens large and small, well cultivated or neglected, some modern and others ancient. We probably have only a passing interest in the history of the place, and what we know has nothing to do with gardening. We may respond sympathetically to the idea of preserving local atmosphere, but inspiration is unlikely to spring spontaneously to mind to help us do anything about it.

Inspiration is always in short supply. It is hard to find and doesn't come from trundling acquisitions from the garden centre round in a barrow, looking for somewhere to plant them. Anyone who thinks so has read too many tales about Vita Sackville West roaming around Sissinghurst, flower in hand, mixing and matching as she went. No doubt – at a very late stage in its development – she did do just that; dotting the i's and crossing the t's of gardening.

But, long before, Harold Nicolson, like a fish out of water, had come to damp, uncongenial buildings in a derelict, almost abandoned farmyard; had looked hard and thought long about what he would like to do with them – after a night picnicking romantically but muddily amongst the buildings, which would have destroyed a lesser man's interest forever – and eventually produced a plan. This plan, partly in his mind, partly on paper, became the foundation for the gardens at Sissinghurst today. It solved the problems of using a variety of separate, ill-aligned buildings to enclose and divide a series of gardens and yet, by vistas and other ruses, retained links between them which produced an overall unity and placed the garden within the setting of the surrounding countryside.

What he did, anyone can do: not by waiting for inspiration but by two processes which we use every day whenever we make a choice of any kind – analysis and evaluation. The first sorts out what we have and what we would like: the second finds the best answer to our needs amongst alternative possibilities.

Keep **analysis** simple by making it personal. Take into account only what you need; how you react to what is already there, and the resources at your disposal.

**Evaluate** alternatives only by your view of their benefits, advantages, merits or limitations.

But keeping it simple does not mean that analyses should be superficial, or that evaluations should be perfunctory. When done well they are likely to lead to quite a different view of what is wanted, and what is possible, than was held at the start, and if the result simply confirms initial impressions an opportunity has probably been wasted. The evaluation should be based on the broadest possible range of alternatives using any relevant information, as well as some which may seem scarcely relevant at all.

This is an opportunity to review every feature that might be a part of the garden, to discover the materials that could be used in their construction – even the most outlandish – and to start thinking about the effects intended. It is a time for fantasy as well as practicalities; for anarchy as well as social responsibility; for wild excesses to offset sober reality; for dreams of exotic effects and plans to cope with day-to-day realities. It is a time for imagination and a time for quiet thought.

The problem is making a start. Looking out of the window produces a blank-filled mind and fellow-feelings for artists staring at unblemished canvases, or sculptors faced with featureless blocks of stone. More significantly the window provides a frame for the garden, suggesting that the whole business is something like painting a picture. This analogy is often made but does not become true for being repeated. Gardens are to be stepped into and walked about in; they are places where length, depth and height are vital and where time is one of the most exciting dimensions of all. The discovery will be made that there is time which moves on relentlessly from year to year and never repeats itself, and another kind of time which spirals through the seasons and returns each spring almost to where it was the year before.

So start by walking about in the space that is to be the garden. There is no hurry – let time pass by and discover how the garden changes, and how the ways it is used change from one time of year to another.

Provide time for second thoughts; brilliant inspirations seldom arrive so perfect that they cannot be improved, and are usually only a step on the way to somewhere else.

## OBSERVATIONS AND REACTIONS
### (Analysis and Evaluation)

#### 1 THE GARDEN'S SURROUNDINGS

A decision which must be made early is, whether to use the setting of the garden as a background and inspiration for the design, the materials and the choice of plants. Features in this section are outside the garden, and it may be impossible to alter them. Their presence may influence what is done, either by providing attractive backgrounds or suggesting themes or, when obtrusive or unattractive, by making it necessary to provide screens.

#### Materials used in neighbouring houses
OBSERVATIONS: Look at the variety of materials used, and their overall effect. Is one material (ie brick, tiles, stone etc) predominant, or is there a mixture? What impressions of colour, texture, mellowness or brashness do they provide?
REACTIONS: Existing materials may provide a guide to those that could be used in the garden. Think about ways that the colours of flowers and foliage can be used to bring out hues in the buildings, and beware of unattractive contrasts; especially when bricks are predominant.

*It is a time for fantasy as well as practicalities: for dreams of exotic effects, and plans to cope with day-to-day realities*

#### Patterns produced by roofs, walls, chimneystacks etc
OBSERVATIONS: Have a look at the overall picture. Is it dominated by vertical features like high gables or chimney stacks, or by horizontal lines like the long, low roofs of bungalows? Are there pronounced interactions between different shapes or just a mish-mash of angles and surfaces?
REACTIONS: Look for shapes and forms beyond the garden, which can act as foils or contrasts for features and groups of plants in the garden. Decide whether features outside the garden should or could be reflected in its lay-out and planting.

#### Shapes and sizes of the spaces between neighbouring houses
OBSERVATIONS: Are the spaces between buildings informal or regimented? Irregular or rectilinear? Conspicuous or miniscule? Do they give the impression that they have happened almost by chance, or by careful planning?
REACTIONS: Small, squarish gardens with promi-

35

nently defined boundaries destroy the informality typical of old villages. Look for ways of planting which do not emphasise boundaries, and try to preserve existing irregularities and spaces whenever possible.

### Materials used to make walls, fences and other divisions

OBSERVATIONS: Is there a wide variety of different materials or virtually only one? Do they appear to be mostly traditional materials which confer a sense of age and maturity, or modern, manufactured materials which present a more up-to-date image?

REACTIONS: Avoid introducing modern, mass-produced products in any locations where traditional materials are prominent. On the other hand, be very wary of the phoney effects which can result if you attempt 'Ye Olde' style by using traditional materials in places where none are already present.

### Levels of noise, disturbance and exposure to view

OBSERVATIONS: Is noise and disturbance a noticeable feature of the place, or does it seem to be peaceful and secluded? What is the nature of any disturbance and how serious are its effects?

REACTIONS: Decide whether anything can be done to reduce annoyance. Hedges, fences, trellises and plants can be used as visual screens, but it is very hard to do anything to reduce noise.

### Neighbouring gardens

OBSERVATIONS: Do you like, or admire, the gardens in the vicinity, and would you say that they fit well into their surroundings, or do they seem to be inappropriate? What plants grow in them? Do they tell you anything about the kind of soil in the area, how hardy plants must be to survive there, whether the ground is fertile or infertile, etc, etc?

REACTIONS: Learn as much as you can about the gardens around, and the plants that are growing well; they may be a good guide for success. Try to identify what it is that you like or dislike about nearby gardens, and what it is about them that fits them to their surroundings. This may help towards ideas which you can use yourself.

### Natural vegetation

OBSERVATIONS: Is natural vegetation an important part of the surrounding scene or is it of little significance? What plants can you see, and do they tell you anything about the nature of the soil or how fertile it is?

REACTIONS: Native trees and plants can be grown in gardens and often with less care than garden forms. It may be helpful to plan to include them, especially when ease of maintenance is important.

### Local litter and domestic paraphenalia

OBSERVATIONS: Are cars, dustbins, telephone poles, overhead wires etc all-pervading or not much in evidence? Are there particular features of this kind which are objectionable and should be taken into account?

REACTIONS: Neighbours' garages, parking places, telegraph poles and wires, and areas where rubbish is dumped are all intrusive, unattractive or unpleasant features which it might be possible to screen when planning the garden.

## 2 THE GARDEN ITSELF

The space where the garden is to be made has qualities which can be used constructively, and will influence the way the garden is laid out. These can be modified to a greater or lesser extent, and the opportunities they offer can be judged and exploited in whatever ways seem most appropriate.

### Character and period of the house and its outbuildings

OBSERVATIONS: Do the house and its outbuildings provide ideas for the design and nature of the garden? What materials have been used in their construction? Does the house appear to be in harmony with neighbouring buildings, or is it made from quite different materials, or in a different architectural style?

REACTIONS: Think about ways that the garden and house can be made to complement one another. The plants chosen and their shapes and colours may contrast or harmonise with the tones and forms of building materials. Garden features may be constructed with materials similar to those used in the house, and in ways which reflect its architecture. Differences or similarities between your house and the neighbours' can be deliberately emphasised, or reduced, by the choice of colours, forms and shapes in the garden.

### Exposure to sunshine and shadow

OBSERVATIONS: Does the garden generally seem to

be markedly sunny or shaded? Are there parts which are persistently either in shade or more or less well lit, and how do these areas relate to the position of the house? Does there seem to be any obvious need to do something about its shadiness or exposure to the sun's heat?

REACTIONS: Finding agreeable places to sit depends on finding places where the sun shines at the right times of day. The ways a garden can be used, and the plants that can be grown, depend on patterns of sunshine and shadow. It may be possible to remove some trees, but shadows cast by buildings may be more difficult to deal with.

### Degree of seclusion

OBSERVATIONS: Is seclusion an attribute of the site, or is it overlooked from any or several directions? Are there parts of it which could be made into secluded corners where it would be comfortable to sit and relax?

REACTIONS: If the garden is overlooked it is likely to be easier to make small secluded areas within it, rather than attempt total seclusion.

### Size of the garden

OBSERVATIONS: Does the garden appear to be large or small? Does its design lead immediately to thoughts of looking for ways to save time on maintenance, or does this seem to be unimportant?

REACTIONS: Large and small are relative terms which depend entirely on how you view the situation, what you want to do with the garden, and what other things you have to do. It is always sensible to plan so that maintenance gets less as you get older.

### Topography and landforms

OBSERVATIONS: Is the garden level or sloping? If sloping, have differences in level already been made to play a part in its layout? Are there any places where it is so steep that it is hazardous, or difficult to cross when pushing a wheelbarrow or on foot?

REACTIONS: Even small changes in level can be used to make a garden interesting, and they can often be created even on seemingly flat sites. Steep slopes provide opportunities for dramatic effects but need careful planning to make them accessible.

### Overall unity or complexity

OBSERVATIONS: Is the garden all of a piece, or is it divided by walls, buildings, hedges, or other barriers to form spaces which have different atmospheres and qualities? Is its shape more or less regular or markedly irregular? How is the house placed in relation to the garden?

REACTIONS: The choice is between a garden with a simple overall form, or one which is divided into areas with different functions and moods. Major divisions of this sort, and the ways that the house relates to the garden, need to be decided at an early stage.

### Existing plants and features

OBSERVATIONS: Is it an empty space or one where a garden already exists? What plants or features such as paths, walls, and structures of one kind or another, are there now? Is it very weedy, and if so do the weeds appear to be annuals or perennials?

REACTIONS: Existing plants and features may be red herrings which bear no relation to new needs. Use them if you really want to, but avoid being dictated to by their presence. If perennial weeds are present in any quantity the first thing to do is to destroy them before any planting is done.

### Condition and type of soil

OBSERVATIONS: Can you tell whether the soil is acid or alkaline; well drained or likely to be water-logged; fertile or infertile? Does it appear to be sandy, an easily worked loam or thick, heavy clay? Do you get the impression that it has been well cultivated and cared for in the recent past, or neglected?

REACTIONS: The soil will be the foundation of all your gardening. It will decide what kinds of plants you can grow, the ease with which you can garden, and the methods you should use. Its merits and limitations must be taken into account both when planning the layout and when deciding what plants to grow.

### Impact of buildings, and vistas beyond the boundaries

OBSERVATIONS: What sort of outlook does the garden have? Which features would you like to screen and which to retain as part of the view? Is the view from any part of the garden or the house a major feature?

REACTIONS: Decide whether you would like to look out on and 'borrow' features in the neighbourhood as part of the garden. If so, the siting of screens and apertures will become a critical issue. Think about any views and balance the pleasure of seeing them with your need for privacy and shelter.

## 3 YOUR OWN NEEDS, LIKES AND DISLIKES

This is your garden, and you will enjoy it only if it fits in with your ideas of what a garden should be, and is right for your lifestyle. This is the time to think about the garden you want and the resources, time and skills which you can devote to it.

### Your interest in gardening in general, and gardening interests

OBSERVATIONS: Are you a dedicated gardener or someone whose other activities don't leave too much time for gardening? Do you have a special interest in any particular aspect of gardening or group of plants?

REACTIONS: Be wary of commitments and complications beyond your needs. Try to avoid the feeling that a garden should be made up of a 'shopping list' of features of one kind or another, and restrict your plot to the features that you really need and which match your interests.

### Time available to look after the garden

OBSERVATIONS: How much time do you want to spend working in the garden, or how much are you prepared to pay for someone else to look after it for you? Do you want a garden where there is always work to be done, or one that can be left to take care of itself when you have other things to do?

REACTIONS: The time needed to look after a garden depends entirely on how it is designed and planted. If you want to restrict the amount of routine maintenance required, this decision should be made early on and provided for by using appropriate plants and simple layouts.

### Reasons that you need/want a garden

OBSERVATIONS: What is the garden for, and what is hoped from it? Are you making it because you feel you have to do something with all the space around the house, and convention suggests that you should make a garden; or do you want the garden as a place to relax in, somewhere for the children to play, a parking space for the car, a hen-run and vegetable patch, a creative occupation, or a mixture of all these and more?

REACTIONS: Make a list of the things that you would like to use the garden for, and try to work out how much space each will need, and how important it is to you. Avoid being tied by conventions – there is no law to say that every garden must contain a lawn. But remember to include unaesthetic necessities like a place for the dustbins, as well as providing for the pleasures such as somewhere to sit and sup, and enjoy the rewards of your work.

### Regard for and sympathy with the garden's surroundings

OBSERVATIONS: Do you feel that the place where you live has particular qualities which should be considered when the garden is being designed, or do you believe that you should enjoy your freedom to do whatever you like in your garden without regard for its surroundings?

REACTIONS: This is not the easy choice between being a conformist or an individualist that it may seem. Paradoxically, if you hang onto your liberties you are likely to end up with a garden much like many to be found anywhere in Britain. But, if you can respond to the nature and special qualities of the garden's situation, there is a very good chance of making something really individual.

Keen gardeners who have ploughed through this appraisal of the garden and its surroundings could reach the end frustrated and disappointed. Where have all the flowers gone? What help is this to someone home from the garden centre with a trolley-load of plants and in need of advice? Plants have scarcely been mentioned, and that is intentional!

Gardeners, plantspersons especially, become so infatuated with their plants that their gardens are little more than shelves on which to display the darlings. An opportunity to make a garden can be completely overlooked in the eagerness to be on with the planting. But the chance will never come again, and it is worth taking a little time to make the most of it.

As ideas begin to form, and a framework for the garden takes shape, the ways the spaces within it will be used become clearer and the plants needed begin to declare themselves; first as impressions, then as intentions which suggest the shapes and colours, heights, textures and forms of the plants needed; and finally as names which fit the hopes, dreams and needs of the garden's creator. But first we will look at the spaces between houses and the boundaries that divide them; the drives and paths that lead into gardens and allow us to move around them, and the steps that link paths, cope with changes of level, and provide focal points.

## THE SPACES BETWEEN HOUSES

Houses in the older parts of villages were placed according to need and opportunity. Villages grew, and often declined, by a mixture of chance and design so that buildings of differing shapes and textures stand side by side, separated by spaces which are often more notable for their irregularity than their order.

These spaces are often nearly as important as the houses themselves, and village developments which ignore these ancient irregularities destroy the villages' character. The gardens around village houses are not simply the private property of the owners of the houses, but often major contributors to the elusive qualities which give atmosphere and style.

Within these spaces are the boundaries between gardens. Once these were defined in ways which brought individual character to different places. Often they were muted; they imposed a patina rather than a pattern on the texture of the spaces between the houses which was secondary to the dominant effect of scattered apple and plum and other fruit trees. But the invasions of the villages in the last twenty or thirty years have changed their function and significance. Formerly low walls, paling fences, chicken wire, corrugated iron, ragged hedges, a row of stones or a turf-covered bank defined the borders of two plots. Even where brick or stone was plentiful, and substantial walls easily made, they were likely to be roughly built, crumbling at the edges, and less than spick and span.

Modest, informal and often untidy barriers of this kind no longer meet expectations when we divide our properties. They do not provide enough privacy, nor protect effectively from invasion by neighbours' children, dogs and footballs. Boundaries have grown higher, and become more prominent. They have become objects of pride, with appearances that must be kept up; and now they dominate the spaces between the houses. They have also become standardised. Mass-produced fencing panels and Castlewellan Gold hedging enclose gardens in villages in Dyfed, in the market towns of Dorset, and in the suburbs of Harrow. They are put up with little thought for what they are meant to do and how they do it, and none at all for their effect on their surroundings.

## THINKING ABOUT BOUNDARIES

The defined boundaries of newly built houses are twentieth-century echoes of the enclosures of a century or two ago. Then well-hedged fields were essential for new ways of farming; today, rigidly enclosed plots with emphatic boundaries are seen as the inevitable way to enclose spaces within which to practise suburban gardening.

These gardens sit within their boundaries like pictures in their frames. No attempt is made to combine the garden and its boundaries in a composition, nor do gardens and their enclosures share common harmonies, tensions or themes. When a fence blows down, it can be – very probably will be – replaced by a hedge with no qualms about its effects on the garden. If so little attention is paid to the ways that boundary and garden interact, it is not surprising that there is seldom any concern at all about the impact of the boundary hedge or fence on the surrounding scenery.

Houses in the countryside, attractively set amongst fields or woods, are isolated from their surroundings by strongly defined fences or hedges, which detract from their appearance. Often these visual blocks are unnecessary and, from a practical point of view, countryside that sweeps right up to the walls of a house can save a great deal of gardening. However, most people would be ill at ease with nothing more than a line on a plan to mark the limits of their domain, and feel a need for more substantial barriers for at least one and probably several of the following reasons.

### SECURITY

*Requirement:* To provide a barrier which deters deliberate illegal entry.
*Response:* The most effective security fence is one which makes entry difficult but provides no cover. High posts and wire, or a water-filled ditch ie moat, are more effective than hedges or high walls.

### PRIVACY

*Requirement:* To define the garden as private property and discourage casual trespass.
*Response:* All that is necessary is some indication of a private rather than public place: change of materials or texture where the drive meets the road, a rope slung between wooden posts, the transition to an obviously gardened place. These are enough to make the point.

### PROTECTION

*Requirement:* To exclude intruding farm animals, rabbits, deer etc which would damage the garden.
*Response:* Physical barriers like hedges (holly and hawthorn), post and rail fences, wire netting etc can be effective. Farm animals with long necks may need a secondary barrier – a single strand of barbed wire slung on posts 1m beyond the boundary. Cats deter rabbits better and more cheaply than fences.

### SECLUSION

*Requirement:* To provide a sight screen to shield the garden from outsiders looking in.
*Response:* Screening is often overdone. It may hardly be necessary during the winter, in the front garden, or in parts away from the house. Internal screens within the garden are usually easier to make, more attractive, and more effective than visual barriers along the boundaries.

### SHELTER

*Requirement:* Protection from the effects of cold winds.
*Response:* Close-knit boundary hedges, and walls, are only marginally effective and produce turbulence. Tall shrubs and small trees within the garden are more effective as wind breaks, and pierced screens, trellises, picket fencing etc can be used to shelter places to sit in.

The quest for privacy and freedom from sudden assaults by the neighbours' children may be temptations to seek refuge behind the Leyland barrier. Before doing so consider how it will look, consider how much time it will take to keep it in order, and above all think about the alternatives.

## APPROACHES TO BOUNDARIES

1 Decide why the boundaries need to be defined, and what purpose hedges, walls, fences and other barriers are to serve; eg privacy, shelter, security etc.
2 Think what can be done with the boundary rather than to it. Parts of it can probably be designed as attractive features in the overall layout of the garden.
3 Avoid the hard assertive lines of fences, walls or hedges that run the length or width of the garden, and meet at an angle. Smudge the lines with clumps of shrubs, variations in material, or features such as a pergola, an arbour or some other structure. Sometimes a sunken fence (a ha-ha) can be used to conceal a boundary and blend the garden with its setting.

4 Avoid narrow beds of plants and shrubs trapped between the boundary fence and a lawn or path.
5 Decide on particular parts of the garden – places to sit, for example – where privacy is important, and provide screening within the garden, or immediately around them, rather than along the boundaries. Internal divisions can be made in many different ways and are flexible and attractive features in gardens.
6 Remember that the need for privacy in most parts of the garden will be much greater in summer than in winter. Deciduous shrubs, climbers, tall grasses and small trees can be used much more flexibly to give all the screening needed, rather than a solid wall, a high boundary fence, or an evergreen hedge.
7 Look at the materials used in the house, and in the vicinity of the garden, and decide whether they provide ideas for materials for boundary walls or fences.

### MATERIALS FOR WALLS AND FENCES

The first signs of neo-rustic incursions are the replacement of chicken wire and corrugated iron stopgaps by Leyland cypress hedges and fences made of light tan, close-boarded wooden panels. The progress of gentrification can be assessed by dividing the yardage of corrugated iron by the total length of newly planted Castlewellan Gold – any value less than 1.0 indicates invasion beyond recovery.

Later, as the boundaries begin to reflect their owners' sophistication and affluence, this simple ratio becomes unreliable. Heraldic creatures appear on gateposts, and walls constructed of various materials including pierced concrete blocks, artificial stone, newly made bricks with rustic finishes, and natural building stone brought from distant quarries, confuse the issue. Their purpose is the construction of barriers which are high enough and dense enough to ensure that nothing can be seen from outside of what goes on inside.

These stockades, totally unlike the more modest divisions used in the past, have become conspicuous features in villages. They appear with no regard for materials already present and have no affinity with their location or the character of the place. They are major elements in the destruction of ancient airs and graces.

*Pierced concrete blocks:* These have many advantages. They are easy to build with, and make screens with almost the ideal proportions of space and solid to filter and slow the wind without causing local whirlwinds in corners around the house. They make effective sight screens, but do not overwhelm as tall, solid walls or fences do. They are excellent supports for plants, which can twine in and out of their spaces in more exciting three-dimensional forms than the two-dimensional strapped-to-the-wires effect of plants or shrubs against a fence or wall. They allow ventilation of shaded spaces beneath pergolas, car ports or in the corners of patios. For all that, the inspiration behind the designs of these moulded blocks of concrete is so crabbed, unimaginative and hackneyed that they line up with *Robinia* 'Frisia', *Rhododendron* 'Pink Pearl', plastic urns and hammerheads of dark asphalt in the drive, in the vanguard of the invasion of a thousand villages by the surburban style.

*Artificial reconstituted stone:* When older houses are surrounded by garden walls of local stone, good intentions suggest that new walls should be made from the same material. Cold reality turns these plans into forlorn hopes when all the quarries which once produced the stone have closed, and estimates come in for building with second-hand stone.

A reconstituted substitute may be suggested, said to reproduce the qualities and appearance of the original but made in conveniently sized modules, which turn building into a simple matter of assembling a large and solid jigsaw puzzle. However persuasively the advantages of the reconstituted stone are pressed, no orders should be made or money spent before comparing the real with the artificial. Few, if any, reconstituted stones possess the complexion and local character of the original, and even the bland, precisely squared blocks from the quarries of Bath or Portland are less than convincingly reproduced by their artificial substitutes. A garden setting – especially one where natural and artificial are used close together – reveals starkly the latter's lack of individuality and inability to weather agreeably.

Like pierced concrete blocks, these twentieth-century blessings for do-it-yourself gardeners fit into rustic settings only when used imaginatively. Caution and very careful selection are essential wherever vernacular materials predominate.

*Bricks:* Colloquially, bricks are dropped. Whatever the distant origins of that phrase may have been, excursions through villages today confirm that their gauche handling still continues.

In Tudor times bricks were lavished on chimneys – partly because they were a practical way to build a fireproof flue, but also because expensive bricks attracted more attention as an elaborate chimney-stack than as a wall. Bricks are still used in these ambivalent ways. They can be the most practical, the most traditional, and the most subtly appropriate of all materials to make a path or build a wall, pergola, outhouse or gazebo. And, they can be used for all those things – just as practically – but also to make an impression.

Choosing bricks is something most of us seldom do, and they present so many alternatives that it is easy to trip into the traps set by multiple choices combined with innocence.

Should the bricks be old or new?
Handmade or mass-produced?
What size should they be?
What finish should they have?
What colour should they be?
What bond should be used to lay them?
What mix of mortar or cement should be used?
How should they be pointed?

The answers to these questions may be lying at your feet or sitting in front of your eyes. Where houses are made of bricks, or features in the garden contain brickwork, there will be samples and patterns to act as a guide. The simplest decision is to match the bricks to be used with those already there; it does not follow that they will be easy to find. The simplest procedure is to use bricks that are readily available; that does not mean it will be easy to match them with the ones already there. Imagination, experience and very sharp discrimination are needed to create friendly unions between bricks of different colours, finishes and, possibly, even sizes.

*Natural building stone:* Eighteenth-century landowners busily emparking had stone walls put up by

Houses in the countryside, attractively set amongst fields and woods, are isolated from their surroundings by strongly defined hedges or fences. Often these visual blocks are unnecessary

the mile. Twentieth-century costs make us more inclined to think in metres. Nevertheless, few garden features are more rewarding than those made of good stone, well used in traditional ways; in villages where stone was the natural and predominant building material of the past it is difficult to find anything to take its place.

Natural stone was once used lavishly. It was readily available, often at virtually no charge, and the labour to quarry, transport and build with it was similarly cheap. High costs have turned it from a staple into a luxury, and created a peculiar problem. It is no longer used as an incidental part of the scene – the easiest, cheapest way to block a hole or put up a barrier – but is reserved for the more prestigious projects and for building special features. The result, even where local stone is used within a setting where the same stone is abundant, can be self-consciously important. The work is too well finished, the results are too contrived, the stones too critically chosen or carefully dressed to match vernacular patterns, which approached these things more casually.

Less forgivably, stone is used blatantly to impress and to convey prestige. Then it is put where it is most visible, and the kinds chosen are those whose dressing, texture, colour and form make sure they stand out amongst their surroundings. This is nothing new. Entrances to grand houses, especially the lodges at their gates, have always been fertile ground for self-advertisement, even a little light lunacy. But what was an occasional idiosyncrasy, and an entertaining feature of the countryside, now becomes a repetitive bore when successive quite modest houses use expensive stonework at their gates to project their importance.

Natural stone was once used lavishly; it was readily
available, often at virtually no cost, and was the easiest,
cheapest way to block a hole or put up a barrier

Bricks can be the most practical, the most traditional,
and the most subtly appropriate of all ways to make a
path or build a wall

## ALTERNATIVES FOR BOUNDARIES

| DESCRIPTION | ADVANTAGES | DISADVANTAGES |
| --- | --- | --- |
| **A Natural Materials** | Many provide settings that are sympathetic to plants, and tend to fit into most gardens easily and effectively. | May not be easy to obtain in standard sizes. Specialised skills may be needed to use them well. |
| *Local stone* | Likely to be complementary to neighbouring buildings and other features. | Can be expensive. May not be easy to obtain or work with. May not weather well. |
| *Imported stone* | Freedom to choose a kind that is well-suited to the purpose, and provides whatever effect is wanted. | Probably very expensive and likely to be obtrusive, and pretentious unless used with skill and sensitivity. |
| *Cleft oak post and rails* | Can be used to make a strong, well-built fence, that fits well into rural surroundings. | Availability regionally restricted. No screening effect. Not a barrier to dogs, children etc unless used with stock wire. |
| *Chestnut paling* | Cheap to transport and widely available in a range of sizes. Flexible and simple to set up. | Can look temporary and jerry-built unless well mounted. Quality may be very poor. |

Garden screens or fences and seats can be made very cheaply from softwood thinnings and split logs and rounds. Materials do not have to be costly to look good – it is thought and imagination which lift this from a cheap job into a feature which strengthens the character of the garden

# ALTERNATIVES FOR BOUNDARIES

| DESCRIPTION | ADVANTAGES | DISADVANTAGES |
| --- | --- | --- |
| *Wooden picket fence* | Versatile; lends itself to individual variations in design and dimensions at reasonable cost. | Traditionally painted, when it will require regular maintenance. Provides only a partial sight screen. |
| *Trellis panels and treillage* | Potentially versatile, can be used to make individual and interesting effects and structures. Excellent support for plants. | Mass-produced, widely available panels look cheap and fragile unless well mounted. Little sight screening. |
| *Wattle panels* | Look at home in country settings, and provide a very sympathetic backing and support for many plants. | Need very strong, firmly based supports. Must be treated with wood preservative to extend their useful life. |

Old floorboards can make a comfortably sturdy, richly textured screen

Picket fencing always looks friendly and welcoming. It defines private space, but makes a chat with passers by or neighbours possible. The tops of the vertical pales can be cut into simple patterns which give individual character to the front garden

## ALTERNATIVES FOR BOUNDARIES

| DESCRIPTION | ADVANTAGES | DISADVANTAGES |
|---|---|---|
| Sawn board panels | Easy to find and available in many sizes and finishes. Make very effective sight screens. Simple to erect. | Mass-production and cost-cutting economies are inclined to lead to poor quality. Very hard to fit agreeably into rural settings. |
| **B Manmade Materials** | Most are widely available, often in a range of sizes, and in forms which make them easy to use. | Often intrinsically unsympathetic to rural settings and to plants. Likely to need imaginative treatments to make them fit in. |
| Artificial stone | Very wide choice of sizes, finishes and effects available, covering almost any requirement. Usually much cheaper to buy and build with than real stone. | Must be carefully chosen and skilfully used to avoid out of place, or brash effects in rural settings. Likely to compare unfavourably if close to natural stone. |
| Bricks | Old and new bricks can be bought in a variety of colours, sizes and textures, to match or complement almost any situation. | Careful selection is vitally important. The colours and textures of some bricks are disagreeably obtrusive in the wrong setting. |
| Pierced concrete blocks | Simple to build with, and provide very effective screens which make good support for plants. | Difficult to combine with traditional or rural settings. Likely to look brash and out of place unless skilfully used. |
| Concrete panels | Need little maintenance and make easily erected, long-lasting sight screens and security fences. | Likely to be ill-set in any traditional village or rural location. |
| Corrugated iron | Widely used in all rural districts to make fences, screens, chicken-runs and stopgaps in hedges. Easy to erect and cheap to buy. | An ugly, utilitarian material that diminishes any setting in which it is used. |
| Wire netting and stock fencing | Makes the cheapest and simplest of stock-proof fences. Not obtrusive if well-sited and supported. | No screening from view or wind. Becomes tatty unless expertly set up and strained. |
| Plastic-covered netting | Useful windbreak and partial sight screen. Can be used to supplement more transparent materials. | A material that does not usually make a sympathetic background for plants in country gardens. |

## SURFACES FOR DRIVES AND PATHS

The gentleman at the front door with an offer of a spare load of tarmac has become one of the characters of the countryside. The load, the story will go, is surplus to a contract up the road. It seldom stretches as far as promised and its arrival invariably depends on the exchange of used tenners. But, dimly aware of the wonderful things that John MacAdam did to make our roads smooth for stagecoaches, we clinch the deal, telling ourselves that a mess of tar and stones rolled flat over the drive is a practical way to cope with mud and weeds and dust and puddles, and that the opportunity offered by the tarry fellow at the front door is too good to be missed.

Being gulled into taking tarmac has become a bit of a habit. We accept it on the driveways, hammerheads and paths around our homes when developers build new houses. We fail to object when local council officials decide on our behalf to spread it over pavements in lanes and side streets where setts, paving and bricks once lent individuality and atmosphere to villages and small country towns.

We comply with proposals to use it down the garden path that leads to the toolshed or the vegetables, the greenhouse or the garage. We accept it because we have been persuaded that it is practical, because we have grown accustomed to it, and because we don't take the trouble to look for alternatives.

If the materials that can be used in a garden to make paths, drives and other surfaces are written down in an order that reflects how well they set off the plants and lawns around them, tarmac comes near the bottom. But we have become so used to this bland, black, featureless substance that we hardly notice it, and in the process have become almost totally undiscriminating and sadly unimaginative in the ways that we use materials for surfaces in general.

This is not because paths and drives are neutral features. They are amongst the most prominent

The materials available for paths and walls, and the ways they can be used, are so enjoyable and rewarding that it is worth considerable effort to search for those that fit the local scene

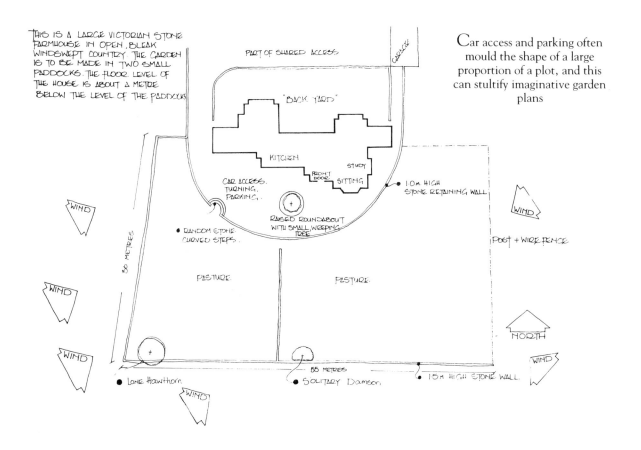

THIS IS A LARGE VICTORIAN STONE FARMHOUSE IN OPEN, BLEAK WINDSWEPT COUNTRY. THE GARDEN IS TO BE MADE IN TWO SMALL PADDOCKS. THE FLOOR LEVEL OF THE HOUSE IS ABOUT A METRE BELOW THE LEVEL OF THE PADDOCKS

PART OF SHARED ACCESS

GARAGE

"BACK YARD"

KITCHEN

FRONT DOOR

STUDY

SITTING

CAR ACCESS, TURNING, PARKING.

1.0 m. HIGH STONE RETAINING WALL

WIND

WIND

• RANDOM STONE CURVED STEPS.

RAISED ROUNDABOUT WITH SMALL WEEPING TREE

POST + WIRE FENCE

30 METRES

PASTURE.

PASTURE.

WIND

NORTH

WIND

• LONE HAWTHORN

55 METRES

• SOLITARY DAMSON

1.5m HIGH STONE WALL.

Car access and parking often mould the shape of a large proportion of a plot, and this can stultify imaginative garden plans

Vehicle access doesn't *have* to be designed like a public road. This layout provides plenty of space for cars without allowing them to dominate the garden

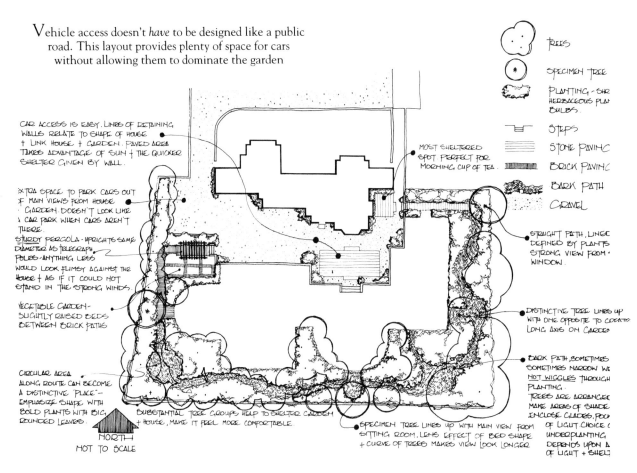

TREES

SPECIMEN TREE

PLANTING - SHR HERBACEOUS PLAN BULBS.

STEPS

STONE PAVING

BRICK PAVING

BARK PATH

GRAVEL

CAR ACCESS IS EASY. LINES OF RETAINING WALLS RELATE TO SHAPE OF HOUSE + LINK HOUSE + GARDEN. PAVED AREA TAKES ADVANTAGE OF SUN + THE QUICKER SHELTER GIVEN BY WALL.

MOST SHELTERED SPOT PERFECT FOR MORNING CUP OF TEA.

STRAIGHT PATH, LINES DEFINED BY PLANTS STRONG VIEW FROM WINDOW.

EXTRA SPACE TO PARK CARS OUT IF MAIN VIEWS FROM HOUSE GARDEN DOESN'T LOOK LIKE A CAR PARK WHEN CARS AREN'T THERE.

STURDY PERGOLA - UPRIGHTS SAME DIAMETER AS TELEGRAPH POLES - ANYTHING LESS WOULD LOOK FLIMSY AGAINST THE HOUSE + AS IF IT COULD NOT STAND IN THE STRONG WINDS.

DISTINCTIVE TREE LINES UP WITH ONE OPPOSITE TO CREATE LONG AXIS ON GARDEN

BARK PATH, SOMETIMES SOMETIMES NARROW WE NOT WIGGLES THROUGH PLANTING. TREES ARE ARRANGED MAKE AREAS OF SHADE ENCLOSE GLADES, POC OF LIGHT. CHOICE UNDERPLANTING DEPENDS UPON A OF LIGHT + SHEL

VEGETABLE GARDEN - SLIGHTLY RAISED BEDS BETWEEN BRICK PATHS

CIRCULAR AREA ALONG ROUTE CAN BECOME A DISTINCTIVE 'PLACE' - EMPHASIZE SHAPE WITH BOLD PLANTS WITH BIG ROUNDED LEAVES.

NORTH
NOT TO SCALE

SUBSTANTIAL TREE GROUPS HELP TO SHELTER GARDEN + HOUSE, MAKE IT FEEL MORE COMFORTABLE.

SPECIMEN TREE LINES UP WITH MAIN VIEW FROM SITTING ROOM, LENS EFFECT OF BED SHAPE + CURVE OF TREES MAKES VIEW LOOK LONGER

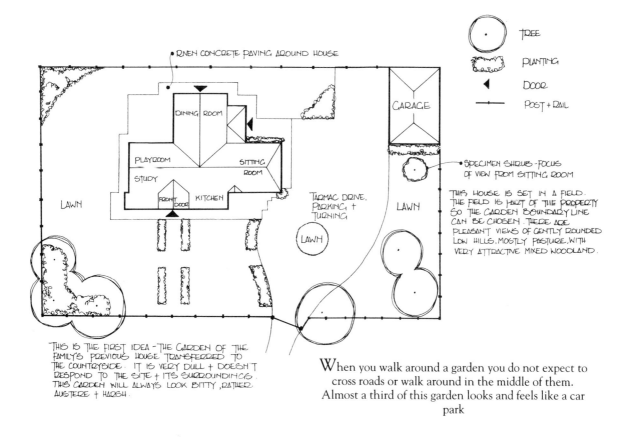

• RIVEN CONCRETE PAVING AROUND HOUSE

DINING ROOM

PLAYROOM  SITTING ROOM

STUDY

FRONT DOOR  KITCHEN

LAWN

GARAGE

TARMAC DRIVE, PARKING, + TURNING

LAWN

LAWN

**LEGEND**

○ TREE

🌿 PLANTING

◀ DOOR

—•— POST + RAIL

• SPECIMEN SHRUBS - FOCUS OF VIEW FROM SITTING ROOM

THIS HOUSE IS SET IN A FIELD. THE FIELD IS PART OF THE PROPERTY SO THE GARDEN BOUNDARY LINE CAN BE CHOSEN. THERE ARE PLEASANT VIEWS OF GENTLY ROUNDED LOW HILLS, MOSTLY PASTURE, WITH VERY ATTRACTIVE MIXED WOODLAND.

THIS IS THE FIRST IDEA - THE GARDEN OF THE FAMILY'S PREVIOUS HOUSE TRANSFERRED TO THE COUNTRYSIDE. IT IS VERY DULL + DOESN'T RESPOND TO THE SITE + ITS SURROUNDINGS. THIS GARDEN WILL ALWAYS LOOK BITTY, RATHER AUSTERE + HARSH.

W̲hen you walk around a garden you do not expect to cross roads or walk around in the middle of them. Almost a third of this garden looks and feels like a car park

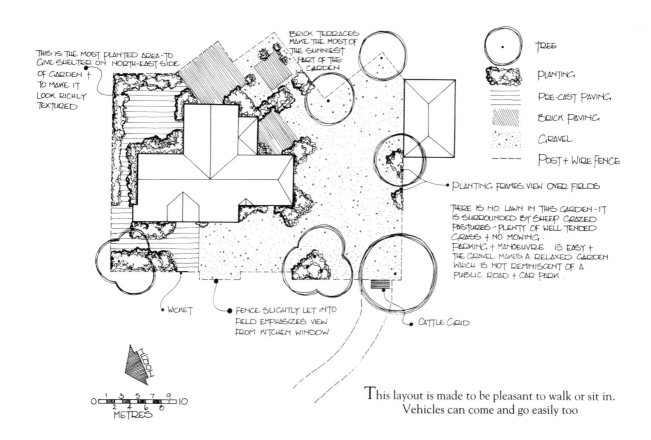

THIS IS THE MOST PLANTED AREA - TO GIVE SHELTER ON NORTH-EAST SIDE OF GARDEN + TO MAKE IT LOOK RICHLY TEXTURED

BRICK TERRACES MAKE THE MOST OF THE SUNNIEST PART OF THE GARDEN

**LEGEND**

○ TREE

🌿 PLANTING

▤ PRE-CAST PAVING

▨ BRICK PAVING

⋯ GRAVEL

--- POST + WIRE FENCE

• PLANTING FRAMES VIEW OVER FIELDS

THERE IS NO LAWN IN THIS GARDEN - IT IS SURROUNDED BY SHEEP GRAZED PASTURES - PLENTY OF WELL TENDED GRASS + NO MOWING. PARKING + MANOEUVRE IS EASY + THE GRAVEL MAKES A RELAXED GARDEN WHICH IS NOT REMINISCENT OF A PUBLIC ROAD + CAR PARK.

• WICKET

• FENCE SLIGHTLY LET INTO FIELD EMPHASIZES VIEW FROM KITCHEN WINDOW

• CATTLE GRID

NORTH

0 1 2 3 4 5 6 7 8 9 10
METRES

T̲his layout is made to be pleasant to walk or sit in. Vehicles can come and go easily too

Cars roll smoothly across many surfaces other than tarmac. They do not need cambered tracks with precisely kerbed edges, and a specification out of a highway engineer's manual

things in the garden, and their appearance affects everything around them, but their importance as major decorative features is seldom appreciated. Their design and materials usually depend on a combination of opportunity, practicality and economy, and the effects on their surroundings are left to chance.

It may be convenient and economical, conventional and functional to surface the path to the front door of a brick cottage with asphalt; to use fragments of old paving stones set in cement to make a crazily paved terrace in front of a house of mortared limestone; to use pink and grey concrete paving slabs in the sunny angle formed by the white-washed walls of a thatched cottage. Local products and materials are often harder to find and more expensive to buy than alternatives which are packaged and marketed throughout the country.

But the use of mass-produced materials in a traditional setting always reduces its individuality, always diminishes its sense of place, and always represents a failure to respond to an opportunity. The materials available for paths and walls, and the ways they can be used, are so enjoyable and rewarding that it is worth considerable effort to search for those that fit the local scene. The range is wide; often one material can be combined with another, not only to create interesting patterns and effects but to blend cheaper products with others that are more expensive.

DRIVES

Cars are demanding, insistent, noisy, smelly, expensive, dangerous and alien to all things rural; they also happen to be one of the greatest single aids to happiness for anyone living in a village or the countryside. They must be pandered to.

Gaps must be made through boundaries to allow them to enter, surfaces laid down over which they can travel and buildings constructed to shelter them, and the neo-rustic lifestyle is such that it will be cars, rather than a car, that need these conveniences. Aesthetics are sacrificed to the geometry of moving cars around, and driveways which are attractive in themselves, or contribute positively to the garden through which they pass, are a rarity.

Firm, well-drained, stable surfaces are essential and these can be expensive to install and to maintain, but there is no reason why drives should be made like mini-motorways. They are conspicuous parts of the garden; the first to be seen and the ones that have the greatest effect on the appearance of the village or countryside around them. They are too important to be left as trimmings chosen by architects and developers, and should always be one of the major responsibilities of the garden's designer.

Currently the unofficial British standard front entrance has factory-made wrought iron gates, painted black, hung on square pillars of mass-produced sand-faced bricks in matching tones, topped with ornamental plastic urns, cement balls

Standard advice for deciding where paths should go is to discover the 'natural routes' by following the tracks made by footsteps in the mud. This very practical approach blandly ignores the impact of well-made, well-designed paths

## MATERIALS FOR PATHS/DRIVES
### and Other Horizontal Surfaces

| MATERIAL | ADVANTAGES | LIMITATIONS |
|---|---|---|
| **Concrete** *Laid in place* *(mix 1:2:4)* | Cheap, easily laid without special skills. Adapts well to awkward shapes and slight slopes. Can be provided with textured surfaces appropriate to uses and surroundings. | Visually uninteresting and can be unattractive. Liable to crack unless the base is very well prepared. Provides a utilitarian rather than decorative surface. |
| *Precast blocks* | Economical and available in a range of complementary sizes to fit different sites and variations in jointing. Can be obtained in a wide variety of surface finishes, colours and effects. | Formal: need to be expertly laid to look satisfactory, on a well-prepared, stable base. Cheaper products likely to look urban or drab. All need great care and imagination if used in informal or rural settings. |
| **Stone** *Precast and reconstituted* | Resembles the effects of real stone more closely than concrete. Cheaper to lay and less expensive to buy than real stone. Available in a range of complementary sizes. Likely to endure frost better than many natural stones. | Usually costs more than concrete blocks. Provides the effect of, rather than being a convincing substitute for, natural stone and seldom weathers so agreeably. Likely to compare unfavourably when used alongside natural stone. |
| *York stone* | Readily available in a range of sizes and finishes, both new and second-hand. Lends itself to informal and attractive jointing patterns. | Can be heavy to handle and very variable in thickness. Likely to be fairly expensive to buy and lay. May be vulnerable to frost, and very liable to become slippery when wet. |
| *Granite* | Hardwearing, and very resistant to weathering and frost. Can be obtained in natural shades of grey, pink and dark green. Combines well with other materials. | Expensive, and demands skilful working to use effectively. Most likely to be available only as setts or small blocks, which limits its range of uses. |
| *Limestones/ sandstones* | Less expensive than most natural stone. Combine well with plants and many other surfaces. Not difficult to lay, and most make non-slip surfaces. Lend themselves to informal paving patterns. | Inclined to be soft and may not weather satisfactorily; some are liable to disintegrate after frost unless expertly laid. |

# MATERIALS FOR PATHS/DRIVES
## and Other Horizontal Surfaces

| MATERIAL | ADVANTAGES | LIMITATIONS |
|---|---|---|
| *Slate* | Hardwearing and very slow to weather. Available in a range of precisely cut shapes, and in a variety of tones. Provides very precise textural contrasts with other surfaces. | Very expensive. Relatively thin and needs careful bedding and expert laying. Liable to become extremely slippery after rain and frost. |
| *Cobbles* | Economical to buy and provide a flexible, varied effect which can be combined with other surfaces to form strong contrasts. Very hard-wearing and long-lasting. | Mostly available as small rounded stones, and can be uncomfortable to walk on. Time-consuming to lay and require a well prepared base. Most suitable for small areas. |
| **Clay** *Tiles* | Available in a wide range of shapes, sizes and colours. Excellent for adding detail and contrast when combined with other materials. | Liable to be very vulnerable to frost. This greatly limits the range that can be used, and the situations where it is practical to use them. |
| *Bricks* | Obtainable in many different colours and textures. Easily laid, and lend themselves to the formation of interesting and varied shapes and patterns. Very flexible in restricted spaces and on gentle slopes. | Liable to disintegrate when frozen so care must be taken to use frost-resistant products. Must be laid on a firm, well-prepared base and kerbed to resist lateral movement. Some become dangerously slippery after rain or frost. |
| **Flexible surfaces** *Gravel* | Cheap and very easy to put down with minimum skill or preparation. Available in a variety of colours, shapes and textures. Adapts readily to odd shapes and sloping sites. Very frost-resistant. | Some kinds fail to produce stable surfaces and are uncomfortable to walk on. Can cause problems when carried onto adjacent lawns. |
| *Asphalt* | Provides clean, trouble-free surfaces at reasonable cost, which are long-lasting and need little maintenance. Very resistant to damage from the weather, and does not easily become slippery. | A material which does not combine attractively with other surfaces, and which does nothing to set off plants. Should be laid professionally on a well-prepared base. Has no intrinsic interest or beauty. |
| *Bark or wood shavings* | Makes an attractive, comfortable surface, which is most appropriate in informal situations. Its resilience and softness make it a good choice for areas where children play. | Can be rather short-lived, unless well bedded and drained. Likely to break down if subjected to heavy traffic. Limited range of effects possible. |

Broad paths can be bold and exciting features, and few qualities are more certain to add distinction to a garden than generosity when specifying the widths of paths

or small moulded lions. The garden on either side is obscured by Leyland cypress hedges: options allow one of the green varieties or Castlewellan Gold, but recent plantings tend to be Gold. Flights of imagination which lead to alternative plants of green and gold suggest confused states of mind in which stylised and eccentric patterns of behaviour are performed simultaneously.

Choosing gates rewards imagination. Simple field gates made of oak or softwood often look good, but it is not expensive to have wooden gates made to a design adapted from something seen elsewhere, or to suit the setting. Metal gates can be wrought to individual designs, handmade by a blacksmith for less than the saving made by forgoing concrete kerbs and a thick layer of tarmac.

Cars travelling slowly roll smoothly across many surfaces other than tarmac. They do not need cambered tracks, with precisely kerbed edges, and a specification out of a highway engineer's manual. The main essential is a firm base to cope with the loads, put down over a permeable membrane to ensure good drainage, and many of the surfaces suggested below for paths can be used ornamentally and practically on drives. These include mixtures of stone flags, paviors, setts, gravel etc, combined in patterns, variations in form, or changes of texture to interrupt the blankness and flatness of the areas which make up drives and the places where cars turn, or stand in waiting.

### PATHS

We use paths to get from one place to another, but in gardens they are also an aid to roaming in comfort while enjoying the plants. Standard advice for deciding where paths should go is to discover 'the natural routes' by doing nothing for a while, and then following the tracks through the mud made by the family going about its daily business. This practical approach takes time and causes a certain amount of inconvenience, even discomfort. It also blandly ignores the impact on a garden of well-made, well-designed paths, and places the gardener's aesthetic capacity on a par with that of a cow walking across a field to the water trough.

The least that should be asked when making a path is:

1 Where should it go?
2 What is it to be used for?
3 How wide should it be?
4 What should it be made of?

A path's destination may not sound like a demanding decision, but it includes the line that the path should follow. The first piece of geometry we are taught, and the last remaining scrap most of us remember, is the theorem that the shortest distance between two points is a straight line. Anyone pushing a loaded barrow, or nipping out on a wet night for a bunch of parsley, is happy to agree and glad to reach journey's end as easily as possible.

Paths that run straight from one part of the garden to another are logically satisfying, and usually visually satisfying too. They raise fears of effects that are too rigid or uncomfortably formal,

but these can be allayed by careful attention to dimensions and scale, by the materials used, and by planting to soften the impact. When straight lines prevail in gardens it is tempting to include curves in paths, and probably also along the edges of lawns and borders. Like all temptations, the ones that incline us to wiggles should be resisted unless surrender is justified by convincing evidence that the rewards will compensate for the fall from grace.

In almost any garden, but especially in large ones, it is a great help to form a 'service network' within the layout of the paths. This forbidding phrase suggests tarmac, kerbs and cambered surfaces on well-engineered, substantially constructed tracks – quite out of keeping with a garden in the countryside. In a gentler sense it means no

Steps provide exceptional opportunities to let our imaginations loose and come up with ideas which not only work well but look good

more than that it should be possible to push a wheelbarrow to all the places where weeds have to be removed, mulches laid, new plants planted, and prunings or leaves collected, without coping with flights of steps, crossing lawns, or pushing past encroaching plants.

The wheel is not an unmixed blessing and wheelbarrows make demands on the design, layout and construction of paths if they are to roll easily. The bonus is that where a wheel runs smoothly a foot finds a firm and pleasant surface to walk comfortably; and the garden becomes more enjoyable and more enticing at any time of the year, but especially when snow, frost or rain make conditions underfoot difficult.

Gardeners have a bad habit of assuming that a lawn is essential and plonking it in the centre of the garden, where it becomes an unavoidable part of any walkabout. The results are bare, muddy entrances where paths and lawn meet, damaged grass after frost, snow or heavy rain, and a choice between wheel ruts across its surface or a ban on the use of the wheelbarrow whenever it is wet. Even in the smallest garden – and even where a lawn is insisted on with great obstinacy – an alternative way is needed which bypasses the lawn with a firm all-weather surface. If stepping stones suggest themselves as the answer to that conundrum, reject the thought and look for more practical solutions which contribute more imaginatively to the appearance of the garden.

The seemliness of paths straight and narrow, and of keeping to them, were drilled into us in our nurseries. They never sounded very comfortable, nor are they. It is the easiest thing to make a path too narrow for comfort, especially when two or three try to walk down it together, and then a minimum of 1.5 or even 2m should be allowed. But paths that are broader still can be bold and exciting features, and few qualities are more certain to add distinction to a garden than generosity when specifying the widths of paths.

In contrast, there are places where paths should be narrow and worm their way from here to there, paths to be traced cautiously, almost on tiptoe, with a feeling of treading through the vegetation in the tracks of some animal. Our sense of order suggests that paths should have parallel sides. But the secretive animal track would be more interesting if its width varied; if it broadened out in places to encourage a pause to look around, and narrowed in others to slip between overhanging plants.

More formal paths, even the most formal, can also be more interesting when they vary in width. They can be composed from squares and rectangles, diamonds and linear shapes, that make a pattern rather than a path and offer alternative ways rather than a predefined track. Materials can be combined to produce a variety of effects, and spaces left where plants provide a third dimension and soften the path's formality.

### MAKING PATHS IN GARDENS

Which brings us to the materials that can be used, the ways paths can be constructed, and the fact that paths are more than skin-deep. A few shovelfuls of gravel, thrown down between lines marking a course across flower beds, and raked smooth, make the skin of a path that can be used in comfort until wet weather and heavy feet squeeze the mud up through its surface, and the path becomes a morass every time it rains.

However constructed, all paths have depth. A light-duty path of wood shavings will be no more than 10cm deep, but bricks or setts and their bed will lie in a trench a full spit's depth. A moment's thought will unearth the fact that this is a trench dug through top soil; the most valuable single asset in the garden. Digging a path releases top soil which can be used to increase the depth of fertile soil in neighbouring flower beds, or barrowed off to be concentrated in a new bed elsewhere. The top soil dug from pathways should never be wasted, and in gardens where thin soils are a problem, making paths can be a handy way to build up fertility in planted areas.

When thinking about making a path, think of it in three parts:

1 There is the **skin** which forms the surface, and which should be agreeable to walk on and preferably attractive to look at. It offers all kinds of alternatives for different treatments, designs and appearances.
2 There is a **supporting layer** or bed, which supplies the mechanical strength to resist the pressure of feet or wheels, and provides channels through which water can drain away from the surface.
3 Beneath both is a **membrane** through which water drains away into the earth below and which prevents mud – the great destroyer of

paths – from being squeezed up through the bed, clogging its drainage channels, and eventually spreading over and spoiling the surface.

The membrane sounds like a complication it would be tempting to do without. In reality it is simple to provide and one of the essentials for success. Woven polypropylene sheet allows water to drain away and prevents particles of clay from moving into and clogging the supporting bed. Polythene sheet is a cheaper, less satisfactory substitute through which holes must be poked to let water drain haphazardly.

The bed is the foundation of paths and drives, and the depth and strength of material needed will depend on:

The stability of the ground beneath the path.

The weight of traffic to be carried.

The material used to make the skin.

A surface of broad paving stones, which distribute the load over a wide area, laid over firm, stable ground, needs no more than a thin layer (5cm) of scalps spread over the membrane to provide a level bed for the flags. Heavy, granite stone setts are similarly undemanding. But a surface made of bricks, which are easily displaced individually, needs more substantial support: 10cm of scalps perhaps, reinforced by an edging or kerb to prevent the bricks moving sideways.

Gravels can be used, preferably those made of flattened stones which support one another or binding gravels held together by a matrix of clay, rather than pea gravels whose rounded surfaces slide past each other to make walking laborious. For most garden paths 10cm of gravel above the membrane is deep enough, but it is more economical to put down a layer of cheap grey scalps, and surface them with 3cm of gravel.

A lorry-load of scalps sounds like a gruesome delivery, but these limestone fragments, ranging from finger-length stones to dust, provide a cheap, easily handled material that makes an ideal foundation for many surfaces, including drives.

A softly comfortable surface to walk on, and one that looks at home in a woodland track or an informal path between trees and shrubs, is made from bark or wood shavings. These last only a short time when laid directly on the surface of the ground, but over a bed of scalps above a membrane they make a serviceable path that need not be renewed for five years or more.

## GARDEN STEPS

At Godspiece Leaze the space for the garden seemed at first to be as level as a croquet lawn. But insignificant wrinkles on the surface were enough to introduce changes in level which added to the garden's interest. Steps need not be grand flights of fancy. A 20cm lift emphasises the change from one part of a garden to another, and 30cm is enough for two or three shallow steps up to a raised platform for a seat, and will turn the view of the garden into a prospect.

Now my garden has banks so steep that falling off them is a hazard. The contrast could not be greater, and instead of trying to discern places where one or two unassuming steps could be formed from a tiny discontinuity the problem is to find anywhere that seems almost level. Few of us are lucky or determined enough to find gardens where the lie of the land provides an ideal balance. Usually we have to scrape and scrimp, literally landscape, to make the most of what we have, and very often this involves making steps to take us from one level to another.

Prosaic and utilitarian in purpose, steps also provide exceptional opportunities to let our imaginations loose and come up with ideas which not only work well but look good: economically or lavishly as the mood or the depth of the pocket may decide.

A rule, perhaps the first rule, of garden planning, should be:

*Always have second thoughts.*

Ideas seldom spring fully formed into the mind. Usually there is a twist or two, or a different approach, that converts half-formed notions into something more interesting or imaginative.

Steps are no exception. The simple, good idea might be straightforward enough – to make some steps from the place where barbecues are held down to the lawn. The thought may be formed at breakfast, and the deed accomplished by lunchtime. A dozen building blocks cemented into place as risers covered with concrete paving slabs to make broad safe treads, and the problem is solved economically and practically.

They may not be beautiful but they seem satisfactory until things that might have been done begin to niggle, and things that are not quite right start to make themselves felt. The steps are a little too narrow, and a threadbare, muddy patch develops where they meet the lawn. They become a natural roost for the family when barbecueing, which leaves no space to walk up and down them. The treads are uncomfortably high, and the paving slabs project a little too far so that a careless ascent leads to a trip or slip. Then their plainness begins to jar; they stick out from the terrace like a jerry-built launching ramp and look hard and obtrusive beside the softness of the grass bank on either side of them. It would have been better if they had been made 2m to the right, when they would have lined up between the French doors and the garden pond to make a short vista down the garden.

Fortunately, hurriedly made steps seldom last long and by the time their shortcomings become intolerable their foundations will have collapsed, and reconstruction will be necessary anyway.

SECOND THOUGHTS WITH STEPS

Steps, like many other features in a garden, provide all kinds of options. They must fulfil the purpose for which they are made, and should do this in a practical way. They should look attractive, and form a pleasant addition in keeping with the part of the garden where they are built. They can be made out of any of a number of materials, and what is used will depend partly on appearance, partly on what is best for the purpose in mind, and partly on cost.

## STEPS: DECIDING ON THE DESIGN

| | PLUSES | MINUSES |
|---|---|---|
| *Treads and risers* | Broad treads and shallow risers are the ideal in a garden. Broad treads are comfortable and feel secure, shallow risers are easy to mount, and the more steps there are the greater their effect on the garden around them. | Steep risers or narrow treads are intimidating, uncomfortable and hard to use safely. They look mean rather than expansive, and can usually be avoided by careful design. |
| *Straights and curves* | Linear designs are simpler to construct, and can be used with almost any of the materials. Curves can be very sympathetic to the garden, and can be used to introduce agreeable shapes and effects. | Straight lines can be very hard, and look uninviting in a garden. Curves are more difficult to build and restrict the range of materials that can be used. |
| *Proportions* | Broad flights maximise the effect of 'opening up' the garden, and allow space for simultaneous use by several people. | Narrow flights look cramped and make little impact. Easily obstructed by people and objects. |
| *Down or across the slope* | Steps running across slopes often look more interesting; extra space may be gained for broad treads. Running down the slope will contribute to a vista, and is a way to provide unity of design. | Crossing the slope takes much more space, and uses more material, which may be uneconomical. Going straight down can result in steep, cramped steps that are neither comfortable to use nor pleasant to look at. |

## CHOOSING MATERIALS

| | PLUSES | MINUSES |
|---|---|---|
| *Bricks* | Easily obtained in a range of colours, textures and finishes. Small and very adaptable, so can be used in many ways. Especially useful for curves. | Have to be well supported with solid foundations to prevent settlement. Care should be taken not to use any which are liable to be slippery when wet, or which disintegrate after frost. |
| *Concrete blocks and slabs* | Easy to find and use. Variety of finishes are available. Most provide non-slip surfaces. Form wide, safe treads which match the scale of broad settings. | Can look very hard; large slabs reduce flexibility of design, particularly on restricted sites. Need very careful use close to traditional materials. |
| *Wood* | Hardwood baulks and old railway sleepers make excellent, comfortable risers, which remain in place with little need for foundations. | Must be treated to prevent wood decay. Rather limited range of effects and uses. Can become dangerously slippery when wet, or in the shade. |
| *Natural stone* | Building stone and setts can tone well with local traditional materials. Adaptable and available in great variety. Combine sympathetically with many plants and with lawns. | Little lateral strength, and good foundations are essential. Likely to be comparatively expensive to buy and build with. Some natural stones become slippery in shade, or when wet. |
| *Gravel* | Can be used very economically and easily to make treads. Combines well with traditional materials and many plants. Never slippery. | Must be well contained by risers. Loose gravels, which pick up on feet and are distributed elsewhere, can become a nuisance. |
| *Poured concrete* | Very easy to use, and flexible, conforming to practically any shape. Non-slip. Textured surfaces can be used to offset drab, unexciting appearance. | Must be well bedded and reinforced to prevent it from settling and cracking; hard and utilitarian unless used with imagination. |

## CHAPTER FIVE

Sunday afternoons were once lazy times when, replete with roast beef and beer, and after listening with half an ear to the discussion of other people's problems on *Gardeners' Question Time*, forty winks in a comfortable chair became the order of the day.

Now Sunday lunch is less of an institution the afternoon is more likely to be spent in pursuit of a good tea. Word has spread that the best can be found at some of the many gardens opened in aid of setaside nurses, emeritus gardeners, the local cottage hospital – if it still exists – and other excellent causes. The tea is the thing, and a chat in pleasant surroundings comes close behind, but few come only for the tea, and most find time to review the garden too.

Some gardens will reveal meticulous planning; others will not only have just happened but still be happening. There will be secret gardens, enclosed and private amongst their plants; some will be practically indistinguishable from the countryside around them. Gardens will be discovered which are nostalgic or innovative; practical or romantic; bright with colour or green and restful; weed-strewn or immaculate; a home for interesting plants or the setting for a lifestyle. They may be part of a country estate redolent of a long-lost muster of gardeners, or tiny spaces behind houses in terraces crammed with the evidence of love affairs with plants.

If you try to earn your tea by attending to the garden; if you do so to get ideas to help you cope with yours; and if you hope to discover the secret ingredients of success, you will probably come away with pleasant memories, a few ideas about plants which looked good on the day, and some inkling of the opportunities before you. You may also be aware of a feeling of helplessness when you compare what you have with what you have seen;

and the solutions to your problems may seem no nearer than before.

The common problem that catches us all out on these visits is that we look at the plants and not the garden. We are carried away by stunning combinations of *Digitalis grandiflora* and *Holodiscus discolor*, *Geranium renardii* and *Sedum spectabile*, and we notice how the spiky leaves of *Acanthus spinosus* emphasise the billowing softness of a clump of *Pennisetum villosum*. We write down all these names; we resolve to improve our own gardens by planting in groups of three or five, and to copy some of the ideas which have taken our fancy.

But the magic properties of plants in threes or fives is an invention – perhaps Beverley Nichols thought of it to lead us up the garden path – and a couple of clumps of a winning combination, even if it behaves as we hope, never made a garden. We saw and noted down ornaments on the mantle-piece, a table lamp, some pictures on the walls, and were so absorbed that we never noticed the walls themselves, the shapes of the rooms and their major furnishings.

We passed from one room to another with our eyes on the ground and never saw how walls or hedges linked the house with the garden and took us from one part to another, or opened up to reveal a view and then closed in again to make a small quiet space. And when we left we had only the haziest idea what plants had been used for hedges, and which trees and shrubs had provided the backgrounds and screens that made the settings for the plants we had been admiring.

Garden visiting is a summer pastime; their owners like to show them off, and we prefer to see them, when bright veneers of colour and foliage add to their attractions. But the structure of the garden and the way it holds the design together may be

# Creating the Garden

Try to measure out vista in kitchen garden, prolonging the paved path, but come up against artichokes and Vita's indignation. Thereafter weed lawn sadly. We have a discussion about woman's rights afterwards.

*Harold Nicolson*

elusive, veiled by the detail. In the early stages of planning a new garden or renovating an old one it is this structure which needs all our attention. The plants, the colour themes and the brilliant juxtapositions we plan to create are things that follow later.

Gardeners suffer acutely from an instinct to shy away from the formalities – many look on them as the pretensions – of design, expressed classically, simply and alliteratively as:

*Form follows function.*

This pre-eminent principle is dismissed by those deeply steeped in the romance of plants as beyond acceptable limits when gardenmaking – a process so creative, so personal, so spiritual even, that it can be done only by fine-tuning intuition to the intimate murmurings of the gardener's psyche. Sitting down with paper and pencil, analysing what is wanted, working out what goes where and making plans, are coldly cerebral activities that should never be a part of gardenmaking.

## THE STRUCTURE OF THE GARDEN

Gardens, like houses, are things of shapes and spaces and creating a garden which is enjoyable and successful has at least as much to do with making comfortable and attractive spaces, as combining shapes imaginatively or collecting an impressive array of unusual plants.

I have likened spaces in gardens to the rooms of houses, but like many comparisons it should not be stretched too far. Spaces in gardens can be limitless or undefined, and interlock or merge with one another in very different ways to the more rigid patterns of rooms, and these possibilities can be used most effectively in country settings.

Spaces and the structural planting which defines them can be used to:

Spring surprises or satisfy expectations.

Form pleasant and comfortable outdoor spaces.

Provide shelter from the house and garden.

Link the house with the garden, and the garden with the landscape.

Create vistas and prospects.

Make appropriate boundaries.

This very simple gate looks welcoming and establishes a distinct character for the garden. This is a DIY gate – style does not have to be expensive

Half a boat, turned on end, makes a shelter for a plank seat. It gives cool shade in hot weather and a cosy nest from which to watch the winter waves

### SPRINGING SURPRISES AND SATISFYING EXPECTATIONS

We are inclined, so I have read, to enjoy gardens more when their design introduces an element of surprise. We enjoy being 'led on' to discover what is hidden around a corner, and are intrigued to reach hidden parts we never guessed existed. Gardens which reveal their all to the first glance are said to be dull and to provide little encouragement for a second look.

That might be true if our gardens were made for explorers, for others to discover rather than for us to enjoy. Leading ourselves on to undiscovered corners of our own gardens poses something of a riddle, and corners and hidden prospects easily become coy tricks, put there in the belief that they are desirable design features. That would not be very exhilarating.

If we are to hide things from ourselves or attempt to lead our visitors on, there must be something round the corner to reward us and humour them when we all take the trouble to go and look for it. It is the garden's structure, including the way it is planted, that produces the most long-lasting effects and can be used most tellingly to make the atmosphere change from one part to another.

A sense of place can be reinforced by the introduction of simple, readily identifiable features, which act as focal points or somewhere to go to:

A pond.
A seat in an arbour.
A pergola leading on to somewhere else.
A roundel of grass enclosed by tall hedges.
A figure carved in wood.
A gazebo or summerhouse.
A bridge over a stream.

---

Features of any kind can be used to form a pattern. It may be a straight line with plants spaced at regular intervals, vertical stems forming a group, a pattern created by a distinctive shrub, or just two trees on either side of an entrance

A sense of place can be reinforced by the introduction of simple, identifiable features, which act as focal points or somewhere to go to

This garden acknowledges, and links with, the surrounding countryside. The field, the hedge and the woodland are as much 'a part of' the garden as the apple tree, the lawn and the shrubs. There is no need to make a solid boundary here – the post and wire fence hardly shows and barely interrupts the view. Post and wire is inexpensive and part of the local scene, so it looks appropriate. It is also practical – the view of sheep and cattle can be enjoyed and, if rabbit netting is also used, the garden is safe from devastation.

The gazebo is made from local reclaimed materials. It is bold and chunky, giving it a feeling of permanence and warmth that most prefabricated garden buildings lack. This garden is very modestly planted – its character is formed by its surroundings, a very few simple shrubs and fruit trees, a relaxed area of grass and the building. A manicured lawn would look sterile in such a friendly setting

On a small island this massive stone throne creates a secure-feeling place to sit and listen to the sea on the shore behind. The stone back and sides also makes a retaining wall. The tree reinforces a sense of warmth and security

Just a few big stones make very effective supports for a slate top. More, but smaller, stones would look fussy unless very expertly arranged. A well-weathered hardwood plank laid over two chunks of stone makes a bench which looks as if it has always been there

It can be done by introducing a predominance of one kind of plant – shrub roses, bamboos, conifers, or trees and shrubs with pinnate foliage. It can be done by the nature of the spaces – in one part hemmed in and small scale, in another expansive and spacious. It can be done with materials – brick or stone or wood can be used deliberately and effectively to mark a part of the garden with a special atmosphere, and make it different from the rest.

As important as surprises is the need to satisfy expectations: hopes raised by the garden should be matched by what the eye encounters. Gardens are not wildernesses, but secure places to wander, sit, relax and garden in! They must convey messages that the place is a garden; that our presence in it is welcome; and that it is there to be enjoyed.

They can be designed and planted to make this obvious, or by small hints or associations that provide an overall unity within the garden and give it a recognisable character and sense of place. This unity is possible even in a garden with many different parts and can be very subtly contrived. It depends on our sense of visual logic which picks out related shapes, colours, textures and forms as patterns that we feel rather than notice, and that tell us the place is as it is by intention, and not the chaos of the wasteland. Visual logic hits us in the eye in formal designs, but in informal gardens the marks of the designer may be very muted.

## LEADING TOWARDS VISUAL LOGIC

| DEVICES | USES |
| --- | --- |

### Symmetry and asymmetry

| | |
| --- | --- |
| Symmetrical arrangements provide very strong visual patterns, which impose themselves on their surroundings and emphasise the hand of the designer. But asymmetry produces understated patterns which create their impressions in very subtle ways. | Symmetry can be emphasised in the ways that paths and other features are arranged, or by regular, ordered and repetitive use of the same plant. Asymmetry is achieved by patterns which offset masses and voids, by one shape beside another, without resorting to close similarities or identities of features, plants, or arrangements. |

### Use of shapes

| | |
| --- | --- |
| Defined angles and curves are not a part of the wilderness and are picked out very readily by the eye, and interpreted by the mind as a sign of deliberate intention. | Any feature – a lawn, a path, a hedge, a pool – whose shape includes straight lines, pronounced curves or defined angles can be used emphatically or subtly to represent order and intention. Plants with pronounced silhouettes – eg topiary, many conifers, and some shrubs and trees – are similarly effective. |

### Introducing patterns

| | |
| --- | --- |
| The eye has a facility for finding patterns and ordered arrangements in recurring features. This can be used to introduce a sense of order, sometimes at very low levels of perception. | A feature of any kind – a plant or group of plants, a colour, texture or form – can be used to form a pattern. It may be a straight line with plants spaced at regular intervals, vertical stems forming a group, a pattern created by a distinctive shrub, or just two trees on either side of an entrance. |

## OUTDOOR SPACES AND ROOMS OUTSIDE

A sheltered corner by the kitchen door that faces east and catches the morning sun is too tempting to ignore, and one morning a table and chairs are set out for an al fresco breakfast. The idea becomes a habit, but shivers when the east wind blows make the thought of shelter appealing. Brown-stained softwood panels provide a quick solution and make the walls of an outdoor dining room. If immediate results were less important, shelter might better have been made by planting a hedge, by setting up a trellis and covering it with climbers, or, less linearly, by surrounding the space with shrubs that would grow tall, laced perhaps with a few trees. If cost was no problem, a brick or stone wall – even concrete blocks or a pierced concrete screen – might have been used. Sitting down to have breakfast in an inviting corner turned out to be the first decisive step towards designing the garden.

Most gardens serve many purposes, and the trick is to find the right place for each one. Some are functional, like where to dump the rubbish; others are part of the garden's role as a playground, or a place to relax in, like the lawn, the sandpit and the terrace. There will be places to garden – borders for flowers and shrubs, raised beds perhaps for vegetables. The first thing to do is to think quietly about how the garden is to be used, and what it will have to provide for: then write down these functions. Some will be space-eaters; others will need no more than a corner.

Then draw a rough sketch plan of the garden – it need not be to scale, and inaccuracies and uncertainties about angles and details will not matter – and cover it with a sheet of tracing paper. Use a felt pen, or some other bold marker equally deterrent to precision or finickiness, and outline places and spaces which the items on the list seem to fit most appropriately. When the first attempt fails, crumple the tracing paper, lay another sheet over the plan and start again. Repeat this – it may be a dozen times – until something about the arrangement of the spaces suggests that the garden is beginning to take shape.

This breaks the ice. It gives an idea of what will be done where, and the structure will begin to emerge. You will see where paths will be needed to link one area with another; where screens of various sorts would hide or shelter or mark a division; where trees or large shrubs would be useful, and where there are spaces which seem right for lawns or drives or pools.

## SHELTER FOR HOUSE AND GARDEN

Buried lumps of concrete, mud and spoilation all around are among the problems bequeathed us when we move into new houses, but even more forbidding is their exposure. There is a pressing need for shelter – from the winds, from passers-by, to sit in the sun and enjoy a snooze.

Unsurprisingly, the immediate response is to set up a fence or buy a hedge, and equally unsurprisingly the defences constructed are inclined to be excessive, and grow to be the most conspicuous part of the domain. In country gardens especially, trees and conifers planted long ago on the boundaries can be grotesquely overdeveloped. They form grey/green ramparts that isolate the garden from the countryside, and their shadows, greedy roots and overwhelming presence leave little scope for gardenmaking.

The fringes of the garden are not the places to set things going, however urgent the need to protect the boundaries may seem. The ideas worked out for the ways different parts of the garden are to be used will suggest the screening needed to make each work effectively, and the space outside the kitchen door that provides a pleasant spot for breakfast is as good a starting point as any.

The first lesson will be the discovery that a 1.6m fence around this little space makes it cosier and more sheltered and private than a 6m barrier on the boundary. Any kind of shelter works best when very close to the place it is intended to harbour. Other spaces in other places will need screens and planting of one kind or another – dividing the garden into useful sections, making one part separate from another, and providing whatever privacy is needed in each, so that the boundaries and the internal arrangements of the garden unite as part of an overall design.

Any kind of shelter works best when very close to the place it is intended to harbour; no one place, let alone an expanse of unshaded paving, provides sunlight or shadow, shelter or screening, at the right moments and in just the right proportions. The most practical way to achieve this is to make several little retreats

## LINKING HOUSE WITH GARDEN AND GARDEN WITH LANDSCAPE

Dreams picture country cottages nestling in hidden valleys, veiled by hedges of sweetbriar, or snuggled into clearings amongst trees on hillsides, when a haze of wood-smoke from the chimney is often to be discerned. Ideal homes in the country do not stick out like lighthouses but form a part of the rural scene around them. Never mind that many fall short of such dreams; the idea of using the garden to link the house with its surroundings is an interesting and worthwhile one to explore.

Walls, trellises, pergolas, terraces and hedges can all be made to reflect the materials or shapes of a house, and link it with the plants in the garden. All can be arranged to form comfortable places to walk about or sit in, shaded on hot days and sheltered from rain and cold winds. But having decided to make a terrace or patio – depending on how you were brought up – there is a danger of falling for the grand design. Impressive sweeps of york stone,

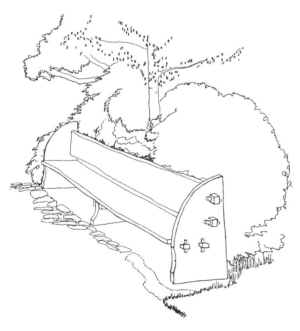

Twiddles and twirls would look weak in a woodland garden. There is no need for decorative flourishes here. This long elm bench can seat seven people – it needs to be strong, and looks solid and reassuring. Being outside all through the year only improves its looks. Don't scrub the green off it – it is in a woodland garden, not on the patio

concrete crazy paving, even fine brick paviors – terraces made in the spirit of promenades along the front of Edwardian mansions – are more likely to leave the house stranded and isolated than link it with the garden, and are less than cosy, inviting places in which to settle down.

There are few idyllic days each year, and very few hours each day, when it is a pleasure to sit out unprotected or unsheltered. But a small sunlit corner, a spot beneath a light canopy of leaves, or a seat in the lee of a screen, will tempt an hour or two's relaxation many times every year and in almost any month of the year.

No one place, let alone an expanse of unshaded paving, provides sunlight or shadow, shelter or screening, at the right moments and in just the right proportions. The most practical way to achieve this is to make several little retreats. The sunlit corner for breakfast by the kitchen door has made its appearance. A vine-clad pergola might make a pleasant place to have lunch, or sit in a chair and read the paper out of the midday sun. A corner backed by a sun-warmed wall, opposite the setting sun, open to the skies but close to overhead cover, could be used for a barbecue or a drink in the evening. Afternoon tea was once an excuse for pleasant dalliance, and the custom might be revived by finding a tea place too. None of these spaces need be large: smallness and intimacy are part of their atmosphere, and each provides inspiration for planting themes which can be extended into the garden as starting points for more distant layouts and planting patterns.

A century ago William Robinson and Reginald Blomfield argued the merits of the formal garden. Robinson championed the natural style and would say nothing in favour of the discipline and order of prescribed forms; and Blomfield as pig-headedly defended the virtues of formality and refused to approve of more relaxed approaches to design. But when Robinson made his own garden at Gravetye Manor, the parts which lay close to the house were as formal as could be. Sir Reginald, moving to a cliff-top house and garden, revealed a taste for informality.

Proponents of the formal and informal in gardens are and always have been two opposing camps; and sometimes one predominates, sometimes the other. Those less involved in the argument than Robinson and Blomfield have proposed a compromise which sometimes appears as a prin-

A homemade gazebo constructed from pressure treated
softwood and mild steel strips – not elaborate or
expensive, just an imaginative use of standard materials.
It is made to look more dressed-up with a small panel of
herringbone brick paving, used rather like a rug on a
cheap gravel carpet. *Vitis vinifera purpurea* makes an
ever-changing roof; small-leaved ivies are grown
underneath and over a seat, as well as up the wall. A
low, clipped box hedge helps to make the corner feel
private without blocking out the view

ciple of garden design. They suggest that the formal parts of the garden should adjoin the house,
and more natural features should be kept away from
it. This feeble compromise cripples the power of
formality and informality to introduce exciting,
contrasting elements in a garden's design. It puts
convention in the place of the tensions and interactions which contribute to mood and atmosphere and a feeling of individuality.

Prejudice, rather than some principle of design,
should be suspected whenever it is suggested that
informal or natural styles of gardening should be
avoided close to the house. It is prejudice that in-
sists that freedom of form and lack of regularity
make untidy settings for homes, and sees trimness,
order and predictability as visible guarantees of the
status and respectability of the occupants.

The same prejudice leads those who judge com-

petitions for best-kept villages to award points
when every grass bank has been neatly strimmed,
every garage is adorned with hanging baskets full of
colourful annuals, and public conveniences are
flamboyantly hidden behind contrasted masses of
crimson and gold berberis and Canadian elder. It is
a prejudice that encourages the invasion of villages
by suburban styles of gardening, and dismisses
idioms borrowed from the countryside around the
village as untidy.

## MAKING THE MOST OF VISTAS AND PROSPECTS

A familiar countryside puzzle is posed by hopes of
preserving an attractive view while providing
enough shelter for life in the garden to be bearable
for its owner and its plants. The choices lie
between seclusion and privacy with compartments
and hidden corners, and openness and accessibility
with connecting vistas and the prospect of the
countryside beyond the fence.

These decisions are fundamental to the nature of
the garden and its atmosphere, and depend on how
it will be used and the owner's personal opinions of
the contribution to health and happiness of
seclusion and shelter, at the expense of the
pleasures of extensive views.

The inescapable problem is that wide prospects
across country, particularly when they face the
direction of prevailing winds or a quarter open to
cold winds, leave the garden exposed. The enjoyment of unrestricted views and sheltered gardens
are mutually incompatible, and decisions have to
be made on which is to be preferred.

1  The view is accepted as the major feature of the
   garden's appeal; designing and landscaping are
   done with that in mind, and plants and features
   suited to exposed positions are chosen.
2  One or two small, enclosed, sheltered areas are
   made as close to the house as possible, but
   elsewhere the view has priority when planning
   and planting.
3  Gardens are made to enclose and shelter most of
   the area around the house, with chosen spots
   where vistas open out to provide wide-ranging
   views across the countryside.
4  Shelter and seclusion within the garden are top
   priorities, and access to the view is restricted to
   points on the periphery – even, perhaps, to windows on the upper floors of the house.

## FORMING THE STRUCTURE

Bulbs in spring or annuals in summer make their point briefly and are gone. Misjudgements are short-lived and effects which are boldly colourful, blatantly flashy or riotously vulgar, and would pall if more permanent, are enjoyable for a short time. The structure planting has to be taken more seriously; mistakes or false starts are more significant and cannot so easily be put right.

A beginning, however tentative, irrevocably influences all that follows, and that beginning becomes a dauntingly fraught step! How should we take it? Sooner or later a survey and the production of a scale plan might be helpful. Sooner might be better than later. But formal plans are inclined to ossify ideas, and this is still a time for generalities and broad principles. At this stage there is no need, for instance, to decide exactly where hedges will run and what they should be made of – better to delay such details and simply attempt to:

1 Identify places where screens of some kind, which might be hedges, are needed.
2 Decide in what directions they should run.
3 Decide how long and how high they need to be.
4 Think about whether they are needed urgently or in due course.

Broad ideas of this kind need to be sorted out wherever changes are to be made, and this can be done with least effort and most freedom on sketch plans, like the one used earlier to decide roughly what should be done where. They should be drawn freehand, quickly and boldly, to represent the shape of the garden; its relationship with the house and its surroundings; its main features – good and bad – and anything else that seems to be relevant.

Perhaps we have a house in mind. Not a secluded cottage in an idyllic setting, of the kind that country-retreaters dream of, but a nineteenth-century product of industrialisation, and the improvements in transport brought by the canals and the railways. Surrounded by a garden of about 0.25ha (2/3 acre) it stands on the edge of a village in the south Midlands. The house is detached,

Afternoon tea was once an excuse for pleasant dalliance and the custom might be revived by finding a tea place too

about a hundred and twenty years old, and made of brick with a slate roof.

Neither picturesque nor unattractive, it conveys a gaunt, manufactured look, which sets it apart from the older houses made of a tawny limestone out of nearby quarries. Until recently it stood on its own beside a lane, but a small housing development during the past two years has destroyed what little seclusion the garden ever possessed. The soil is a fertile, water-retentive heavy clay loam, but drains adequately and is never waterlogged; it has a high pH which makes it unsuitable for plants which dislike lime. The ridge on which the village stands is about 100m high, exposing it to east winds but providing the benefits of freedom from spring and autumn frosts, and a long growing season.

The house has recently been sold, and its owners feel the presence of the new houses overlooking them from the other side of the lane; they suffer the chilly effects of their exposed position on the ridge when the east wind blows; and they are dissatisfied with the uninteresting appearance of the garden.

They have made a sketch plan to help them work out the structure of their new garden. Walking about in the garden has given them the feeling of distinct sectors, which have their own problems and provide their own opportunities. The key decision has been made to build on these differences and develop the garden as three separate but interlinked areas.

### AREA ONE

This area faces east with long views across country and is very exposed to the east wind. It is overlooked by the windows of the kitchen and breakfast room and contains only a few neglected, rather uninteresting plants, in addition to the semi-mature trees shown on the plan. A dilapidated old field hedge provides little shelter.

### AREA TWO

The second zone lies between the lane and the north side of the house on each side of the drive. It provides the outlook for the dining room windows, but is overlooked by the new houses across the lane. A stone wall running along the boundary with the lane is an attractive feature but too low to act as a screen. The garden on each side of the drive consists of lawns and borders filled with roses, various shrubs and herbaceous plants. A greenhouse stands in one corner.

AREA THREE

The French doors of the sitting room on the west side of the house lead onto an apology for a lawn, embellished by three old apple trees and bounded by a five-year-old Leyland cypress hedge. Beyond the hedge there is an ancient, slightly run-down orchard, and in the middle distance an attractive view of some of the older houses and the church in the village.

All that is wanting now are flights of fantasy to fuel the inspiration that will set off the planning processes. Instead we look blankly at the garden. If we are rash enough to be doing this with our spouse, disagreements start even before there is anything to disagree about, and the few ideas that had begun to emerge grow feebler and less inspirational by the minute. Something is needed to get things going and the most likely way to do that is to ask questions that are easy to answer, but lead on to others which have to be thought about a bit, and eventually to more searching ones which hold the key to the ideas which are so elusive.

Start with something practical. Planning a

garden consists of finding a balance between ideas which will make the garden beautiful, and the day-to-day practicalities which will make it possible. The practicalities are more likely to be familiar ground. Phrase the questions so that they lead to responses which comment on the situation and clarify what is wanted, rather than to a mere 'yes' or 'no'.

Questions that might helpfully be asked are shown below, with comments on their implications. Sometimes situations will be very precisely defined by the responses and pinpoint the few plants with the particular qualities needed. Other responses will leave more freedom of choice. Possible responses shown below are labelled A, B, C and D, and in each set A indicates situations that would most restrict the variety of plants meeting the needs expressed; subsequent letters indicate progressively more flexible situations.

HOW MUCH TIME CAN BE SPENT LOOKING
AFTER THE GARDEN?

This is a time for realism – there may be better things to do than garden, advancing years may

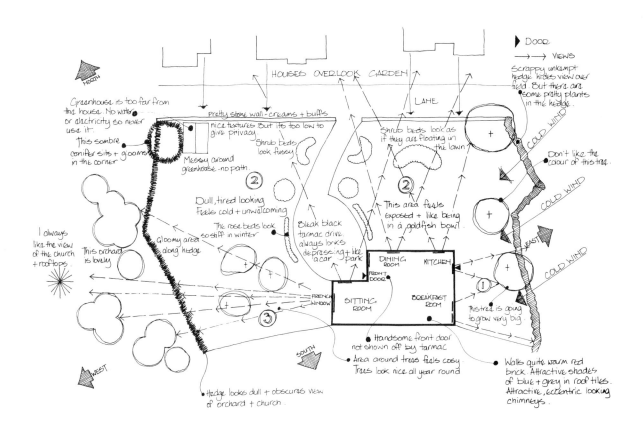

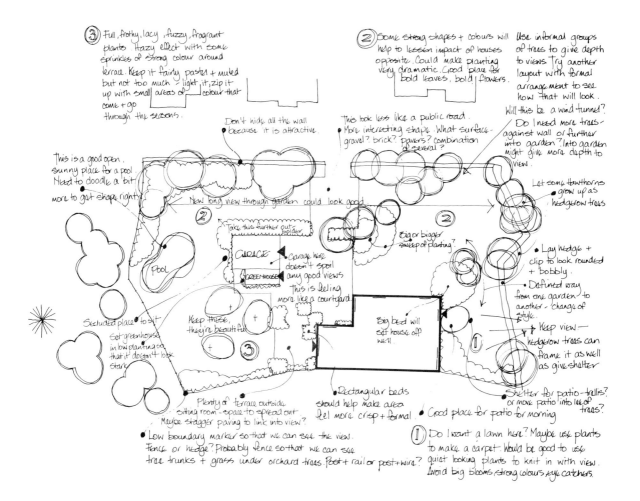

③ Full, frothy, lacy, fuzzy, fragrant plants. Hazy effect with some sprinkles of strong colour around terrace. Keep it fairly pastel + muted but not too much, light it, zip it up with small areas of colour that come + go through the seasons.

Don't hide all the wall because it is attractive.

This is a good open, sunny place for a pool. Need to doodle a bit more to get shape right.

② Some strong shapes + colours will help to lessen impact of houses opposite. Could make planting very dramatic. Good place for bold leaves, bold flowers.

This look less like a public road. More interesting shape. What surface - gravel? brick? pavers? combination of several?

Use informal groups of trees to give depth to views. Try another layout with formal arrangement to see how that will look. Will this be a wind tunnel? Do I need more trees - against wall or further into garden? Into garden might give more depth to view.

Let some hawthorns grow up as hedgerow trees

New long view through garden could look good

Take this further out

Garage here doesn't spoil any good views. This is feeling more like a courtyard.

GARAGE

GREENHOUSE

Big or bigger sweep of planting?

Lay hedge + clip to look rounded + bobbly.

Defined way from one garden to another - change of style.

Keep view — hedgerow trees can frame it as well as give shelter

Secluded place to sit. Set greenhouse in low planting so that it doesn't look stark.

Keep these, they're beautiful

③

Pool

Big bed will set house off well.

①

Shelter for patio - trellis? or more patio into lee of trees?

Plenty of terrace outside sitting room - space to spread out. Maybe stagger paving to link into view?

Rectangular beds should help make area feel more crisp + formal.

Good place for patio for morning

Low boundary marker so that we can see the view. Fence or hedge? Probably fence so that we can see tree trunks + grass under orchard trees. Post + rail or post + wire?

① Do I want a lawn here? Maybe use plants to make a carpet. Would be good to use quiet looking plants to knit in with view. Avoid big blooms, strong colours, eye catchers.

make gardening no easier, and the trouble and expense of paying someone else to look after the garden may be unwelcome. Should some parts, or even the whole garden, be deliberately designed to be as easy as possible to look after?

A Very little time available. All plants should be able to grow with the least possible care and attention.
B Limited time available and the amount of care needed will be very significant when choosing plants.
C Sufficient time available to look after a number of plants which will need special attention of one sort or another from time to time.
D Amount of care and attention required will be of no significance when choosing which plants to grow.

## DOES THE GARDEN NEED SHELTER OR SCREENING?

Plants, walls, hedges etc can provide visual screens, shelter from the wind, divisions within the garden, and backgrounds to planted areas. Are any of these needed? Where, and how high/dense should they be?

A Substantial screens are essential, and take precedence over all other needs.
B A major need for which provision must be made, subject to visual impact within and beyond the garden.
C Some screening or shelter to be included as part of the garden's design.
D Screening or shelter not needed or even undesirable.

## HOW IMPATIENTLY ARE RESULTS REQUIRED?

There will be parts of the garden where the need for effective structure planting is urgent; others where delays are less important. If priorities can be established they will lead to decisions about how the work should be organised and the kinds of plants needed.

A Rapid development with the least possible delay a first priority.
B Effects required quickly and time to maturity a significant point when choosing plants.
C No pressing need to include plants with other than average rates of growth.
D Rate of growth much less important than achieving the visual effects required.

## HOW PERSISTENT AND DURABLE SHOULD THE PLANTS BE?

If the garden is very exposed, in a frost pocket, by the sea etc the plants have to be restricted to those able to survive the conditions; when low maintenance is a priority, plants which are likely to need constant replacement should be avoided. In more favoured situations, or where more time is available, persistence and durability may not be important.

A Above average longevity, total hardiness and disease resistance are qualities of first importance.
B Plants should be reliably hardy, long-lived and easily grown.
C The plants chosen might include some with less than average persistence, if otherwise suitable.
D Longevity and persistence much less important than other qualities, particularly appearance.

Once answers to these practical problems have been found, thoughts can turn to what the garden might look like – not in detail, but in terms of the general impression that is intended. For instance:

## DO EXISTING FEATURES PROVIDE A GUIDE FOR THE FUTURE?

The garden itself, or its surroundings, may have a character and atmosphere which should be preserved and taken into account when planning the new planting. There may be existing features which could be emphasised; others might be better played down.

A A situation where it is very important to choose plants which complement or enhance existing features.
B Local atmosphere significant and should not be diminished by the planting.
C Responding to 'the spirit of the place' desirable, but not at the expense of other objectives.
D No reason why the location of the garden, or its surroundings, should influence the choice of plants grown in it.

## WHAT OVERALL EFFECTS ARE WANTED?

The garden might be designed to make a striking, dramatic impression with strong contrasts of colour, shape and scale; or something quieter might be appropriate, in which the effects depend on harmonies and matching colour themes and forms.

A Striking and dramatic with strongly defined, and often contrasting, shapes, colours and textures.
B Strong forms, including some contrasts. Intended to create an emphatic and positive impression.
C A few contrasts between forms and textures, but the overall impression would be of harmonies rather than contrasts.
D Harmonies prevail to provide an overall feeling of quiet unity, and a generally understated background to the plants in the garden.

The answers to the questions should identify problems and effects which are wanted, and tell us what qualities will be needed by plants in different parts of the garden. The result is a profile which can be used to match the qualities needed with the plants that are available. Profiles for the three areas of the garden around the brick-built house in the south Midlands appear on pp76–7. The letter at the beginning of each paragraph refers to the responses to questions in the earlier analysis.

## THE GARDEN EMERGES

The garden is beginning to take shape. Much of the detail is still obscure, but as we might just discern a crocodile in a murky pool from the curve of a tail, the scaly texture of its body and glimpses of a bright eye that glints ominously from time to time, so we can now tell where hedges or screens could be placed, identify spaces where grass and formal planting might be effective, and foresee some of the problems that lie ahead.

Each area has a profile describing:

How it will be used.
The qualities needed by the plants.
What it is going to look like.

And that is what we need to fill in the features and structures that will give the garden its shape and character.

### AREA ONE: THE VIEW TO THE EAST

This space between the house and the old field hedge on the east side of the garden begins to look quite straightforward. The profile calls for simple, self-sufficient planting to link the garden with the countryside. The plants must be hardy, lime-tolerant and long-lived, and some must be able to grow in dry, infertile positions under trees. Brilliantly exotic effects are not called for, and this is a suitable place for casual, natural styles of gardening using native species of trees and shrubs, with some exotics to lift the planting.

The neglected field hedge looks like a problem. It would be a major undertaking to grub it out and plant a new hedge in its place. But it is at one with the countryside and fits the profile for this part of the garden, provided it can be restored to health and vigour. It will be cleaned out, topdressed with fertiliser and, if possible, brashed or laid. If it is too far gone, it will be cut to the ground and encouraged to produce new shoots that can be laid in a few years time – in the meanwhile it, and the garden, will be protected by a post and rail fence and sheep netting. Once the framework of a good hedge has been re-established it will be formed into a round-topped, close-knit hedge kept in shape by an annual short-top-and-sides.

The three trees, planted – or just allowed to grow – by a previous owner, are good-looking healthy trees beyond adolescence and bordering on a vigorous middle-age, but they are dubious assets in spite of these qualities. Left where they are they would grow to dominate this end of the garden, shutting out much of the view and reducing the ground beneath them to a semi-desert of dry shade. These prospects bear no resemblance to the profile for this part of the garden. The choice lies between keeping them and giving up the options identified

in the profile, or removing at least two of them and going ahead with the plans for the garden.

There remains the question of the breakfast spot! Somewhere very close to the house, facing east or south-east for the morning sun, and sheltered. The place exists; the south-east corner of the house beside the kitchen is ideal and might be paved. The shelter does not, and a small enclosure would have to be made here; perhaps with creeper-covered trellis around it, and a screen of taller shrubs beyond the trellis.

### AREA TWO: BESIDE THE LANE

This will be an important part of the garden with bright, colourful planting and scope for doing things and trying out new ideas. But before those pleasures become possible, it has to be sheltered from the east wind and screened from passers-by.

The drive is a problem. This graceless splodge of threadbare tarmac divides the area and laps against the house, providing an unobstructed view from outside into the heart of the garden. It was a hasty and unconsidered adjustment to the arrival of the car during the 1930s, when, flanked by lawns and rose beds, it embodied the stereotyped front garden of the time. As it is, it destroys all hopes of making the place inviting.

The remodelling of the drive, the choice of plants to form a sight screen along or close to the wall by the lane, and the need for shelter from the east wind are practical problems. But the ways they are dealt with will have major visual effects on an important part of the garden, and must combine gracefully and attractively.

Overlooked until now is the greenhouse. Like many of its kind it has no proper path to it, no electricity supply, no supporting facilities such as cold frames, and no source of water apart from an inadequate water butt. Is it needed? Is it needed where it is, can it be fitted into the profile for this part of the garden, and can its deficiencies be remedied?

Its presence is no argument that it should remain where it is. Somebody else put it there, somebody else may have made a mistake, somebody else may have had reasons for putting it in that corner. Those reasons no longer apply, and have nothing to do with whether it will be in the right place in the new garden, whether it will be easy to reach and practical to run, and whether it is wanted at all.

## AREA THREE: LOOKING ACROSS THE ORCHARD TO THE VILLAGE

This brings us to the grass on the west side of the house, the three old apple trees and the thriving, dog-legged Leyland cypress hedge, which even in youth almost conceals the village houses and church beyond the orchard. Whatever may have been the reasons for planting it and for its distinctive layout, it is clear from the profile that the hedge is no longer needed. It should be removed as soon as possible, and replaced with a see-through boundary – perhaps squared oak posts with cleft rails. The garden itself will be allowed to take shape during the next two or three years, making the most of the old apple trees and responding to a setting in which the shapes of the houses in the village are an attractive feature.

The garden will have a formal structure based on a grid of straight paths at right angles to each other, leading from a small terrace outside the sitting room door. The beds between the paths will be filled with plants: particularly hardy perennials, shrub roses and smallish shrubs; and among them many herby, aromatic things that spill out over the paths and intermingle with one another to offset and soften the formal patterns of the paths.

The new owners of the garden had hoped to find space for a pond. The removal of the Leyland hedge makes room for one between the old orchard and the formal garden to the west of the house. This is a good place; the lie of the land is right, and a pond with a more or less regular bank along the side nearer to the garden and a more irregular outline on its far side will link the strong grid of paths with the more casual forms of the orchard. It would

## PROFILES FOR THE THREE AREAS OF THE GARDEN

| AREA ONE | AREA TWO | AREA THREE |
|---|---|---|
| | *Time available to look after the garden* | |
| A Everything possible should be done to reduce maintenance in this area; partly because it needs to be kept open to preserve the view, but also to provide time to spend in more interesting parts of the garden. | D This is to be the 'gardened' part of the garden, and its design and layout should provide scope to try out new ideas and new planting schemes. | B A feeling of permanence and tranquillity is needed here. So far as possible the plants in this area should be capable of achieving this without repeated or constant care. |
| | *Shelter from wind and screens from view* | |
| C The view from the kitchen window is more important than protection from the wind. A small, sheltered nook is needed close to the house for breakfast on sunny mornings. | B Effective screening urgently wanted close to the wall to provide more privacy for the whole of the front garden. Protection from the east wind also essential. | D The view across the old orchard to the village is peaceful and rural, and the existing Leyland hedge disrupts an attractive scene. The situation provides sufficient privacy without the hedge. |
| | *The time taken to grow large enough to be effective* | |
| B This part of the garden is dull and depressing. It does not need a great deal done to improve it, and the sooner it is attended to the better. | A Something is wanted very quickly indeed to reduce this area's goldfish-bowl quality. This is the area where most of the gardening is to be done, but at present it is too public to make that much fun. | D This is already quite a pleasant corner, in which new effects and new planting can be gradually introduced and allowed to develop without any need for urgency. |

also add the security of a moat against intruders – animal or human – from that direction, without obstructing the view.

## MAKING A SCALE PLAN

Armed with a profile, with ideas beginning to flow, and the layout starting to take shape, the question crops up once again – what about making an accurate scale plan?

It is easy to put off the idea, and succumb to the temptation not to bother. Plans need skilful interpretation, and garden plans demand leaps of imagination to extract even a hint of the appearance of the gardens they represent. The lines on the page have little obvious connection with the subtle combinations of colour, texture and shape that make a garden, and the imagination, or experi- ence, needed to interpret them limit their value as an aid to garden design.

The short answer to the question of whether it is worth making a scale plan is, 'Probably yes'.

But it may be worth first spending a little time doing other things, which make it easier to visualise the heights and contours of the planned planting. The simplest is to go back into the garden and spend time in it – time on site – getting the feel of it, poking into its assets and limitations, finding out exactly where and when the sun shines strongest, and all the other things introduced in previous chapters, but now with new ideas in mind.

A hosepipe is the design aid most frequently ad- vised during this stage: it can be laid on the ground and used like an enormous French curve to trace the course of future flower beds. It is advice that

---

### PROFILES FOR THE THREE AREAS OF THE GARDEN

| AREA ONE | AREA TWO | AREA THREE |
|---|---|---|
| | *Persistence and durability of the plants* | |
| A  Exposure to the east wind makes very hardy plants essential here. The need for low maintenance demands that time is not spent replacing losses. | C  The major screening plants must be permanent. Otherwise, this is an area for attractive plants which may occasionally have to be replaced. A balance must be reached between maintaining a feeling of seclusion, and the need for a visually exciting garden. | B  The intention here is to develop a garden where defined shapes and forms are predominant. This will take time to achieve, and will become effective as it matures. Longevity and reliability are important qualities when choosing plants for this area. |
| | *The need to pay attention to existing features* | |
| B  The views across country are to be preserved, and plants and forms of planting which do not disrupt them must be used. | D  The gardens of neighbouring houses already make a piecemeal, disjointed effect, and there is no need to take account of the setting or existing features in this area. | A  The garden here is adjacent to, and could be a part of, a village scenario full of atmos- phere and style. This must be a major influence guiding the way the garden is laid out and planted. |
| | *The overall appearance of the garden* | |
| D  Quiet, natural planting, which blends the garden with the country beyond. An emphasis on harmonies of shapes and textures, with contrasts of scale to provide variety. | A  This is the place for colour and bold effects which hold attention within the garden, and offset its north-facing aspect. Strong colour contrasts in foliage of shrubs and trees could provide the desired effects. | B  A mixture of formality and informality, in which a structure of strong shapes and a firm design to set off the view of the village will combine with soft planting (including the old apple trees). Traditional forms based on yews and box brushes would fit well. |

should be resisted. Hosepipes have wilful natures that incline them to bend only according to their own preferred patterns of arcs and curves, and to impose their own geometry on the shape of a garden. Their uses are limited. On the flat surface of a lawn they may achieve an elegant kidney-shaped bed: on broken ground or amongst shrubs, and in places where hedges or walls intervene, they make little impression and are easily led astray.

Far better to obtain a bundle of bamboo canes and a large roll of brightly coloured polypropylene twine, and outline new paths, borders, hedges and walls by canes driven into the ground with twine between them.

Try to visualise ideas by making sketches too. Freehand sketches, however inexpertly done, of views across the garden from different places within it focus dreams and turn them into projects. The sketches need not be artistic affairs with delicate shading. Instead tape large sheets of paper to a piece of hardboard and use felt pens – coloured ones as well – to mark in boldly what is there and, even more boldly, overlay those outlines with the shapes and masses of the garden you have in mind. Spend a morning making pictures from here, there and anywhere – none may merit framing but it may be a surprise to discover how enjoyable the exercise is, and what a font of ideas it releases.

A sense of place can be reinforced by ornament. This stone sculpture, lying in a woodland garden, is called Fallen Leaf

Now! Back to that accurate plan and why, even if attempts at sketching have revealed unimagined artistic abilities, it is still worth the trouble to make one. It will help to:

*Visualise spaces in the garden:* The spaces in a garden, which are such a vital part of its composition, are the one element in its design which are easier to visualise on a two-dimensional plan than in any other way.

*See it as it might be, rather than as it is:* Features already present in a garden can make it almost impossible to imagine the place without them. When plans are drawn features can be included or excluded at will.

*Try out alternatives quickly and easily:* Any number of alternative possibilities can be tried out on a plan. Use overlays of tracing paper, and draw in ideas to find out which seem most appropriate.

*Compose details of layout and design:* A plan shows exactly how much space there is for the features which are to be included. These can be arranged and rearranged, and their dimensions adjusted, to find the most convenient and agreeable ways to fit them in.

*Plan vistas and arrange prospects:* Existing features – trees, walls, buildings etc – may obscure possible views through the garden, which can be traced more easily on a plan.

*Prepare detailed planting plans:* Whether planning a noble avenue or a simple bedding scheme, details of which plants should go where are easily worked out on a plan. In particular, it provides a quick and easy way to try out variations and different effects.

*Estimate costs of ideas and alternatives:* The numbers of trees and shrubs; the number of square metres of herbaceous plants, paving, or paths; and the amount of walling that will be needed can be read off a plan and used to estimate costs.

A plan can be drawn to scale only after surveys have been done and measurements obtained. How much easier it would be to use an Ordnance Survey map or, if one is handy, a plan produced by a builder or an architect. Sometimes these suffice, but other people's plans may not be quite what is wanted. Gardeners are interested in details which often do not appear on them at all; it can be practically impossible to work with them effectively, making changes, adding or taking away one thing or another; the scale may not be convenient for planting plans; and they may be out of date. Sundry plans from architects and builders, whose interests lie in houses rather than gardens, can be imaginative productions, even though they carry no little notes in their remoter corners saying 'Here be Dragons'.

Far better to take the plunge, do a survey and make a plan. It's not difficult; it's interesting to do, and the result is very, very useful. An accurate way to survey a garden, which can be done without calling for help from a press-ganged partner; is described in Appendix A.

## THE PLANTSMAN'S CON

A garden is the space around the house; a space which is there to be used in whatever way most appeals to the house's occupants. But during the twentieth century we have all been conned into believing that a garden has to be a place for plants.

This idea has been spread by dedicated gardeners

Winter evening classes can provide highly individual and practical garden ornament. These fellows can be picked up by their ears

This garden is very easy to care for. Nearly all the planting and maintenance is done by the farmers, woodmen and livestock who occupy the surrounding countryside. The table legs are made from blue half-round coping bricks

– collectors of plants who measure their own, and others' success by the variety and rarity of the plants they grow and cannot imagine any other possible reason for having a garden. The idea is also spread by books and magazines with pictures and approving descriptions which point the way to the garden beautiful.

Approval plays its part too in peer pressures, which persuade the owners of gardens crowded together in the suburbs that their plots are places for lawns and flowers. These make less noise than children playing; are less threatening than hives of bees; more socially acceptable than cars and bits of engines; and less dubious than rabbits, chickens or pigeons.

There is no need to garden the space around the house at all. In many parts of the world houses are simply set in the surrounding landscape – or villagescape – and are often all the more attractive for it. It may be that a few vegetables are all that is wanted, and time spent growing flowers seems wasted effort. In northern France many small country gardens are like that – a few rows of cabbages or leeks within a wooden paling fence.

Gardens are safe places for children to play. Yours may be the only such place – then make it a playpen, and remember that playing involves activity and romping when balls are kicked and bicycles ridden, without regard for fragile flowers, and that a layer of bark over a well-drained bed makes a safer, better surface than a lawn.

The space around the house provides somewhere to relax and enjoy the company of friends. The swimming pool, a tennis court, somewhere to have a barbecue, or sit around and chat may be higher priorities than spending time looking after flowers. In that case reduce the plants to no more than are needed to provide a pleasant setting for the fun, and make time to enjoy being sociable.

Remember, when you create your garden, that it is a place for you. Don't be conned into believing that a garden has to be just a place for plants.

Oak half barrels are very versatile. Wood is good insulation against frost, so roots and compost need less protection than when using clay or plastic. The big barrels can be very boldly planted, and will happily accommodate quite large shrubs or small trees, as well as perennials and seasonal plantings

The wildwood – so potent and so sinister in folklore – is not far away and its power still haunts us. Memory recalls a small boy thrilled by the shapes and shadows, the bulk and strength and stillness of trees standing together. How a small wood stretched out and became a great forest: and then, how quickly excitement changed to terror when my companions hid and I was alone and overawed amongst the trees.

Even the tame trees in gardens have dryads lurking in their branches. They seem a challenge to our control and admiration readily gives way to a sense of threat – to us, to our houses, to other plants in the garden, to our drains. We resort to heavy-handed lopping and mutilation to limit their power, and assure ourselves that we are still in command.

This 'pruning' goes on everywhere suburban gardens cluster together. It is a brutal butchery paying no thought to the natural forms of the trees, their contribution to the appearance of gardens and the opportunities provided by their shade and shelter. It ignores more constructive ways to manage or shape trees, and cuts them down to size, literally and figuratively. This reduction has nothing to do with gardening, or the needs of the garden, and everything to do with atavistic fears of the wildwood and its ancient hidden forces.

Shade has a reputation as one of the problems of a garden and the phrase 'sunlight and shadow' reveals the instinctive warmth of our responses to the image of light and life produced by the first word, and the feelings of gloom and chill evoked by the latter.

These reactions ignore the longing for shade when the sun beats down on an unprotected garden, or the discomforts of open spaces exposed to driving rain and cold winds. They forget the warmth within the shelter of a group of trees when the sun shines in early spring, or the relief from the heat and dust and glare on hot summer days from a canopy of leaves – not just for humans looking for somewhere to sit and relax, but for plants as well. They take no account of how shadows in a garden balance and contrast with sunlit spaces, and the feeling that shade provides of stepping into another world, an alternative garden, quite different from the one where plants bask in the heat and dazzle of sunshine.

This is the world of the spinney, created within the shelter of deciduous trees, whose inhabitants are numbered amongst shrubs and perennials from woodlands throughout the temperate world.

The sheltered space beneath a single tree can be a spinney to its inhabitants. Or a spinney may be formed by three or four small trees clustered in a group; or by the beds beside a path flanked by apple trees; or by a pergola. It may be larger; the far end of a garden – perhaps the whole of a small garden – planted with trees to form a woodland glade which hides the boundaries, and brings the countryside across them. Where there is space, its size may entitle it to be called a wood, either newly planted, or made within existing woodland. These are places where shade and shelter become a part of the garden, and where trees form the walls and ceilings of outdoor rooms.

Trees hold a special place amongst the native plants – and so the scenery – of any country. Their height and bulk make them the largest living objects most of us ever encounter, and are certain to make impressions in gardens. When plans are made and trees are chosen, thoughts should turn to what they do as much as to how they look. Amongst other things, trees in a garden:

# Gardening with Trees

I fear those grey old men of Moccas, those grey, gnarled, low-browed, knock-kneed, bowed, bent, huge, strange, long-armed, deformed, hunchbacked misshapen oak men that stand waiting and watching century after century biding God's time.

*Francis Kilvert*

Provide structural features.
Introduce variations in scale.
Contribute to management.
Provide shade and shelter.
Act as screens.
Are beautiful to look at.
Support wildlife.

In any woodland the interactions of one plant with another establish a kind of stability. It is a stability under pressure from the changing seasons, from severe frosts or droughts and the occasional hurricane; continually modified by the ageing, senility and death of the plants. From time to time it breaks down, only to be re-established, perhaps in a slightly different form.

Adverse reactions to shade take no account of the feeling that it provides of stepping into another world, an alternative garden, quite different from the one where plants bask in the heat and dazzle of sunshine

A spinney might be the fragment of a copse formed by three or four small trees clustered in a group

The woodland pattern can be adapted as a way of gardening that depends very little on intervention by the gardener, for gardening with trees should never aim to arrest development. This is neither possible nor desirable, and to attempt to prevent all changes, to hold the planting in a steady state, would be to lose sight of opportunities and return to the suburban style. The woodland approach is also distinct from the Jekyll style, in that interactions between the plants themselves – rather than the gardener's art and craft – decide which plants play their parts successfully.

The major performers in these balancing acts are the trees. The shade they cast, their height and density and the seasonal growth cycles of their leaves and roots control the vegetation that can grow and thrive beneath them.

This garden was planted in the late nineteenth century. It has lost its intended style and character, becoming an amorphous mass of jaded deciduous shrubs and sombre, gloomy evergreenery – mostly common laurel, Portugal laurel, box and yew. Enormous *Philadelphus* and *Corylus* are choked with dead and collapsing stems. Young horse chestnuts are everywhere. *Robinia pseudoacacias*, suffering from a lot of die-back, are shedding large branches. Thin, sad-looking, over-mature *Chamaecyparis* promote an air of dereliction and testify to years of neglect. The summerhouse sits on top of a grassy slope, looking as if it has just landed there

Some of the barns and outbuildings on this farm are being converted into dwellings. The approach to the farmyard is rather raw and bleak, so what can be done to make a welcoming approach? Ideas can only be developed if the scene is first criticised or analysed in detail. This view shows some attractive features, and some which are less appealing!

To revitalise the planting, work in stages:

1  Remove all dead and dying trees and shrubs
2  Remove all trees and shrubs that you don't like. If there are plants which you cannot decide about, put off your decision until after stage 5
3  Cut back all the tangled *philadelphus* and *corylus* to approximately 30cm above the ground
4  Prune out all dead stems and branches so that you can see the framework of healthy wood
5  Remove the young horse chestnuts, keeping only those which you may want to grow on
6  Prune and thin shrubs to create an attractive framework of stems. This takes time – time to observe and to understand the innate character of the plant and to enhance it by pruning. Do not give the shrubs a 'haircut'

This pruning and thinning will radically alter the microclimate of the area, letting in more light and moisture. The overgrown planting gives a very limited range of extremely difficult conditions – very dark and very dry. The new range of growing conditions gives the opportunity to make a much more interesting garden

The new planting is chosen and sited in a direct response to the criticisms in the first sketch. Planting will help to tie the site into the surrounding hedgerows, fields and woodlands. A good proportion of the plants should be native trees and shrubs. The entrance can be given extra distinction by using simple, understated plants boldly in order to soften hard edges, anchor buildings to their surroundings, screen ugly features or reduce their impact by breaking up their outline

An option is to abandon attempts to grow flowering plants, and rely on the ability of mosses to survive and do well under these conditions

## COPING WITH SHADE

Mature trees cast a heavy shade, and their roots remove water and nutrients from the upper layers of the ground beneath them, depriving lesser plants of light and space and sustenance. They may be attractive to look at, but their cramping effects on gardening are often grudged, and large trees are easier to enjoy in the further corners of neighbours' gardens than in our own.

Few plants, wild or cultivated, survive beneath the dense and spreading canopies of large horse chestnuts, beeches, planes, sycamores, limes and others like them, and scarcely any thrive. The line of least resistance is to lie back, enjoy the trees and accept gracefully that it is their taming influence on the vegetation that provides the time to do so.

An option then is to abandon attempts to grow flowering plants, and rely on the ability of mosses to survive and do well under these conditions. Gardening with mosses is a great deal easier now than it was. Many of these plants tolerate paraquat, and repeated sprays of this herbicide can be used to destroy grasses and herbs attempting a wispy appearance beneath the trees, leaving a carpet of moss to develop in their place.

However, provided conditions are not too extreme, there are a few plants able to make a living under trees. Gardeners are inclined to label them as dull and use them reluctantly, only because they feel forced to do so. That is a pity. Periwinkles, London pride, the Japanese laurel, Gladdon iris, ivy, cyclamen and butcher's broom are all thoroughly serviceable garden plants – all have excellent foliage, and several have very attractive flowers. The usual fault is to plant half-heartedly and dot plants about, widely spaced and haphazardly placed, so that they look as mean as the spirit that put them there. They should be thickly planted, with mixtures to make full use of their foliage and give the eye something to muse on.

Many bulbs do well in these dry areas. They grow through the winter, flower in the spring and retreat underground before conditions become too hard in the summer. But if colour and dazzling brilliance are wanted, they are possible: busy lizzies provide the means. These little plants, that came to us from Zanzibar and are annuals in our climate, are remarkably, almost unbelievably, tolerant of the shadows and droughts close to large trees. They cannot endure cold, but planted during late June

Trees and houses make an equivocal mix

they will paint the dullest shade with scarlet, pink, magenta and white until, dissolved by the first frosts, they disappear, leaving scarcely a trace behind them.

However, not all trees grow heavy, dark and greedy. The more open canopies of many provide protection and shelter for plants growing below them. Their roots leave space in the fertile upper layers of the soil for lesser plants to find a living, or go deep into the ground where they scarcely compete at all. These are the ones to use in spinneys to reproduce the four-tiered matrix of trees, shrubs, herbaceous plants and bulbs that is the foundation of the balance of forces in natural deciduous woodlands.

Gardeners are born thrawn. They make rock gardens where there is no hill for miles. They pursue the ideal of the herbaceous border, knowing full well how hard a creature it is to control, and fill their rose gardens with varieties whose ancestors grew most happily in Turkestan. When they garden on chalk or limestone they long for rhododendrons and make beds of peat to grow them in, but in a country where climate, soils and topography combine to ensure the success of deciduous woodland they have little or no notion of making a spinney and describe shade as a problem.

## TREES IN SMALL GARDENS

Trees and houses make an equivocal mix. Houses have drains and trees have roots and the affinity which one holds for the other leads to trouble when they meet. Trees provide a frame and a setting for houses but grow large and heavy, and dwellings close to them seem threatened and vulnerable. Trees shelter a house from winter storms but in summer cause clay soils to shrink, so that walls move and crack, and doors swing open in their frames. Trees produce shadows which make houses dark and gloomy but keep them cool in a heatwave. Trees keep out cold winds and make a sun-trap in one garden, but take the light from neighbours in another. Trees are sacrosanct; they should never be cut down, and may even be protected by preservation orders, but the destruction of a large tree frees a garden from a tyranny which restricted every imaginative development. Gardens without trees are barely furnished, but trees that make their presence felt are resented for taking over.

These contradictions lead to problems, and in small gardens objections of one kind or another to trees mean that the options thought acceptable have become very limited and the ways they are grown even more limited.

By convention trees are grown as specimens. Each is an isolated ornamental feature, bound and staked, with trimmed stems to leave space beneath for other plants, or room to pass with the lawnmower. Most are planted as standards or half-standards and grown very formally, and since there is little space in a small garden those that are diminutive by nature are preferred. It is firmly believed that a tree is a fixture which should never be cut down, but sooner or later they grow large and become a problem. Then they are either tolerated but resented, or disfigured by inexpert lopping.

To find the trees the problem is to stand the situation on its head. It is the ways they are used which cause the problems, and the solutions depend on adapting the ways we grow them to their natures: to use them as screens, structural backgrounds, and providers of shelter and shade to other plants. These solutions have little to do with conventions which decree that trees should be planted as specimens and focal points.

Specimen trees depend for their effect on viewing space, which is bound to be in short supply in a small garden. At best their flowers look stunning only briefly, and as an alternative colourful foliage, which steals the scene for longer, has become a selling point. But this makes a literally monotonous spectacle, that is not enlivened when the same weeping silver pears, golden acacias, crimson or variegated acers, and purple-leaved plums and beeches turn up as the stars in half a dozen other gardens along the road.

When grown as screens and backgrounds, trees play less obtrusive but nonetheless vital roles complemented by lesser plants which add to the garden's attractions, and vary the picture from week to week and season to season. The first step is to ditch the gardener's conviction that trees are inviolate fixtures, every one of which must be nurtured and cosseted until in due course it develops into a majestic specimen of its kind.

Long ago our ancestors discovered that trees could be grown within useful and productive limits. The methods they used can be seen wherever the art of coppicing is still practised, and in woodlands and beside motorways where trees are invari-

Looking north across the new garden of a restored farmhouse, the prospect is rather
depressing. The concrete edge to a pool and the post and rail fence dominate the middle
ground. Dead trees and an ugly farmbuilding catch the eye before the softer fields and trees.
The foreground is open, and looks stark and unwelcoming

The new planting is planned to screen the bad views and frame the good ones. Carefully
positioned trees also make the garden more sheltered. Most of the shrubs are low – it is
possible to look out over them. Some trees with several stems are used to give a more relaxed
style than is possible with single-stemmed trees

The colours, textures and patterns of bark can be a very large part of a tree's appeal, and there are many with bark which makes individual trees an asset in any garden

ably planted close together and progressively thinned out. Gardeners have never felt they had much to learn from foresters, and close planting followed by thinning·or coppicing are techniques which they have scarcely adopted.

Many broad-leaved trees – evergreen and deciduous – respond well to coppicing and this technique, based on cutting back to ground level at intervals, provides for an almost perpetual cycle of growth and renewal. It is ideally suited to the needs of gardens, including small gardens. Not only does it keep the trees where they are wanted, but it maintains variety during the different stages of growth and renewal, and provides conditions which encourage the growth of herbaceous and other ground-covering plants under the trees.

The stems of young trees are especially signifi-

cant, and coppicing draws attention to them, making the most of their attractions. After a few years the colours, textures and patterns of bark can be a very large part of a tree's appeal, and there are many – birches, snake-bark maples, stuartias, parottias, the Tibetan cherry, some rhododendrons and Corsican pines amongst them – with bark which makes individual trees an asset in any garden. Occasionally – *Betula papyrifera* is an example – an attractive bark compensates for an otherwise graceless tree. The strongest, most striking effects result from coppicing or planting close together to form groups or groves of one kind, and then the repeated stems form patterns and shapes that connect the canopy of leaves above with the planting on the ground below.

Birches do not coppice well, but their outstandingly beautiful bark makes a dramatic impact when trees are set irregularly in groups, with no more than a metre or so between some of them when first planted. Seedling plants, with slight variations in colour and other characteristics, look better than uniform clones and are much cheaper to buy.

Progressive thinning weakens the effects of the clustered stems, and will eventually reduce a group to a few specimens. There comes a time when the decision must be made either to remove those that are left, and start the process again, or to rely on the impact made by the maturing trees. When space is short and maximum effect is needed, quite short-term cycles of growth, thinning, total removal and replanting are most likely to give the best results.

## ALTERNATIVES TO CHERRIES

Blossom on trees, like froth on a pint of Guinness, is part of the product – not unimportant, but not what it is bought for. No amount of froth makes a bad pint good, and spectacular blossom for two or three weeks on a large, obtrusive plant is a poor reward for a minor contribution during the rest of the year.

Yet, when garden centres are visited to buy trees and choices are made, the first question is 'Does it flower?' The questioner will not be happy with references to academic, technical flowers like the catkins of hazels and alders, the bright but small tassles of ashes, or the subtleties of colour and shape of many maples. They must be proper flowers – and lots of them too, double if possible – with petals and colour. They should be flowers which hang in bunches and cover the entire tree.

Prominent in the customer's mind will be the Japanese cherries. Almost oblivious to these novelties until around the turn of the century, gardeners had no immunity when they encountered them and fell for them completely. Within a few years a flowering cherry, usually one with sugar-pink double flowers, became the universal representative of freedom in suburban gardens and streets, and a prime choice for an ornamental tree practically anywhere else – even on the village green!

Gardeners have succumbed so wholeheartedly to this infatuation that, for seventy years and more, these cherries have set the standard for garden trees. It is a standard based solely on the splendour, flamboyance or vulgarity of the plants in flower, that takes no broad view of what is needed. The more modest attractions of *Prunus serrulata spontanea* and *Prunus x yedoensis*, preferred in Japan and also to be bought in Britain, make little impression compared with the blatant displays of 'Kanzan', 'Amanogowa' and Mr Cheal's hunch-backed little weeping cherry.

The results are a devastating lack of imagination in the way trees are used, particularly in small gardens, and a depressingly scant variety to choose from at all but the most specialist sources. This miserable choice contrasts strikingly with the rich variety of trees which could be planted if imagination rather than infatuation decided what we wanted.

For sheer sumptuousness and shameless vulgarity, no trees compete with *Prunus* 'Kanzan' on the right day, apart from some of the large rhododendrons and magnolias; but the specialist tastes of some of those rule them out as widespread, popular choices. Alternatives are judged on their ability to approach the display of 'Kanzan', and inevitably the choice falls on those with a profusion of flowers, or golden, crimson, variegated or silver foliage. A very small coterie of these have now become programmed in our minds, and on the software of computerised landscaping systems, as small specimen trees acceptable for starring roles in gardens everywhere.

## CHERRY VICTIMS – UNDERVALUED GARDEN TREES
### (excluding native species)

Our choice of trees for gardens is limited much more by what is readily available than by what exists. There are a great many trees that could be grown in gardens, including small gardens, but which are seldom found for sale except by specialist sources. Some of these are introduced and briefly described below.

The list does not include native species and their garden forms; the popular varieties, which make up the great majority of the trees planted today; tender species, or varieties which can be grown only under special conditions, or with a great deal of care; and trees which are not available through well-known commercial sources.

The list is biased towards trees that do not grow large, since these are likely to be the most sought-after for gardens. Some, marked *, have a natural tendency to grow as shrubs and need early training or pruning to establish a tree form, but make satisfactory small trees when this is done. Evergreen species and varieties are marked (E). Those that need lime-free or neutral soils are marked (A).

# ACER

The maples are one of the most valuable of all tree groups for gardens. Commonly represented by varieties of the Norway maple, the sycamore, the box elder and two Japanese maples, other species tend to be neglected. Many grow into beautiful small/medium trees with very attractive bark, and lend themselves well to close planting or coppicing to make full use of their stems. They cast light shade, have sparse roots and provide good growing conditions for plants in their shelter.

| | |
|---|---|
| A. capillipes | Small with striped bark and good autumn colour. |
| A. cappadocicum 'Aureum' | Medium with yellow-flushed foliage. |
| A. cappadocicum 'Rubrum' | Medium with colourful immature foliage. |
| A. davidii 'George Forrest' | Small/medium with attractively striped bark and good autumn colour. |
| A. forrestii (A) | Small with striped bark, and beautiful foliage and young stems. |
| A. griseum | Small/medium, cinnamon-coloured flaking bark and brilliant autumn foliage. |
| A. hersii | Small with striped and marbled bark, and fine autumn colour. |
| A. nikoense | Small/medium graceful tree with brilliant foliage in autumn. |
| A. opalus | Medium, rounded tree with conspicuous soft yellow flowers in early spring. |
| A. palmatum | Excellent small, multi-stemmed tree with elegant form and attractive autumn colour. |
| A. pensylvanicum (A) | Small, with finely striped bark, and clear yellow autumn foliage. |
| A. rufinerve | Small/medium with beautiful bark, and brilliant autumn colours. |
| A. saccharinum laciniatum | Medium/large elegant tree, with finely lobed leaves. |
| Aesculus pavia 'Atrosanguinea' | A small buck-eye with spikes of crimson flowers in June. |
| Alnus incana 'Aurea' | Medium sized grey alder with yellow-flushed immature foliage; can be coppiced. |
| Amelanchier asiatica* (A) | Small, with white, pink-flushed flowers in spring and fine autumn colours. |
| Arbutus x andrachnoides (E) | Small/medium, winter-flowering strawberry tree with peeling tan-coloured bark. |

# BETULA

The birches include some of the most popular and most beautiful of all trees. They are grown particularly for their bark, and look most effective in closely spaced groups or when grown as multi-stemmed trees. Popular, widely grown species and varieties are those with intensely white bark, but others, just as striking, have bark in various shades of cream, cinnamon and chestnut. None are at their best on strongly calcareous, base-rich soils. Most produce finely coloured yellow foliage in autumn.

| | |
|---|---|
| B. albo-sinensis septentrionalis | Medium, with pink/copper bark overlaid with a glaucous bloom. |
| B. costata | Medium/large, with pure white bark peeling to expose a creamy lower layer. |
| B. ermanii | Upright and tall, with bark pink-flushed on trunk and copper-coloured on branches. |
| B. lenta | Medium/large, with polished mahogany bark. |
| B. lutea | Medium/large, with peeling creamy-orange bark and fine autumn colour. |
| B. nigra | Medium/large, with dark, peeling frayed bark, grows well on damp ground. |
| Buxus balearica* | A box tree with upright growth forming a fine stem, and relatively large leaves. |
| Caragana arborescens 'Pendula' | Very small, weeping tree; immature foliage suffused yellow-green in spring. |

# CARPINUS

Hornbeams are pleasant, easily grown trees, tolerant of exposure to wind and able to grow well on most soils. Never showy, they form excellent settings for other plants and combine well with native species of woodland trees.

| | |
|---|---|
| C. caroliniana | Small/medium, with upright branches arching at the tips, and fine autumn colour. |
| C. japonica | Small, with broad spreading form and eye-catching catkins. |
| C. turczaninowii* | Small tree with brightly coloured immature leaves in spring. |
| Carya ovata | Medium/large; shagbark hickory with leaves like a walnut, clear yellow in autumn. |
| C. tomentosa | Medium/large; big-bud hickory with large, fragrant, pinnate leaves. |
| Catalpa fargesii | Medium, showy spikes of pale pink flowers in midsummer. |
| Catalpa speciosa | Medium, with attractive spikes of white, purple-spotted flowers in July. |
| Cercis siliquastrum 'Alba' | Small, the white-flowered form of the Judas tree. |

# CORNUS

The shrubby dogwoods are well known and widely grown. Even more striking, but much less often seen, are some of the tree species which are mostly small/medium in size with very graceful forms, and memorable clusters of flower-like bracts.

| | |
|---|---|
| C. alternifolia* | Small, with broad, rounded form and attractively layered branches. |
| C. controversa | Medium, with upright growth and layered spreading branches; fine autumn colour. |
| C. 'Eddie's White Wonder'* | Outstanding form, covered with clusters of white 'flowers' in spring. |
| C. florida* (A) | Small rounded tree, white/pink flowers in spring; outstanding autumn colour. |
| C. kousa chinensis* | Small with layered branches covered with white 'flowers' in midsummer. |
| C. mas | Small, rounded, bushy tree producing masses of yellow flowers before the leaves. |
| C. mas 'Variegata'* | An attractive form with brightly variegated leaves. |
| C. nuttalii* | Medium, outstanding upright but rounded tree with conspicuous white 'flowers'. |
| Corylus colurna | Medium/tall, the Turkish hazel; an upright, very symmetrical specimen tree. |
| Cotinus obovatus* | Small/medium, the American smoke bush, with brilliant autumn colours. |

# COTONEASTER

Some of the large, evergreen cotoneasters make very valuable small trees, which look especially effective when laden with berries. They are, unfortunately, susceptible to fireblight.

| | |
|---|---|
| C. frigidus* | Small with wide-spreading branches, weighed down by berries in autumn. |
| C. frigidus 'Fructoluteo' | A form with light yellow berries. |
| C. x watereri 'Cornubia'(E) | Small/medium, a very vigorous grower with exceptionally large fruit. |
| C. x watereri 'John Waterer'* (E) | Small and wide-spreading, with heavy masses of red berries. |
| C. watereri 'Rothschildianus'* (E) | Small and wide-spreading, with bunches of yellow berries. |

# CRATAEGUS

The thorns include a large number of very useful small/medium trees apart from the widely grown 'Paul's Scarlet'. Almost all can grow well under difficult conditions and are tolerant of shade and exposure to cold winds. They are attractive in flower, in fruit and in autumn colour, and provide good shelter and conditions for plants growing beneath them.

| | |
|---|---|
| *C. arnoldiana* | Small, with exceptionally large bright red haws. |
| *C. azarolus* * | Small, produces pear-shaped edible fruits and brilliant autumn colours. |
| *C. crus-galli* | Small rounded tree; shining leaves, with brilliant colours and conspicuous haws in autumn. |
| *C. laciniata* | Small, with deeply lobed leaves and large vermilion haws. |
| *C. laevigata* 'Plena' | A small round-headed tree with beautifully formed double white flowers. |
| *C. laevigata* 'Rosea Flore Plena' | Similar to the last, but with pink flowers like tiny rose-buds. |
| *C. x lavallei* | Small round-headed tree with glossy foliage and persistent orange fruits. |
| *C. mollis* | Medium, broad tree, with large clusters of bright red haws. |
| *C. pinnatifida* 'Major' | Small with divided leaves, very bright haws and brilliant autumn colour. |
| *C. prunifolia* | Small/medium round-headed tree; glossy foliage, bright haws and fine autumn colour. |
| *Davidia involucrata* | Medium upright; the handkerchief tree is hardy and grows well on most soils. |
| *Elaeagnus angustifolia* | Small/medium upright silver-leaved tree; very wind-tolerant and hardy. |

# EUCALYPTUS

These exotic-looking trees do not usually appear at home in a country setting, and none are bone hardy. Apart from *E. gunnii* and *niphophila*, which are widely grown, the following may be worth a try – particularly if coppiced repeatedly and grown primarily for their foliage.

| | |
|---|---|
| *E. dalrympleana* (E) | Medium, very fast-growing with brightly mottled bark. |
| *E. parvifolia* (E) | Medium, tolerant of chalk soils, and very hardy. |
| *E. pauciflora* (E) | Small, with long pointed leaves and white bark. |
| *Eucryphia glutinosa* * (E), (A) | Small/medium; narrow, upright growth and white flowers in late summer. |
| *E. lucida* * (E), (A) | Small, with fragrant drooping flowers after midsummer. |
| *E. x nymansensis* 'Nymansay' (E) | Small/medium, with masses of white flowers in later summer. |
| *Franxinus chinensis rhyncophylla* | Medium/tall, with graceful leaves and clusters of fragrant white flowers. |
| *F. mariesii* | Small, with clusters of fragrant creamy white flowers during midsummer. |
| *F. ornus* | Medium; manna ash makes an attractive ornamental tree with fragrant white flowers. |
| *Genista aetnensis* * (E) | Small, upright with open form and masses of yellow flowers after midsummer. |
| *G. cinerea* * (E) | Small, upright with rounded head, covered with fragrant yellow flowers in summer. |
| *G. tenera* * (E) | Small, rounded head, densely covered with fragrant yellow flowers during July. |
| *Gordonia axillaris* * (E), (A) | Small, with glossy leaves and white flowers during the winter. |
| *Halesia monticola* (A) | Small, wide-spreading tree with masses of white bell-shaped flowers in spring. |
| *H. monticola vestita* (A) | Small, produces larger flowers. |

# HAMAMELIS

The witch hazels are a group of large shrubby trees, most of which provide a great show of flowers during the late winter and then settle down as well-shaped attractive settings for other plants. Many have fine autumn colour, and all provide useful shelter for plants growing beneath them.

| | |
|---|---|
| H. japonica 'Arborea' | Small; wide-spread, almost horizontal branches and fragrant yellow flowers. |
| H. japonica 'Zuccariniana' * | Small, upright growth and pale yellow, strongly scented flowers. |
| H. mollis 'Brevipetala' * | Small, with upright shape and clustered, very fragrant deep yellow flowers. |
| H. virginiana * | Small, wide-spreading, covered in autumn with small, fragrant, yellow flowers. |
| Hoheria glabrata | Small, with attractive leaves and masses of shining white flowers in summer. |
| H. lyallii | Small, lightly hairy leaves and white flowers after midsummer. |
| Idesia polycarpa * | Medium, with distinctive leaves and clusters of small green flowers; red berries. |

# ILEX

Hollies are amongst the most distinctive and valuable of all evergreen trees. Many excellent garden forms have been derived from I. aquifolium, the native species, and are not included in this list.

| | |
|---|---|
| I. latifolia * (E) | Small, with large, very distinctive leaves, and masses of orange/red berries. |
| Juglans ailantifolia | Medium; a walnut with unusually large, elegant pinnate leaves. |
| Ligustrum chenaultii * (E) | Small; distinctive long 'privet' leaves and large clusters of flowers in summer. |
| L. lucidum * (E) | Small, with fine, large glossy leaves, white flowers in bunches during autumn. |
| Liriodendron tulipifera 'Fastigiatum' | Medium; tulip tree making a broad column with attractive foliage. |
| Maackia amurensis | Small, with distinctive pinnate leaves and clusters of faintly blue-rinsed flowers. |
| Maclura pomifera | Small/medium, the osage orange; female trees produce large orange-like fruits. |

# MAGNOLIA

These include some of the most spectacular, and elegant, of all garden trees. Varieties of M. x soulangiana and M. x loebneri are most frequently found in gardens, but many other excellent plants are rarely seen except in large collections. Most are vigorous, hardy, easily grown plants that thrive in neutral and acid soils.

| | |
|---|---|
| M. acuminata | Medium/large; distinctive large leaves and curious elongated fruits after the flowers. |
| M. 'Charles Coates' * (A) | Small, with rounded form, and fragrant white flowers during early summer. |
| M. macrophylla (A) | Small; has enormous, broad leaves and large ivory-coloured flowers in early summer. |
| M. obovata (A) | Small/medium, with handsome leaves, large flowers in summer and attractive fruits. |
| M. salicifolia * (A) | Graceful small tree; narrow leaves, white flowers in spring and fragrant bark. |
| M. sargentiana robusta (A) | Medium, extremely showy with rosy-crimson flowers in early spring. |
| M. sprengeri (A) | Medium, one of the most outstanding with large rose red flowers and fine leaves. |
| M. tripetala | Small/medium; large broad leaves, fragrant flowers in June and attractive fruits. |
| M. x veitchii 'Peter Veitch' (A) | Medium; vigorous grower with fragrant white/pink flowers in April. |

# MALUS

A few varieties of crab apple, including John Downie, Golden Hornet, the Japanese crab and some of the purple-leaved varieties, are widely grown. Other small/medium sized trees are seldom seen. Practically all are tough, easily grown specimens which are able to tolerate exposure to cold winds, although scab can be a major problem.

| | |
|---|---|
| M. baccata mandschurica | Small/medium with rounded shape, fragrant white flowers and small fruits. |
| M. hupehensis | Medium; an upright tree, with large, pure white fragrant flowers and small fruits. |
| M. 'Katherine' | Small; rounded twiggy crown; semi-double pink flowers and bright red fruit. |
| M. x robusta 'Red Siberian' | Small/medium, with white/pink flowers and masses of cherry-like red fruits. |
| M. x robusta 'Yellow Siberian' | Small/medium; like the previous variety but with golden-yellow fruits. |
| M. spectabilis | Small upright tree, with apple-blossom-pink flowers in late spring. |
| M. toringoides * | Small wide-spreading tree, fragrant white flowers and showy red/yellow fruits. |
| Nothofagus antartica (A) | Medium/large fast-growing tree; attractive small leaves and good autumn colour. |
| N. dombeyi (E), (A) | Medium/large, a very useful fast-growing evergreen with small shining leaves. |
| N. obliqua (A) | Medium/large, very fast-growing tree. |
| Nyssa sylvatica (A) | Medium, slow-growing tree that prefers moist soil; exuberant autumn colour. |
| Osmanthus yunnanensis * (E) | Small but fast-growing evergreen with broad leaves and white fragrant flowers. |
| Ostrya carpinifolia | Medium, an upright tree with catkins in spring and hop-like off-white fruits. |
| O. virginiana | Small upright or rounded tree with attractive leaves and good autumn colour. |
| Paulownia fargesii | Medium/large with broad heart-shaped leaves and panicles of showy lilac flowers. |
| P. fortunei | Small, with creamy-white and lilac flowers, with purple markings. |
| Phellodendron amurense | Small/medium with beautiful pinnate leaves and conspicuous corky bark. |
| Phillyrea latifolia * (E) | Small, with olive-like dark green glossy leaves, and off-white flowers in spring. |

# PHOTINIA

A useful but almost neglected group of small trees, which includes some evergreens. P. x fraseri 'Red Robin', best known for its brilliant red immature leaves, is often seen for sale, but is usually a less than successful garden plant. Susceptibility to fireblight can be a problem with the deciduous species.

| | |
|---|---|
| P. beauverdiana | Small; flat bunches of white flowers in May; autumn colours and red berries. |
| P. davidiana * (E) | Like a very stylish cotoneaster; combines autumn colours with evergreen foliage. |
| P. davidiana 'Fructoluteo' * (E) | A form with bright yellow berries. |
| P. serrulata * (E) | Small with broad leaves, crimson when young, and bunches of red berries. |
| P. villosa * (A) | Small round-headed tree, with conspicuous berries and bright autumn colours. |
| Populus lasiocarpa | Medium/large, with very big leaves with bright red veins. |
| P. 'Serotina Aurea' | Medium, broadly erect tree with yellow immature leaves turning yellow/green. |
| P. violascens | Large, with very broad leaves similar to P. lasiocarpa. |

# PRUNUS

The cherries include many good garden trees, besides the outstandingly showy double and semi-double forms of the Japanese cherries and the pink form of the winter-flowering *Prunus subhirtella autumnalis*, which are such popular choices. Many have very splendid displays of autumn colour.

| | |
|---|---|
| *P. cerasus* 'Rhexii' | Small/medium; long-established form of the morello cherry with double white flowers. |
| *P. conradinae* 'Semiplena' | Small, with white, pink-flushed flowers very early in spring. |
| *P.* 'Hally Jolivette' * | Small, elegant tree covered with very light pink, semi-double flowers in spring. |
| *P. incisa* * | A very floriferous small tree, producing single white flowers and autumn colour. |
| *P.* 'Kursar' | Small, with masses of deep pink single flowers in early spring. |
| *P. maackii* | Small, with polished golden-mahogany bark, and single white flowers in April. |
| *P. mume* 'Beni-shi-don' * | Small; produces deep pink, fragrant flowers in very early spring. |
| *P. mume* 'Pendula' | Small weeping tree with light pink, mostly semi-double flowers in early spring. |
| *P.* 'Pandora' | Small upright tree covered in early spring with lightly shaded pink flowers. |
| *P. serrulata pubescens* | Medium upright tree, covered with white/pink single flowers in late April. |
| *P. serrulata spontanea* | Medium, broadly spreading tree with single white or light pink flowers in May. |
| *Ptelea trifoliata* * | Small/medium; distinctive leaves, sweetly scented flowers and hop-like fruits. |
| *Pyrus nivalis* | Small upright tree, with silvery woolly leaves and clusters of white flowers. |

# QUERCUS

Oaks are seldom grown as garden trees, with the possible exceptions of the evergreen holm oak and the American red oak. This very large group contains a number of species and varieties which make valuable additions to a garden.

| | |
|---|---|
| *Q. castaneifolia* 'Green Spire' | Medium/tall, forming a robust columnar tree. |
| *Q. frainetto* | Large tree with big, deeply lobed leaves and deeply fissured bark. |
| *Q.* x *ludoviciana* (A) | Large vigorous tree; semi-evergreen with fine autumn colour. |
| *Q. palustris* (A) | Large tree; deeply lobed, glossy green leaves and fine scarlet autumn foliage. |

# RHODODENDRON

Amongst the most showy of all trees grown in gardens when in flower, but almost all need some pruning and training to convert them into trees rather than large, rounded shrubs. Many have attractive stems, which with their fine foliage can make them distinctive additions to a garden.

| | |
|---|---|
| *R.* 'Albatross' (E), (A) | Fragrant trusses of white, pink-flushed flowers. |
| *R. auriculatum* * (E), (A) | Trusses of fragrant, white, trumpet-shaped flowers in August or later. |
| *R.* 'Aurora' (E), (A) | Fragrant rose-pink flowers in April/May. |
| *R. barbatum* (E), (A) | A large, rounded form with peeling bark and dense, rounded heads of scarlet flowers. |
| *R. calophytum* (E), (A) | Broad, upright growth with large leaves and trusses of white/pink flowers. |
| *R. decorum* * (E), (A) | Fine foliage and large, funnel-shaped white/pink fragrant flowers. |
| *R. falconeri* (E), (A) | Striking foliage and large trusses of sulphur-yellow flowers in April. |
| *R. fictolacteum* * (E), (A) | Large, impressive leaves and open, creamy white flowers in April/May. |
| *R. fortunei* * (E), (A) | Open trusses of bell-shaped, fragrant pale pink flowers during May. |

## RHODODENDRON

| | |
|---|---|
| R. 'Fulgarb' * (E), (A) | Deep crimson flowers as early as February, in compact trusses. |
| R. 'Ivanhoe' * (E), (A) | Brilliant scarlet flowers during April. |
| R. 'kewense' (x loderi) * (E), (A) | Fine deep green foliage; trusses of fragrant white/pink flowers. |
| R. 'Polar Bear' (E), (A) | Pure white, trumpet-shaped, fragrant flowers during July and August. |
| R. sinogrande (E), (A) | Large deep green leaves; trusses of creamy white flowers with crimson centres. |
| R. thomsonii * (E), (A) | Rounded leaves and smooth cinnamon bark; fine deep crimson flowers. |
| R. yunnanense * (A) | Upright growth with masses of slender, funnel-shaped pink flowers in May. |
| Rhus trichocarpa * | Small; very fine pinnate leaves, apricot-pink when immature and yellow in autumn. |
| Robinia x ambigua 'Decaisneana' | Medium, with attractive pinnate leaves and large trusses of pink flowers. |

## SALIX

The willows include many species, varieties and cultivars which play a useful part in gardens; nearly all, apart from weeping forms, respond particularly well to coppicing or pollarding. Many are varieties of native species and therefore are not included on this list.

| | |
|---|---|
| S. exigua * | Small, very elegant tree; conspicuously bright silver leaves on slender stems. |
| S. magnifica | Small, most unusual willow with extremely broad almost laurel-like leaves. |
| S. matsudana 'Pendula' | Small weeping form which grows well in any reasonable garden soil. |
| Sambucus canadensis 'Aurea' * | Small round-headed elder with soft golden pinnate foliage, and white flowers. |
| S. canadensis 'Maxima' * | Small broad-topped tree with large pinnate leaves and huge heads of flowers. |
| Sophora japonica | Medium/large round-topped tree; pinnate foliage, clustered white flowers. |
| S. japonica 'Pendula' | Small with attractive pinnate foliage and pendent branches. |

## SORBUS

The rowans are a large group of mostly small trees, whose berries, foliage and autumn colours provide plenty of interest in gardens. By far the most commonly grown are the whitebeams, varieties of the mountain ash and Sorbus hupehensis, a Chinese species with foetid flowers. Others as good or better are available. A drawback of the whole group is its susceptibility to fireblight.

| | |
|---|---|
| S. cuspidata | Medium upright whitebeam with large silver/white leaves. |
| S. discolor | Small upright rowan, with fine pinnate leaves and very rich autumn colours. |
| S. domestica | Medium/large with pinnate leaves and small, pear-shaped, edible fruits. |
| S. insignis | Small upright rowan; attractive pinnate leaves; large bunches of pink berries. |
| S. latifolia | Small/medium whitebeam with peeling bark and tawny yellow, brown-spotted berries. |
| S. pohuashanensis | Small/medium broad-headed rowan; orange-red berries and intense autumn colour. |
| S. sargentiana | Small/medium distinctive rowan; large sticky buds and huge bunches of red berries. |
| S. scalaris | Small, spreading rowan with fern-like leaves, red berries and fine autumn colour. |
| Staphylea colchica * | Small/medium upright tree; green/white flowers followed by lantern-like fruits. |

| | |
|---|---|
| *S. holocarpa* 'Rosea' * | Small, spreading tree with pink-suffused flowers during April and May. |
| *Stewartia koreana* (A) | Small/medium tree with flaking bark and outstanding autumn colour. |
| *S. pseudocamellia* (A) | Medium, with colourful peeling bark, white flowers and bright autumn colour. |
| *S. serrata* (A) | Small, with polished brown bark, white solitary flowers and fine autumn foliage. |
| *Styrax hemsleyana* (A) | Small, open-centred tree with clusters of pure white flowers during June. |
| *S. japonica fargesii* * (A) | Small, spreading tree with hanging bell-shaped flowers during June. |
| *S. obassia* * (A) | Small; distinctive large leaves and hanging clusters of fragrant white flowers. |

## SYRINGA

Lilacs, even the larger ones, have a tendency to shrubbiness and some training is usually needed to encourage a tree-like form. A very few varieties of the formerly abundant hybrids are now found repetitively in gardens, but there are numerous alternatives – mostly with rather more interesting foliage.

| | |
|---|---|
| *S. josikaea* * | An upright small tree with large trusses of fragrant purple flowers. |
| *S. pekinensis* | Small tree with long pointed leaves and dense panicles of white flowers. |
| *S. reflexa* * | Small, usually multi-stemmed tree with very large leaves and rose-purple flowers. |
| *S. reticulata* * | Small round-headed tree with dense clusters of white flowers in June. |
| *S. tomentella* | Small, usually multi-stemmed tree with mauve-pink, fragrant flowers from late May. |
| *S. yunnanensis* 'Rosea' * | Multi-stemmed, small tree with slender trusses of fragrant mauve-pink flowers. |
| *Tamarix gallica* | Small, spreading tree with fine blue-green foliage, and tassels of pink flowers. |
| *T. pentandra* 'Rubra' * | Small open-headed tree, with pink/red flowers in May and June. |
| *Tetradium (Euodia) daniellii* | Small/medium with very attractive, large pinnate leaves and fragrant flowers. |
| *T. hupehensis* | Medium, with pinnate leaves, off-white flowers and large bunches of red fruits. |
| *Tilia mongolica* | Small/medium with densely twiggy rounded crown, and good autumn colour. |
| *T. tomentosa* | Medium/large with big silky, white-backed leaves and fragrant flowers in July. |
| *Toona (Cedrela) sinensis* 'Flamingo' | Small, with large variegated, white/pink/green pinnate leaves. |
| *Xanthoceras sorbifolium* * | Small, often multi-stemmed, with fine pinnate leaves; panicles of white flowers. |
| *Zelkova serrata* | Medium/large spreading elm-like tree, fine autumn colours. |
| *Zelkova* 'Verschaffeltii' * | Small, round-headed tree with attractive bark and small, toothed leaves. |

Trees make bold and effective impressions in gardens. Other plants can be used to provide complicated interactions of colour, texture and form, and for subtle details. The trees lend themselves to simple treatments that do not strain for attention, and should be chosen for easily understood reasons. Everyday qualities and commonplace adjectives that describe how trees grow and what they are to do are more likely to be helpful when making choices than botanical terms and imaginative descriptions going into details of minor importance.

A specification for a tree could be expressed in such a way as: 'It should be small but not grow too slowly; rounded rather than upright. It should look natural, thrive in places where the sun shines strongly, and be tough enough to survive cold weather. It should be attractive in spring and autumn, and not cast too much shade.'

## SIZE

| | |
|---|---|
| Very small<br>Small<br>Medium<br>Large<br>Very large | It is very often helpful to think about size in stages: ie after five, ten or fifteen years. Very few gardens have space for a mature cedar, a plane or even a Norway maple or tulip tree, but each of these and many others are beautiful as young trees. There is no good reason why they should not be planted and enjoyed for a decade or two, and then replaced when they outgrow their space. Think also about systems of management which restrict development and make it possible to control size eg coppicing, pollarding, pleaching, heading back, and (skilful) pruning. |

## RATE OF GROWTH

| | |
|---|---|
| Very slow<br>Slow<br>Moderate<br>Fast<br>Very fast | Time becomes a critical dimension when choosing trees. Many grow slowly and steadily, taking years to develop the characteristics for which they are chosen. Very often these can be planted amongst other, faster-growing kinds, which produce a more immediate impression and can be removed as time goes by. Nurse trees of this kind will protect and encourage the growth of those which are slower. Where space is restricted, think too of the possibilities of using selected compact varieties which grow less rapidly than the species itself. |

## SHAPE

| | |
|---|---|
| Columnar<br>Weeping<br>Rounded<br>Spreading<br>Conical<br>Flat-topped etc | The opportunities for using variations in shape are very often not used as imaginatively as they should be. The interactions of different shapes are especially important when planting trees in groups. Many of the trees that are planted in gardens can be obtained in a variety of forms, which provide much more choice than is generally realised. Note that shapes change as trees mature, and that the characteristic, often characterful, silhouettes of many kinds of mature trees may take many years to develop. |

## OVERALL EFFECTS

Natural
Gardenesque
Subdued
Neutral
Flamboyant
Sombre
Leafy
Ethereal
Open

Trees have massive impact, and the qualities they possess inevitably have major effects on their surroundings. Visual impressions are formed by the stance of the tree; its proportions; the interplay between foliage, twigs, branches and trunk; the density, tone and texture of the foliage; the colour, texture and patination of the bark, etc, etc. The impressions these qualities make will be different depending on the maturity of the tree and the season of the year. They all play their part in the garden, and can be used as exciting and positive elements in its design. It is worth taking time to assess and try to visualise them as clearly as possible.

## LIKES AND DISLIKES

Exposure
Cold
Drought
Water-logging
Shade
pH of soil
Warmth
Sunshine

Like all other plants, trees grow better in some conditions and situations than in others, and it is important to try to match their likes and dislikes with the qualities of the place where they are to be planted. Many trees grow naturally in woodland communities and may not be at their best as isolated specimens, whether in gardens or parkland or on village greens. The stresses of isolation are greatly increased when trees are set amongst grass growing right up to their stems. Newly planted trees should be allowed at least a square metre of grass-free space to themselves.

## TIMES WHEN THEY LOOK BEST

Spring
Summer
Autumn
Winter

Trees are large and conspicuous throughout the year, and there is no season when dramatic effects cannot be achieved from them. In small gardens in particular the trees chosen should make a positive contribution in as many different seasons, and in as many different ways, as possible. Beware of attaching too much importance to a single brilliant quality, and be aware of the subtle, understated attributes which many trees possess – 'third-party' qualities including their appearance when covered with hoar-frost, or the extent to which they attract birds.

## LEAFINESS

Dense canopy
Light canopy
Spreading
Upright

This is the quality which makes trees useful or otherwise as screens, and which decides whether a wide variety of other plants can be grown in their vicinity, or whether the choice will be limited to the few which are able to withstand the effects of heavy shade or greedy surface roots.

## SPACING AND PLACING

The well-ordered manners of suburban gardening pay strict attention to spacing. Trees, shrubs, perennial plants – even the humble daffodil – all have their regulation distances within which each should live without tangling with its neighbours. Interlacing stems and branches show that something must be done and that control should be restored by cutting back or removing one of the offenders. These spacings are the fundamentals of the garden's layout, and as a result small gardens have space for very few, very small, trees.

This view of trees as plants which grow in isolation, widely separated from one another so that each can develop steadily into a fine specimen of its kind, is a gardener's concept. It is a notion which gets in the way of imaginative use of trees in gardens and, although hallowed by usage, pays little attention to the conditions to which trees respond best.

Trees are creatures of woodland or scrub, likely to start life in the shelter, if not the shadow, of their elders and in company with other immature trees at various stages of development. They combine to suppress the growth of competing grasses, and make what use they can of gaps in the canopy above them. They benefit from the shelter around them, and develop a root system below ground in preparation for a rapid response when opportunities occur.

Their natures are less well suited to isolation, particularly in competition with the ever-present roots of a grass sward, and to positions where they have no protection from grazing animals, or must endure cold, drying winds, and the unshadowed heat of the sun. Few allowances are made in gardens for these problems and, more often than not, trees are left to struggle. Sometimes they are given help:

*By killing the grass surrounding newly planted specimens*
An area approximately 1m square should be kept clear of all grass and weeds for at least two or three years after planting.

Glyphosate can be used to kill vegetation, and a mulch or repeated sprays with paraquat will keep it clear of weeds after that.

*By staking and protecting*
Stakes should only be used on exposed sites, on sandy soils, and when planting large trees. They should be as short as possible, securely fixed so that they cannot rub against and damage bark, and must be checked regularly. Young trees, particularly nursery transplants, whips and maidens, establish better and grow quicker when guarded from rabbits and deer and sheltered from cold winds by plastic tree-protectors.

*By mulching and feeding*
Mulches conserve water and prevent regrowth of weeds. The simplest can be made from squares of polythene or woven polypropylene, kept in place by turf or soil turned over their edges. Applications of fertiliser during the first three years will encourage rapid early development.

*By watering*
Trees need quantities of water even when young. Their needs are more easily met by conserving water with mulches, destroying competing grasses, and encouraging vigorous root growth than by going round with the watering can.

When conventions are ignored and trees are planted close together, they do not persist in growing as individuals. Each is influenced by the presence of its companions and moulds itself into a part of a clump, which in turn develops an overall shape that takes its form from the nature of the trees within it, and their surroundings. This can be seen in any copse or wood, in places where trees cluster in neglected corners, in hedgerows and in the planting of many new towns. Clumps of trees are also a common enough sight in gardens, where they are thoughtlessly deplored as examples of careless planting.

Trees in a group, whether of a kind or mixed, cease to star as individual prima donnas. They become part of the overall impression of the garden, and their effects depend on their combined shapes, tones and textures. The scale is larger and the effects more significant but the principles are the same as those we think about when planting shrubs and herbaceous perennials.

When conventions are ignored and trees are planted close together they do not persist in growing as individuals. Each is influenced by the presence of its companions and moulds itself into a part of a clump

The virtuous gardener, so we are told, always stakes newly-planted trees and, when buying trees from a well-run garden centre, will be reminded of this path to virtue. Not that trees will fall over unless they are staked – in most situations and in most soils this will not happen if they have been planted with any care at all – but the garden centres preserve the myth because it persuades a good customer to become a better customer by accompanying each tree sold with a stake and tie. At best these hold a tree upright in light soils or exposed positions; at worst, stakes and ties cause damage unless carefully placed and checked frequently to make sure they are not rubbing or chafing the stem. Even when well placed and tended, their reassuring presence may discourage the development of the roots and delay establishment.

Trees held erect, accurately aligned with vertical stems, look smart and trim and are an assurance that the gardener is in control. They go with standard roses, concrete posts and well-founded panelled fencing, and other precise features of the suburban style. In country gardens their formal stance is less agreeable, and a more haphazard arrival at the patterns formed by their slanting stems contributes better to the sense of place. Here old habits should be abandoned, and instead of buying trees several years old, pre-formed into standards and half-standards, young maidens should be planted which will grow into shapes compliant with their surroundings.

## FRUIT TREES:
## ORNAMENTAL AND USEFUL

Ornamental trees are anachorisms in cottage gardens, embellishments that depend on leisure and refinement. What cottager would have been content with a cherry that never produced fruit? That may seem archaic and academic when most of us no longer depend on our gardens for essential provisions. Why should we feel regretful that fruit trees have ceased to be part of every garden in villages and in the countryside, now that Santa Rosa plums, Golden Delicious apples and Packhams pears are on the shelves of every supermarket?

But could anyone not share those regrets who visits Herefordshire in the early spring, and is reminded of the wonderful beauty of old standard pears in full bloom? The sight of those enormous fruit trees towering erect above the farmhouses, with their dark wood and pure white flowers echoing the black and white houses beneath them, causes astonishment that today practically nobody plants these trees at all, and they have become almost unobtainable. Even when reminded that standard pears worked on seedling stocks can take years to come into flower, and that the trees we see in Herefordshire are perry pears, their loss is still a sacrifice we should never have been prepared to make.

The regrets become more pointed when attempting to eat a Santa Rosa plum, a Golden Delicious apple or a Packhams pear picked in some distant part of the world weeks before it reached the shop where it was sold. It will be one of tens of millions of identical fruits whose standardised qualities of sweetness, crunchiness or aroma have just the blandness and predictability that sells products whose sales depend on never, ever risking the surprise aroused by unexpected qualities of character or individuality.

Holidays during a wartime youth were spent in a house whose walled garden was crammed with apples and pears and plums planted during the first decades of this century. From July to September I was an enthusiastic, persistent sampler of these fruits and, because each tree had a label with a name impressed on it, and because I happened to be interested as well as greedy, I learned their names and the differences between them. And I discovered that the joy of eating fruit lies in its variety, and the interest and pleasure it gives us depends on each having its season, so that when those we eat in August pall we look forward to making new acquaintances in September.

Fruit trees are among the very few garden plants that come close to creating vernacular styles characteristic of villages and country gardens in different parts of the land. The pears of Herefordshire have already been mentioned, and orchards of ancient cider apples are still conspicuous in parts of that county; as they were until recently in Somerset, where now they are a fading memory replaced by modern, more regimented orchards. Cherry trees growing on the brick earths of parts of Kent, with sheep grazing beneath them, beside oast houses for hops, confer an immanent sense of place. In the Carse of Gowrie alongside the Tay, and elsewhere, gnarled old apple trees preserve only faint memories of earlier, more fruitful times, but the hills through which the Teme flows in Worcestershire still carry a white mist of plum blossom in springtime. Apart from these regional associations, there once were villages throughout Britain noted for their apples or plums or pears or damsons; many are still commemorated – though often only just – by a variety which bears their name.

These trees are no longer planted, and when groups of executive houses go up in Leigh Sinton, as anywhere else, they may be black and white pastiches of traditional buildings in Worcestershire but their gardens owe nothing to the fruitful countryside around them. Their trim lawns, bush roses, rockeries and flowering cherries are mindless repetitions of suburban gardens to be seen all over Britain. No fruit tree is planted in a garden for its blossom – not even an apple as beautiful as Arthur Turner, whose flowers have earned it the RHS Award of Garden Merit. Not even sweet cherries with their white flowers, dark wood and fine autumn colours – and certainly not tall, majestic, dark and white standard pears.

If anyone doubts it, suggest an apple or a pear or a plum to a customer in a garden centre who has come to buy an ornamental tree. The response will be a firm statement that a flowering, *not* a fruit tree is wanted, and the suggestion will be disregarded because fruit trees are planted only in parts of the garden scheduled for useful plants – amongst vegetables, or in groups referred to as the orchard. If the suggestion is pressed it will be dismissed as impractical. It is well known that fruit trees grow and crop satisfactorily only when sprayed and pruned, and cannot be properly looked after amongst garden plants.

These responses conceal deeper reservations. Fruit trees have been wrested from the wildwood and tamed – more than other trees they have been tailored to the needs of androcentric gardening. Their sizes can be precisely controlled, they can be pruned and trained to any shape. The seasons when they crop and the ways their fruits are used are well known, and the patterns through which one pollinates another are understood.

Fruit trees are no longer allowed to make their presence felt as trees; to set them free would be to put the clock back a century or so. The merits of dwarfing root stocks and of small trees for small gardens – even for large gardens – have been triumphantly proclaimed for fifty years, and we

have almost forgotten their virtues grown as half-standards; even if we want one, we can scarcely buy a standard tree.

Bush trees, we are told, and cordons even more so, are easy to pick, easy to prune and spray, and will not embarass us by producing so much fruit that some falls and lies unused on the ground. For fruit lying unwanted is a reproach and an embarrassment – it leads to accusations of wastefulness. But nothing is wasted when unneeded apples are left to be eaten by birds, insects, and other creatures that can make a living from them during the autumn and into winter.

Fruit trees planted in gardens like any other tree do remarkably well if left to take care of themselves. Unpruned, they grow in youth into graceful, natural shapes, and in maturity and beyond into trees with a character that enhances any garden. Unsprayed, they acquire a fauna of their own – amongst which anthocorid bugs, ladybirds, predatory mites and lacewings ensure that most pests never develop to be a plague. The apples will lack the surface gloss of *le crunch*; the plums will not be so round and red as Santa Rosas, and some of the pears will be smaller and less interestingly pale than a Packhams. But see which are preferred in a tasting trial, and eat them knowing that regular drenches with poisonous chemicals to protect a skin-deep beauty have played no part in their production.

APPLE ROOTSTOCKS

All apples are grafted, put together from parts taken from two plants with entirely different qualities: the scion and the stock. The scion is a shoot from a particular variety, and it is this which grows into the branches of the tree from which the fruits are picked: it is the part everyone thinks about when they buy an apple tree. The stock develops into the root system and, as in the way with roots in general, is more or less out of sight and out of mind.

Buying apple trees involves us in pleasant thoughts about whether cookers or eaters are needed, what they will taste like, and when they will crop. A good deal of care is taken to choose varieties with appealing qualities. It is almost equally important to think about the stock on which the variety is grafted, and make sure that it too is suitable for what is in mind. It irreversibly affects:

The size the tree will reach at maturity.

Its vigour and rate of growth.

The time it will take to start to bear fruit.

The weight of crops the tree will carry.

The stock which grows into the roots beneath a tree should be as much a part of the descriptive information in catalogues or on labels as the name of the variety which forms its top. It seldom is. Nor is it widely known that varieties of crab apples are also worked on these stocks, and they too can be bought with built-in tendencies to grow large or small – depending on their rootstocks.

| SUMMARY OF THE QUALITIES OF APPLE ROOTSTOCKS | | |
|---|---|---|
| No. | Vigour* | Recommended uses |
| M27 | 4 | Very dwarfing stock that produces compact, early-bearing bush trees. These are ideal for small gardens, are long-lived, develop good root systems and usually need no staking. |
| M9 | 6 | A dwarfing stock that produces early, very fruitful small bush trees which will usually need to be staked throughout their life. Likely to be short-lived and often used as a filler between larger trees that start to fruit later. |
| M26 | 8 | Semi-dwarfing stock used to produce heavy crops on bush and single cordon trees where space is short. On most types of soil root development is sparse and the trees need permanent support by stakes. |
| MM106 | 10 | General-purpose stock for producing half-standard, bush and cordon apples. Trees will start to crop well after only a few years under average conditions, and usually maintain a good balance between growth of the shoots and the crops carried. |
| MM111 | 12 | Slightly more vigorous general-purpose stock which can be used on poor soils, or when large half-standard or bush trees are needed. Early cropping is light but trees will begin to crop well within about five years. |
| M25 | 15 | Very vigorous stock used to produce large half and full standard trees that will need room to develop. Cropping is light during the first few years, but trees on this rootstock are very long-lived and able to carry extremely heavy crops for many years. |

* The vigour of trees grown on these stocks is shown here in relation to trees grown on MM106 – rated at 10.

ORCHARDS

Orchards have country-appeal. They conjure images of gnarled and ancient apple trees, and busy bees amongst the flowers in spring; even of lambs gambolling on the grass beneath them. Or their appeal may have more to do with the ordered and efficient appearance of trees in lines, emphasised in recently planted commercial orchards. If so, before surveys are made and grids set out to mark planting positions, return for a moment to the good habit of having second thoughts.

Commercial orchards almost invariably contain a very few different varieties of one kind of fruit, usually planted in a large rectilinear field. Their regular shape and layout makes it easier to apply sprays and carry out mechanised activities efficiently.

Orchards made to form a pleasant part of a garden are more likely to contain several different kinds of fruit trees. It would not be ambitious to want to grow plums, pears, apples and damsons, and possibly cherries, quinces, medlars, bullaces and walnuts too. Most people would want to in-

Gardens do not have to look trim and organised. In this garden the thatched cottage looks almost as if it has grown up with the plants. The meadow under the apple trees is cut three times a year – this change of grass management has transformed the atmosphere of the garden in just one season. An old field hedge of hazel, dogwood, hawthorn, blackthorn and holly gives a constantly changing picture. Ivy and hart's tongue ferns make an attractive evergreen carpet on the hedgebank – only revealed after the leaves have fallen. There is no need to spoil this garden by feeling obliged to garden it

clude several varieties of at least some of these, and plums, apples and pears could contribute a dozen to twenty different kinds between them. Very often the space for this kind of orchard is neither very large, nor very regularly shaped. These thoughts are all of a kind which suggest that the strict symmetry of a commercial orchard would be out of place, and that the aim should be to use informality and irregularity to make a small orchard a peaceful and secluded feature in a garden.

Conventionalists will, as a last fling, insist that fruit trees must be spaced out with text-book distances between each, but like other trees they can be planted in groups. Three or four half-standard and standard plums or a group of apples, even pears, put in only a few feet apart will turn into a little fruitful grove, each tree protecting and pollinating the others. This can be a way to fill a corner or make a screen; it can be a way to put in a few extra varieties, beyond the number that strict spacing would allow.

In recent years it has become fashionable to complain that different kinds of apples, pears and plums are hard to find. It is said that our choice has

*The aim should be to use informality and irregularity to make a small orchard a peaceful and secluded feature in a garden*

become limited to a few well-worn varieties. Cox and Bramley are the apples most often mentioned, Williams and Conference pears, and Victoria and possibly Czar for those who want plums.

It is ironic that, amongst these varieties, only Conference pears and Victoria plums rate highly as good choices for those who want to grow their own fruit, while the range currently available is enough to satisfy the most ardent and acquisitive orchardist. Some of the best-known wholesale nurseries in the country regularly grow a total of about a hundred different varieties of apples, pears and plums – not between them, but each – and no garden centre would have any difficulty in making arrangements to stock a comprehensive, interesting range. The problem is not that the varieties are limited, but that demand is overwhelmingly concentrated on a few familiar kinds. A more open and inquisitive approach by customers would reveal unexpected

A modest gravel drive to a cottage looks unobtrusive and friendly. It is practical and economical and much more fitting than blacktop edged with concrete kerbs. The hedge is made of gooseberries and currants – edible, practical and pretty, it makes the over-used cypress seem very poor value. The trees are apples

richness of choice, including many recent introductions as well as worthy old-timers.

## CIDER APPLES

There are those whose consciences could never leave an apple to rest unneeded on the grass, let alone the quantities that even modest orchards of large trees produce. No amount of reassurance that fieldfares and butterflies, blackbirds and badgers will make good use of the fruit can shake their conviction that that would be waste on a wicked scale. There is another answer – to grow cider apples.

These too are now planted commercially as much smaller trees than the large standards of the past, under which cattle could graze. But these large trees can still be bought, and are an attractive way to restore the traditions of old-style orchards when using up the fruit is a problem. Cider apples, provided they are from the right varieties, can be collected in sacks and sold to cidermakers, or, by making other arrangements, exchanged for cider. The ease with which this can be done depends on how far away the nearest cidermakers are, but in many parts of the country this is a practical and productive way to dispose of the produce from a small orchard.

## CIDER APPLE VARIETIES

The most important qualities in cider apples are sweetness, acidity and the content of tannins. Each has a vital bearing on the quality, taste and character of the cider the apples produce. The great majority of ciders are made from the juices of several different apples, blended together to produce an agreeable balance between these qualities. Some varieties can be used on their own to make individual, vintage and often very characterful cider.

**Ashton Bitter.** Late September; moderately vigorous, upright tree; good crops of medium-sized apples; average-quality cider, useful for blending.

**Brown's Apple\*.** Late October; very vigorous spreading tree; crops heavily, medium-sized fruit of low sugar content; makes a fragrant, fruity cider.

**Dabinett\*.** Early November; moderate to weak-growing, making a spreading tree; very heavy, regular cropper with medium-sized apples; average sugar content, makes a palatable, full-bodied cider of above average quality.

**Dymock Red\*.** Late September; moderately vigorous, spreading. Average sugar content; makes a high-quality cider.

**Ellis Bitter.** Late September; vigorous, round-headed tree; moderately heavy cropper, with large apples; reasonable quality cider from low-acid, mildly astringent juice.

**Harry Master's Jersey\*.** Early November; moderately vigorous, making a small, compact tree; biennial tendency, moderate crops of medium-sized apples; above average sugar content; produces reasonable cider.

**Kingston Black\*.** Mid-October; moderate, spreading growth; moderate crops; makes a full-bodied, high-quality cider with a distinctive flavour.

**Major\*.** Late September; medium-sized, spreading tree; regular crops of medium-sized apples; average sugar content; makes excellent, slightly astringent cider.

**Michelin.** Late October; moderate to weak growth, making an upright tree; regular crops of medium-sized apples; good quality cider for blending.

**Reinette o'bry\*.** Mid-October; moderately vigorous, compact tree; a regular heavy cropper; dessert-character apples make a good-quality cider for blending.

**Somerset Redstreak.** Early October; moderately vigorous, rather brittle branches; makes a good-quality cider for blending.

**Stoke Red\*.** Late October; slow-growing, moderate-sized tree, which produces heavy crops; above average sugar content, aroma and flavour; makes excellent cider.

**Sweet Alford\*.** Late October; vigorous grower making a large spreading tree; moderate cropper; above average sugar makes very useful well-flavoured cider.

**Sweet Coppin\*.** Early November; moderately vigorous, growing into a large tree; biennial, but heavy bearer; average sugar content, makes good blending cider.

**White Jersey\*.** Late September; moderate to weak growth forming a spreading tree; heavy but biennial cropper with small apples; average sugar, produces a moderate-quality, low-acid, blending cider.

**Yarlington Mill\*.** Early November; moderately vigorous, very heavy cropper with medium-sized fruit; above average sugar content; makes excellent well-flavoured cider.

\* These varieties produce juices with the qualities needed to make vintage ciders.

A small cider orchard at the end of the garden is not an industrial enterprise, with rows of trees standing uniformly aligned, but a place to recapture the atmosphere of the farmhouse orchard with trees of different sizes and shapes scattered or informally placed on whatever piece of ground can be spared.

## CONIFERS IN COUNTRY GARDENS

Native conifers number only three, none of which is a very noticeable feature of large areas of the countryside. Yet conifers are to be seen in every part of Britain. Conspicuous by a presence – conferred by their shapes, their dark masses and their textures – they stand out from, and often stand above, the rounded forms of more characteristically native deciduous trees.

All but a handful – the most notable exception is the larch – came here first during Victoria's reign.

Everyone with a place in the country during the second half of the nineteenth century, whether peer or parson, dignified it with specimen trees of fashionable wellingtonias, noble and Douglas firs, and *Arbor vitae*. Later Lawson's cypress became popular as a cheap and easy hedge and Monterey cypress was tried for a time, but cold winters made life impossible for this Californian in most parts of the country. Then, during the 1950s, gardeners discovered Monterey's bastard offspring, and seized on its power to grow a metre in a year as the closest thing to instant vegetable screening that God could bestow on suburban man.

Leyland cypress may be a recent phenomenon; it is not such a new plant. To be accurate it is not 'a' plant at all but the name given to hybrids of the Monterey and Nootka cypresses. The first happening occurred near Welshpool in 1888; and was not the diffident appearance of a single seedling but, forebodingly, the descent of a small gang of six. Since then other seedlings have appeared and those who buy Leyland cypress may be offered any one of fifteen or more different clones, variable in their colour, leafiness, ability to stand up, growth rate and a dozen other qualities.

For sixty or seventy years these plants attracted little attention. Then, with the age of plastics, its merits became apparent; not just as a screening tree for which it has quite convincing qualifications, but, much more dubiously, as a plant to make a hedge. It is not a conifer which can be propagated easily from cuttings, and the most suitable clones for garden use are not those which are most easily propagated. Plants labelled simply 'Leyland Cypress' should be regarded with some suspicion, and money parted with only for those which are identified as one of the recognised and better clones. These include Leighton Green, named after the estate where the seedlings originated; Haggerston Grey, after Mr Leyland's castle in Northumberland; Naylor's Blue – not truly a blue conifer but a green one with a glaucous cast to its foliage; or, for those whose rash courage convinces them that they can fit anything into a country setting, that plant of slightly different origin – Castlewellan Gold.

Native Scots pines, yews and junipers are all instantly noticeable in the places where they grow naturally. It is not surprising that alien conifers inevitably bring exotic qualities to their surroundings which are obvious to everybody. They are

This hotchpotch of a garden is in south Shropshire. It is set in a modest village in soft, attractive hill country. This planting is at odds with the character of the place – it is in a prominent position and so imposes itself upon far more people than just the residents of the house. Over the next few years it will grow and stop looking like a very nasty rash – gradually it will develop into a harsh, sombre, monotonous mass

In this alternative idea plants have been chosen to complement the softness of the surrounding countryside and vegetation. This garden will be much more varied and interesting through the seasons. It is a far friendlier looking place and is not demanding to care for

trees which can provide dramatic and exciting contrasts in gardens and in the landscape; used without thought or caution they are intrusive and all-pervading. Their shapes, textures and forms invariably contrast with the rounded, softer-textured and lower-profiled shapes of native trees and shrubs, and when wrongly set they become discordant elements in country scenes.

Conifers have the same distinctive impact whether as part of the broad scale of the countryside, as specimen trees in a large garden, or as dwarf and miniature forms on a rockery. They are plants which inevitably declare themselves wherever they appear. Great care is needed to ensure that their presence contributes positively and satisfyingly to their surroundings, and planting them casually, thoughtlessly or unperceptively should be resisted by stinging fines and drastic retribution.

Conifers have the same distinctive impact whether as part of the broad scale of the countryside, as specimen trees in a large garden, or as dwarf and miniature forms on a rockery

Apple-cheeked biddies whose gardens are admired by everyone do not just have pretty faces. Behind those sweet looks are wills of iron, for gardening is a gentle craft that conceals absolute control. Concealment is barely skin-deep in androcentric suburban gardens where straight rows of vegetables, and borders where every plant is separated from its neighbours by clean-hoed soil, proclaim their owner's care. But it is there in the gardens of followers of Jekyll and Sackville West, and often exercised with such subtlety that innocent visitors think that little planning and less work makes these gynocentric displays look as they do!

But even in the best-regulated gardens there are forgotten corners where ivy, London pride, bergenias, periwinkle or yellow archangel find a haven and establish communities, which are more like the alliances of wild flowers than the ordered plantings of a garden, and thrive on the gardener's neglect.

# Fitting in the Plants

And when I am asked what qualities I consider most necessary in a gardener wishing to have and keep a good collection of plants, I name without hesitation these three – patience, liberality and a catalogue.

*Canon Henry Ellacombe*

her garden for the plants she wanted to grow. One of these places she called the ditch garden, and I first saw it during a visit to East Lambrook Manor about fifteen years after the death of its creator.

By that time the plants she had chosen to put there had merged into semi-natural alliances which had many of the qualities found in wild communities. Numerous smaller, less resilient plants had failed to survive, but those that remained had formed a complex mixture of leaves and flowers and stems; a matrix within which they lived, and through which they were able to resist invasion by outsiders. They had re-arranged themselves in patterns different to those that had been there originally but the impression they created was a very agreeable one, quite unlike the desolate disorder of a neglected garden.

A more familiar phrase to describe these close communities of plants would be ground-cover; and the worthiness of ground-cover has become an accepted article of gardening faith. The phrase promises a garden which needs little or no maintenance, and it is a promise which often disappoints. Sometimes the plants chosen are unsuitable but more often they are used in the wrong way.

Heathers have become the epitome of ground-cover but these plants, and ling in particular, cast a false trail across the scent. They are naturally inclined to grow in great drifts – often by the square mile – where little else but heather exists. This makes them an easy model to copy but provides a misleading pattern for other, more sociable plants, which combine in mixed communities. The ditch garden at East Lambrook Manor was, and is still, an example of a community of plants in alliance together, and is as good a place as any to try to discover how such communities can be

## GARDENING WITH ALLIES

These tucked-away communities reveal another face to gardening: one that depends on the inborn abilities of plants to form mutually dependent alliances. Then control has less to do with fighting weeds and holding plants captive, and everything to do with learning how to assemble and look after groups of plants so that they can form the partnerships by which they hold their ground and keep weeds out.

It is not only in forgotten corners that this happens. It goes on as a matter of course in many gardens. Margery Fish was a great and original gardener, who understood that plants do well only when planted in the places that suit them, and who went to great trouble to find just the right spots in encouraged to establish themselves successfully.

The plants must be *compatible*: Margery Fish had originally planted many different kinds, and some of them had been overwhelmed by stronger neighbours.

The plants must be *adapted to the conditions*. This had been taken into account; nevertheless many of the plants were not well-matched enough to survive seasons when frost, drought or cold winds were extreme, and in competition with other plants.

A *matrix* must be formed by the foliage of the plants – at ground level and above – which makes it difficult for unwanted plants to get in. The surviving plants had mingled together forming a dense matrix, beneath a light canopy of willows whose overhead shade reinforced the cover provided by the herbaceous plants.

There must be *time* for development. The ditch garden had been planted many years previously, and for several years before my visit had been less meticulously maintained than the owners might have wished. This allowed the plants to redistribute themselves and find the niches needed to build up a balanced community.

### PLANTING COMPATIBLY

Plants that are incompatible merit permanent separation, just like people who cannot get on, although the idea, being no part of the human condition, is less familiar. Plants that are to grow amicably side by side must be more or less equally vigorous, and few garden for long before they discover the effects of a mismatch. A familiar resurrection occurs each spring when alpines are set out for sale on garden centre benches. Alyssums, aubrietas, phloxes, saxifrages and androsaces all seem equally diminutive, vulnerable and cherishable in their little pots, and are bought naively to share a corner of the rockery together. Once planted the fragility of the first three fades to a memory, as they submerge the creeping androsaces and saxifrages before establishing a robust balance one with another, which may persist for years – demonstrating a compatibility founded on their mutual ability to resist intrusion, which the smaller, less assertive plants lacked.

### MATCHING THE PLANT WITH THE PLACE

Matching strength with strength is a straightforward balance that all gardeners learn to think about every time they put different plants close together. More complex is the need to match their likes and dislikes.

A combination recommended from time to time for a vivacious effect is purple sage and *Alchemilla mollis*. Both have remarkable tolerances which enable them to survive in a variety of situations in gardens, and contribute beautifully. But they grow naturally under such different conditions – the sage on hot, dry, stony slopes, the ladies' mantle on cool, moist Caucasian meadows – that they make an uneasy pair even in the protected setting of a garden, and sooner or later their different predispositions will destroy the partnership.

Many gardeners would argue that it is part of the gardener's craft to grow plants where they are wanted, whatever their nature; and that half the fun of gardening is devising ways to do that. But anyone who hopes to garden by encouraging the plants to form successful alliances, and develop as more or less balanced communities, must choose very carefully and be very aware of their natural adaptations.

The matchmaking gardener has to work partly by instinct, partly on information received, to find partners that will be compatible. First, by balancing abilities to encroach or resist encroachment:

Vigour.
Rate of growth.
Size and stance of leaves.
Seasonal patterns of growth.

Second, by matching preferences and aversions:

Full sun; light shade; deep shade.
Drought; constant moisture; aquatic.
Acid/calcareous soils.
High fertility; low fertility.
Exposure; shelter.

Most plants will react critically to only one or a few of these conditions. In other respects they will be content with 'average garden conditions' – a comfortably vague term, which nevertheless makes practical, widely understood sense.

Choosing successful plant alliances depends on the same imagination and experience as finding wild flowers. We look for cowslips amongst unploughed, unfertilised grass – formerly in old meadows, now more probably on the banks of

Even in the best-regulated gardens there are corners where garden plants of many kinds find a haven and establish communities, which are more like the alliances of wild flowers than the ordered plantings of a garden

It can be hard to believe that a plant as ethereal as a blue poppy comes to us as an unchanged, unimproved, unspoilt wild flower

motorways. We hope to find ragged robin in corners of damp fields or ditches. We search for them in different places because we recognise that each has different natural adaptations which enable it to make the most of conditions where it lives.

This reasoning seems less obvious in gardens. The most popular, brightly bred garden flowers like roses, dahlias, delphiniums, peonies and daffodils appear to be archetypal plants of the garden, far removed from whatever wild things they ever were. We take it for granted that they have become adapted to garden life and will have forgotten the natural preferences they once had. Even candelabra primulas, rhododendrons, viburnums and many herbaceous perennials, whose wild ancestry is less remote, become garden plants in our minds as soon as we become familiar with them in our borders. It can be hard to believe that a plant as ethereal as a blue poppy comes to us as an unchanged, unimproved, unspoilt wild flower. But past gardeners, and more recently plant breeders, who change the outward appearance of plants with patience but without too much difficulty seldom even try to alter the internal arrangements which

The ditch garden at East Lambrook Manor was, and is still, an example of a community of plants in alliance together

govern their likes and dislikes. Lettuces and potatoes have been cultivated for far longer than almost any of the flowers we grow, but lettuce seeds still refuse to germinate when high soil temperatures remind them of the dangers of doing so during arid summers in their ancient Mediterranean home, and the plants still run to seed during the long hot days when we need them most. We fear for the young shoots of early potatoes on frosty nights in spring, because these have never lost their wild ancestor's susceptibility.

The natural conditions under which garden plants grew when they were wild remain the best possible guide to where they will be most at home in our gardens. Fortunately gardeners and those who write about gardening take more notice today than hitherto of whence plants came and the conditions in which they grew, and descriptions of plants in encyclopaedias and elsewhere very often include information about their origins, likes and dislikes.

### FORMING A MATRIX

If gardening and farming ceased and the countryside was left to itself, there would be a brief post-revolutionary period of anarchy as grasses and annuals, perennials and a few surviving cultivated plants competed for space in fields that had been arable. Within a year or two perennial grasses and broad-leaved meadow plants would take over, and very soon afterwards sapling trees, seedling shrubs and brambles would begin to grow through the grasses, restrained but not excluded by rabbits, deer and other grazing animals.

Gradually the trees and shrubs would grow larger and transform the grassland into scrub, and then into open woodland where young trees, shrubs and climbers and a thick ground-cover of broad-leaved plants crowded out the remaining meadow grasses and herbs. Eventually the leaves of mature trees would form an overhead canopy each summer, beneath which only those shrubs, perennials and bulbs able to make a living when the leaves had fallen, or find sunlit spaces in temporary glades, would survive.

The natural dominance of deciduous woodland looks like some arcane point of academic interest in agro-chemical landscapes produced by farmers encouraged to grow a handful of crops, sustained by heavy applications of fertilisers and the ruthless chemical control of weeds, pests and diseases. But even under these conditions it could happen again, and for those who garden – hopefully without too much effort – it is something very practical indeed. The gardener who copes with weeds by grassing down the flower beds, and then makes spinneys of the lawns, is starting on the same course that the countryside would if left to itself.

The grasses in a lawn resist invasion by annual weeds. Competition is permanent and the matrix formed by the leaves of the grasses and herbs is almost complete for much of the year, offering few unoccupied niches. From time to time grass wears thin, or worm casts cover the surface, and seedlings have opportunities to establish themselves. It is notable that most of these intruders will be perennials – chances of an entry are too few and far between to throw away success by not hanging on to a space once it has been found. Later, when looking at ways to make a meadow in a garden, we will come back to the problems of gaining an entry to an established grass sward.

Deciduous woodland – the spinney in the corner formed by one or two small trees – possesses the even stronger defences of a three-dimensional matrix. Plants in woodland communities benefit from each other's protection and shelter, but they compete for light and water and nutrients, and only those naturally adapted to take the chances and endure the hazards of this balance can survive.

Articles in magazines, programmes on television, garden lore handed on in allotments or saloon bars, make much of the problems of shade but when the right kinds of plants are used – the woodland flora of the world provides ample scope for imagination – it is one of the simplest environments in which to set up self-sufficient, long-lasting alliances between plants.

## PLANTS THAT DO WELL IN THE SHADIER PARTS OF GARDENS

The genera listed below all include a number of species which grow well in the shade of deciduous trees. The list should not be interpreted uncritically: often the range of plants referred to here covers only a part of the diversity of the genus as a whole. Thus Campanula refers to the tall woodland species: Lonicera, to the climbing honeysuckles: Saxifraga is almost restricted to the species which are akin to London Pride: and Viola refers to those which gardeners know as violets.

*Acanthus.* Large perennial plants from the Mediterranean, grown for their distinctive spiky or broad, rounded foliage, as well as their flowers; they do surprisingly well even in dry shade.

*Acer.* Popular small trees, or large shrubs, some with crimson or dissected foliage, that grow best in sheltered, lightly shaded positions on neutral or acid soils. Young plants must be protected from late frosts in the spring. Many have very attractive bark.

*Aquilegia.* Valuable, easy, colourful, self-seeding perennials, that colonise well and will seek out spaces in which to grow.

*Anaphalis.* Among the few silver-foliaged plants that grow well in light shade; also useful because their white flowers are produced during late summer.

*Aralia.* Tall shrubs grown for their imposing leaves and dramatic effect; easy to grow in most soils and situations. The forms with variegated leaves make striking specimen shrubs.

*Arum.* The wild arum is a distinctive plant in ordinary or dry shade; the Italian arum's marbled leaves make it a valuable space-filler in winter/early spring.

*Aruncus.* Tall perennial with strong plumes of ivory flowers, suitable for most soils in light shade.

*Asarum.* Ground-hugging matrixmakers; happy in dense shade, and should be planted thickly as weed suppressors between and beneath taller plants.

*Astilbe.* Colourful plumes of flowers and attractive foliage; needs moist soils to grow well, enjoys light shade. Very long-lived, persistent plants.

*Astrantia.* Long-lived, easily grown, tolerant plants. Varieties, including a variegated form, of A. *major* are widely available and good. A. *maxima*, less common, is well worth finding, and spreads gently but persistently by rhizomes.

*Aucuba.* Shrubs notable for their shining evergreen foliage, glossy red berries and ability to endure dry shade; worthy of less ascetic situations.

*Bergenia.* Very persistent, easily grown evergreen

perennials, planted for their broad, leathery leaves; newer varieties have better colours and foliage than some of the old stand-bys.

*Brunnera.* A perennial forget-me-not with handsome, broad leaves, able to establish itself in light, quite dry shade, where it may colonise actively.

*Caltha.* Marsh marigolds do well in light shade in moist/boggy places. The white form is particularly attractive; all but the double form self-seed in the right place.

*Campanula.* Several tall species are good woodland plants; outstanding are *C. latiloba* and *latifolia* in moderate to deep shade, and cultivars of *C. persicifolia* in light, dry shade. White-flowered forms are particularly valuable as shade enlighteners.

*Clematis.* Attractive, often showy, climbers with beautiful flowers, and great covering power; many of the species are easily grown in semi-natural woodland. One kind or another is in flower throughout the year.

*Convallaria.* Lilies-of-the-valley are good colonisers able to succeed on dry calcareous soils, even in quite deep shade beneath other plants and in competition with their roots.

*Crataegus.* Easily grown small/medium trees that tolerate exposure, shade and drought; several are outstanding for autumn colours or fruits, or both.

*Daphne.* Most are intensely fragrant small shrubs tolerant of light shade; several, including *D. mezereon* and *D. laureola,* are able to grow in deep shade. Both will self-seed in the right conditions.

*Darmera.* Strong perennial for moist places, with persistent ground-enveloping rhizomes. Pink flowers in late spring on naked stems, followed by large round leaves.

*Dicentra.* *D. spectabilis* and its white form are spectacular even in dry, dense shade; forms of *D. eximia* and *formosa* infill enthusiastically between shrubs and taller plants.

*Dryopteris.* The male fern, amongst others, has attractively contrasting foliage; all are long-lived, easily grown plants, even in dry shade.

*Duchesnea.* A creeping infiller with yellow flowers and strawberry-like, but unenjoyable, fruits. It tolerates deep shade and drought, but does much better in damper conditions.

*Euonymus.* Deciduous species make large shrubs with dramatic fruits and some have fine autumn colours; they grow best in light shade and fertile soil. Evergreen species are good ground-coverers amongst other shrubs.

*Epimedium.* Very long-lived, easily grown herbaceous perennials, holding their ground tenaciously to resist weeds; fine, almost evergreen foliage.

*Euphorbia.* Forms of the wood spurge including 'Purpurea' and *robbiae* are valuable in flower and foliage for light, or even deep, shade.

*Fatsia.* A tall shrub with massive, glossy, evergreen leaves which benefits from shelter. It does well in the shadow of deciduous trees and walls.

*Filipendula.* Pink or white-flowered relatives of the meadowsweet, that grow best on moist soils in light shade; golden-leaved and variegated forms are available.

*Gaultheria.* Densely foliaged, evergreen shrubs that fill spaces between taller plants on sandy, acid soils. They have purple/black berries in the autumn.

*Geranium.* Large genus with many excellent low-growing, ground-hugging species, hybrids and cultivars; many are long-flowering and shade-tolerant. Easily propagated, and first-rate for forming a matrix.

*Hedera.* Ivies make useful infillers between shrubs and trees, and ground-cover amongst perennials and bulbs; tolerant of dense shade once established and resistant to some herbicides.

*Helleborus.* Persistent, easily grown perennials; *H. foetidus* grows in dry shade; *HH. orientalis* and *corsicus* are better in more fertile, lighter positions amongst shrubs.

*Hemerocallis.* Long-lived clump-forming perennials; thrive in light shade on rich, moist soils; their upright, linear foliage contrasts with broad-leaved perennials.

*Hosta.* Popular perennials with broad leaves forming tenacious, weed-excluding clumps; best in light shade and fertile conditions which do not become too dry; a great many forms are grown for their foliage qualities.

*Hydrangea.* Valuable late-flowering shrubs for lightly shaded, fertile, and preferably not dry situations; colours may depend on soil acidity.

*Hypericum.* Tolerant, easily grown shrubs and low ground-cover; persistent; *H. calycinum* may not be easy to remove once established in the wrong place.

*Ilex.* Hollies are useful evergreen large shrubs/trees; tolerant of shade, prefer fertile, water-retentive soils; female or hermaphrodite forms are needed for berries.

*Iris.* *I. foetidissima* is a handsome, evergreen foliage plant that does well even in dry shade and bears striking fruits; 'Citrina' best for flowers; there is also a variegated form.

*Kalmia.* Medium-sized, evergreen shrubs with glossy foliage and pleated pink buds and flowers. Tolerant of light shade on acid, sheltered soils which are not too dry.

*Lamium.* Valuable perennials with attractive foliage that fill spaces between shrubs and taller plants; easy to grow, easy to propagate and tolerant of a wide range of conditions.

*Leucobryum.* A dense, velvet-surfaced moss forming rounded cushions that make a most attractive surface cover in dry, dense shade; resistant to paraquat.

*Ligularia.* Large, often coarse-leaved perennials with bright orange or yellow flowers; do well in light shade, on constantly moist soils.

*Liriope.* Evergreen tufts of grass-like foliage with clustered spikes of flowers similar to grape hyacinths in the autumn; tolerant and easy to grow on neutral and acid soils.

*Lonicera.* Climbing honeysuckles; many are fragrant, especially at night; will grow in dense shade, but need to reach sunlight to flower well.

*Lunaria.* Honesties make attractive spring-flowering biennials and perennials; the former are likely to self-sow and colonise well. Both are grown for their seed pods as much as their flowers.

*Lychnis.* *L.coronaria* is a silver-leaved, short-lived, self-seeding perennial which does well in dry, light shade; colours range from white through pink to deep magenta.

*Mahonia.* Evergreen shrubs with striking foliage; M. *Japonica* notable for fragrant flowers and large, infertile berries; most flower during the winter or in early spring.

*Matteucia.* Rhizomes form shuttlecock-shaped clusters of fronds; a beautiful plant that is very shade-tolerant but needs fertile, constantly moist soil to do well.

*Meconopsis.* Welsh poppies are excellent spontaneous colonisers in places which suit them; others require humid locations on moist humus-rich soils to do well.

*Milium.* Bowle's golden grass, a variety of the wood millet, grows easily in light shade on dry to moist soil; self-seeds without making itself a nuisance.

*Pernettya.* Small, prickly evergreen shrubs make dense thickets on acid soils. Grown for the conspicuous clusters of large white, pink or cerise berries.

*Phyllitis.* A number of forms of the hart's tongue fern exist; all provide useful evergreen foliage in contrast to other plants; tolerant of dry shade and calcareous soils.

*Polygonatum.* Solomon's seals are active, graceful colonisers in light or moderate shade on ground which does not become too dry.

*Polygonum.* Varieties of the knotweed include long-flowering P. *affine* for dense, low cover in light shade, and P. *campanulatum* for infilling between and under shrubs.

*Primula.* Primroses and relatives do well on good soils in light shade, and many candelabras take light shade on soil which is constantly moist.

*Polypodium.* Evergreen ferns which will colonise under deciduous trees even in deep, dry shade. In humid parts of the country they will grow epiphytically on trunks and branches of trees.

*Polystichum.* Ferns with large, exceptionally beautiful fronds, contrasting well with broad-leaved plants; best in light shade on moist, fertile soils, to make the most of their foliage.

*Pulmonaria.* Persistent, easily grown perennials; self-sow and colonise well; now available in a wide range of varieties, many with striking foliage.

*Rhododendron.* Evergreen and deciduous shrubs for acid soils; a great variety of sizes, colours and flower forms; many have extremely attractive foliage, and beautiful bark and buds in spring.

*Rodgersia.* Large-leaved perennials for light shade on ground which does not dry out; strikingly effective in flower and foliage throughout the summer.

*Ruscus.* Small, upright prickly shrubs that form dense thickets and do well even in dry shade; berries are unusual and depend on presence of male and female plants.

*Sarcococca.* The sweet boxes are a group of small, evergreen shrubs, with flowers that scent the air in winter; most tolerate heavy, dry shade in summer.

*Saxifraga.* London pride and relatives grow and persist well even in dry shade; forms of S. *cor-*

*tusifolia* flower in autumn and need humus-rich positions, which do not become too dry.

*Smilacina.* Close relative of Solomon's seal; needs fertile, relatively moist, acid soil in the light to moderate shade provided by deciduous trees.

*Tellima.* Densely-foliaged woodland plant; 'Purpurea' produces rounded hummocks of crimson leaves in winter; easy to propagate and easy to grow under most conditions.

*Trollius.* Herbaceous perennials with brilliant flowers, which tolerate light to moderate shade provided the ground is fertile and never becomes too dry.

*Viburnum.* A large group of evergreen and deciduous flowering and berrying shrubs; the majority are easy to grow, many are fragrant and most tolerate light shade.

*Vinca.* Periwinkles are excellent colonisers; *V. minor* is easily controlled and tolerates dry shade; more invasive *V. major* needs more fertile conditions.

Many of the candelabra primulas take light shade on soil which is constantly moist

*Viola.* Violets do well even in quite dense shade and many are fragrant. Most seed themselves freely; purple-leaved *V. labradorica* is particularly useful.

## COPING WITH SUNSHINE

When chores mount up, hard-pressed gardeners toy first with drastic solutions that include burying the garden beneath loads of ready-mixed concrete. Less desperate second thoughts, or well-meant advice from friends and neighbours, suggest that making lawns out of most of the flower beds and filling the remainder with shrubs would cut down gardening and leave more time for other things.

But borders filled with shrubs look dreary for much of the year, and only partially solve the problem of too much work. Lawns never saved anyone hard work – although lawns and areas of roughly mown grass place maintenance on the familiar footing of so many cuts per week, per month or per year and can be done by taking the mower out of the shed and getting on with the cutting. Knowing what should be done is the attraction of grass, and a very great attraction it is. So much so that the lawn could be the logo of the suburban style, and provides a refuge for males standing by uneasily in Jekyll gardens, who grasp the mower as a lifeline to take them from the quicksands of weeding amongst unfamiliar plants to firmer ground.

But shrubs without the intervention of trees and the ground support of perennials form incomplete matrices whose spaces invite invasion by other plants. Many of these will be grasses, at home wherever gaps appear and the sun shines strongly. The result is a perpetual struggle against the dogged determination of the border to turn into scrub – the natural step on the way to full-blown forest.

Scrub is a word to avoid when describing the gardening efforts of friends; few would think it a complimentary description of their new mixed border. But like it or not, mixed borders are garden portrayals of the mixture of shrubs, grasses and herbs that grow naturally on sandy wastes or on steep, dry banks. Scrub persists only where soils are so infertile or liable to drought that grasses and herbs grow sparsely and trees can gain no foothold. These limitations are seldom found in gardens, where higher than average fertility and abundant water supplies are more probable. Combined with sunlight, these create opportunities which grasses and the more ebullient weeds are well adapted to use to their advantage.

When trees are not wanted but shrubs are, the alternatives are either to form as complete a matrix as possible with few spaces where outsiders can gain a roothold; or, to find some way to keep weeds out of spaces which invite their entry. A matrix can be formed by:

1 Reproducing the conditions that lead to natural scrub development.
2 Using plants – and mixtures of plants – to form as complete a matrix as possible in the absence of trees.
 Weeds can be kept out by:
1 Using mulches, repeatedly and effectively, wherever gaps appear between shrubs.

2 Using contact and systemic herbicides to destroy all existing weeds, and repeated sprays of pre-emergence herbicides to prevent reinfestation from germinating seeds.

## REPRODUCING NATURAL SCRUB

Hawthorn bushes on ancient commons, and acres of gorse; blackthorn on steep dry banks, and broom on sandy slopes; the wayfaring tree and wild privet on downland chalk, rhododendrons and heathers on thin layers of peat above sandy soils. These are models for mixed borders. In each, impoverished, infertile soils – often periodically drought-stricken – enable shrubs to hold their ground amongst grasses and herbs, and resist invasion by trees, which need more ample provisions.

Gardens with similar conditions are places where the right plants, put in the right places, will establish alliances of shrubs and sub-shrubs that can form a matrix without overhead tree cover, and with only sparse support from ground-covering perennials. Shrubs that succeed under these conditions are those that grow naturally in hot, dry, sunny places. Many will be members of the pea and mint families, or be aromatic and silver-leaved shrubs and sub-shrubs from parts of the world with Mediterranean climates. The broad-leaved viburnums, spindles, forsythias and loniceras are natural allies of trees; they are much less drought-tolerant and less likely to be happy in exposed, unshadowed and parched places.

Most gardens are not natural settings for scrub. Successful settlements that grew up to become villages and small towns were most often those founded on fertile ground, where loam and clay soils hold the nutrients and water that encourage grasses and trees to grow well. These are situations where shrubs have difficulty holding their own, and traditional gardening does little to make things easier for them – for traditional gardening includes the traditional jobbing gardener.

Many of these characters understand shrubs much as they understand Brussels sprouts and potatoes, and the need to keep lawns shorn almost to the roots. They understand that when shrubs are planted each needs room to develop, and a forsythia, a deutzia or a weigela will be given 3m or so in which to flourish, flower briefly and form a dense green mass. They understand that the ground between shrubs should be forked every winter to break it up, destroy other forms of plant life, and ensure that dressings of artificial fertilisers reach the roots. They understand pruning – but not as a skill, rather as a curb involving close cropping with a pair of shears to keep spaces clear between the shrubs in which to fork, weed and feed. But when Dick or Bob or Wilf or Jack is laid low with a bad back for a month or two, the shrub border's vulnerability to invading grasses and other weeds, encouraged by the forked-over, fertile open ground, becomes all too obvious.

A matrix can be built up based mainly on shrubs, reinforced with perennial plants, grasses and ferns. This package carries a more familiar ring as the mixed border, and has become as notable a feature of late twentieth-century gardens as herbaceous borders were when Edward reigned and Jekyll ruled.

The aims should be:

1 To plant thickly – partly to crowd out weeds, partly to hold some of the soil fertility in the vegetation, and partly to establish a balance which keeps them all in check by making plants compete for limited resources.
2 To plant shrubs so that they form clumps or citadels emerging from the lower-growing perennials, either as individuals or as close-set groups.
3 To use the perennials, grasses and ferns as a close cover between and even under the shrubs, so that every square inch of the soil's surface is occupied.
4 To avoid disturbing the soil, breaking up the roots or adding concentrated fertilisers.
5 To improve soil structure, and add modestly to soil fertility when necessary, with top dressings of organic matter worked down amongst the plants.

### GRAVEL GARDENS

Much more drastic measures are possible to re-create scrub. Bearing in mind that low fertility and restricted supply of water are the conditions that encourage scrub, and that it develops naturally on sandy, gravelly soils, the obvious answer is to make a garden out of gravel.

In principle and practice this is remarkably easy. It need be nothing more than a deep layer – 15 to 30cm – of gravel above the surface of the ground. A deaf ear should be turned to inner promptings, or

neighbours' suggestions, that a little soil, leaf-mould, peat, bark, compost or anything whatever should be added to the gravel to make life easier for the plants, and these should be installed with roots as near bare as possible. Flattened gravels are preferable to rounded ones because they are more pleasant to work with and to walk on, and un-washed gravels with a thin coating of clay on every stone provide roots with all the support and sustenance they need.

Gravel gardens are planted like any other garden. This is easily said but less easily done, for gravel refills a hole almost as fast as it is dug, and burying the roots of even small plants becomes a furious scrabble against gravity. The roots grow through the layer of gravel and down to the soil below, and usually need no more watering or care than they would if planted straight into a regulation flower border. The gravel provides an undemanding, easily maintained surface, and an environment which many plants find extremely congenial – particularly the evergreen, aromatic sub-shrubs from hot dry parts of the world.

Paradoxically, this is a most practical and successful way to deal with heavy, sticky, sporadically waterlogged, seasonally hard-baked, often highly fertile clay soils. In their natural state these are frustratingly difficult to cope with: making life hazardous every winter for plants whose survival depends on good drainage, and drying brick-hard each summer with cracks that tear roots apart. Bury the clays beneath 20cm of gravel, and forget it.

### SHRUBS FOR SCRUBS

In a very broad way shrubs can be divided into two groups: those that emerge and those that smother.

Emergent shrubs insinuate themselves amongst grasses or through other shrubs, or form a layer within the shadow of trees. They either produce clusters of tall stems from ground level, or construct a framework of branches on which the leaves gradually shade out most of the grasses and herbs beneath them, and thus hold a space amongst neighbouring shrubs and small trees. They exist in close-knit associations with the plants around them, and survive by forming a balanced matrix with their companions. In sunlit parts of gardens, especially on fertile soils, they are open to infiltration by other plants including grasses and weeds of all kinds.

Mixed borders are garden portrayals of the mixtures of
shrubs, grasses and herbs that grow naturally on sandy
wastes, or on steep, dry banks

Smothering shrubs grow where the ground is dry at certain seasons, and on acid, nitrogen-deficient soils. These are places where essential resources, water or a vital nutrient, are in short supply, and survival depends on gaining more or less exclusive use of what is available. Each plant spreads out to exclude competitors and hold a bit of ground. These shrubs are effective weed-smotherers wherever the balance is tipped in their favour; but fertile soils which remain consistantly moist make it easier for grasses and other weeds to penetrate their defences.

### EMERGENT AND SMOTHERING SHRUBS

**Emergent:** Should be planted as part of a matrix of shrubs, perennial plants, etc which can form an interlocking and mutually dependent community. Likely to do well in fertile borders, often in association with trees.

| | | |
|---|---|---|
| Abelia | Amelanchier | Aralia |
| Aronia | Berberis | Buddleia |
| Callicarpa | Chaenomeles | Chimonanthus |
| Clethra | Cornus | *Corylopsis |
| Corylus | Cotinus | Cytisus |
| Deutzia | Elaeagnus | Euonymus |
| Forsythia | Fuchsia | Hibiscus |
| Hippophae | Indigofera | Kerria |
| Kolkwitzia | Leycesteria | Ligustrum |
| Lonicera | Magnolia | Neillia |
| Osmanthus | Paeonia | Perowskia |
| Philadelphus | Photinia | Potentilla |
| Pyracantha | Rhamnus | *Rhododendron |
| Rhus | Ribes | Rosa |
| Rubus | Salix | Sambucus |
| Sorbaria | Spartium | Spiraea |
| Stachyrus | Staphylea | Styrax |
| Syringa | Tamarix | Viburnum |
| Weigela | | |

The essential qualities which enable scrub to persist are
low fertility and a restricted supply of water – and the
obvious answer is to make a garden out of gravel

123

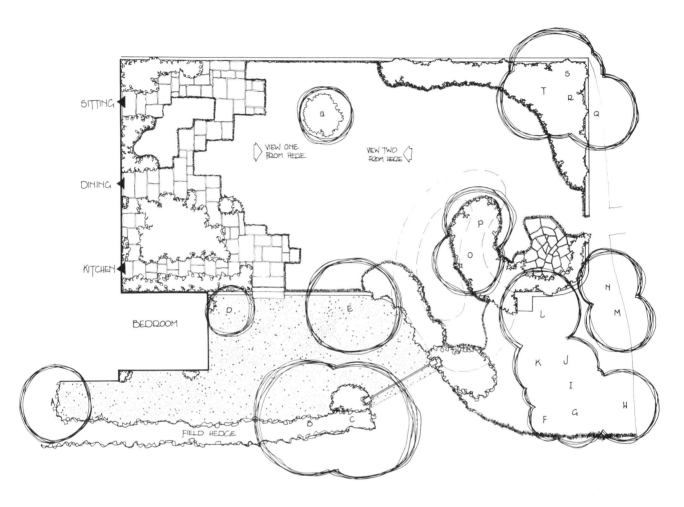

From cowhouse to bungalow. The garden is not overlooked; the views out over the fields are simple and pleasant, and the site is sheltered. With no need for screening or shelter, the garden can include its surroundings.

| | | | |
|---|---|---|---|
| A | Existing *Acer campestre* | L | Existing *Salix alba* |
| B | Existing *Fraxinus excelsior* | M | Existing *Corylus avellana* |
| C | Existing *Fraxinus excelsior* | N | Existing *Corylus avellana* |
| D | New *Amelanchier lamarckii* | O | New *Acer davidii* |
| E | New *Fraxinus ornus* | P | New *Acer davidii* |
| F | Existing *Corylus avellana* | Q | Existing *Fraxinus excelsior* |
| G | Existing *Corylus avellana* | R | New *Acer campestre* |
| H | Existing *Corylus avellana* | S | New *Acer campestre* |
| I | Existing *Corylus avellana* | T | New *Acer campestre* |
| J | Existing *Corylus avellana* | U | New *Amelanchier lamarckii* |
| K | Existing *Quercus robur* | | |

View one. The planting within the garden is arranged to lead the eye gently out
to the avenue of trees beyond. A secluded place to sit can be glimpsed through the coloured
stems of the *Acer davidii*

View two – the house is long and low. The planting in the garden emphasises the horizontal
line by using a lot of spreading, carpeting and mound-forming plants accentuated by the tree
stems, clumps of sword- and strap-shaped leaves, and occasional tall spikes of flowers

**Smothering:** Succeed as individuals, each planted where it can form a self-maintaining, weed-resistant clump of foliage and stems. Many are very suitable for hot, dry, sunny banks; gravel gardens; or gardens on acid sands or peat soils.

| | | |
|---|---|---|
| *Andromeda | *Arctostaphylos | Artemisia |
| Ballota | Buxus | *Calluna |
| *Cassiope | Ceanothus | Cistus |
| *Cyathodes | *Daboecia | Dorycnium, |
| *Erica | Euryops | *Gaultheria |
| Genista | Halimium | Hebe |
| Helianthemum | Helichrysum | Lavandula |
| *Ledum | *Leucothoe | Myrtus |
| Olearia | *Pernettya | Phlomis |
| *Phyllodoce | *Pieris | *Rhododendron |
| Ruta | Salvia | Santolina |
| Skimmia | Thymus | Ulex |
| *Vaccinium | Vinca | |

\* Genera which contain a high proportion of acid-loving species, many occur naturally on moist, nitrogen-deficient soils.

Rhododendron appears under both headings. Some species in this genus are compact, rounded shrubs that occupy the place of heaths above the tree-line on mountains; others are upright shrubs, deciduous and evergreen, that grow amongst woodland at lower altitudes.

## ROSES FOR COUNTRY STYLES

Tucked away amongst the long list of emergent shrubs is the genus *Rosa*, which includes the ancestors of all garden roses, and a great many species which have played little or no part in gardens. It is ironic that gardeners have chosen to grow these most sociable shrubs in dedicated beds, often strictly isolated from other plants. The habit has become so ingrained that there is a widespread belief that roses are bad mixers.

Of all our shrubs, roses are amongst the most capable of holding their own whether with plants growing on the ground beneath them, or in an aerial network of stems and leaves

Wild roses are amongst the pioneer species of natural scrub and it is no coincidence that they, and other pioneers like brambles, blackthorn and hawthorn, are armed with sharp points to fend off the muzzles of animals grazing the grasses through which they make their entry. But these adventurers also survive by forming impenetrable thickets, in which different species intertwine and support and protect one another. Of all our shrubs, roses are amongst the most capable of holding their own whether with plants growing on the ground beneath them, or in an aerial network of stems and leaves.

And that is fortunate, because for much of the year roses look uninteresting at best and forlornly tatty at worst. Modern bush roses are extreme examples of attaching so much importance to a striking flower that almost all the other qualities for which plants are valued are sacrificed. This penalty is paid *in extremis* when roses are grown on their own; mixed with other shrubs and plants their shortcomings are veiled.

Roses, like conifers – but for entirely different reasons – impose themselves on their surroundings. Not just when grown in rose gardens, when that is inevitable, but also as part of a more general planting. Our reactions to their flowers and their stance make them stand out, and infuse a garden with their presence. But they have no strong structure or other features which can be used to make patterns or a definable impact, and there is little variety in the impressions they create. Gardens of roses skilfully planted with perennials and other shrubs can be very beautiful, and to many are the essence of the ideal country garden, but it is hard to find ways to give them a feeling of individuality and the sense of place that distinguishes one garden from another.

It is frequently pointed out that only a very few species, out of the many that exist, have been hybridised to produce our garden roses and it is certainly true that the most popular varieties display only a small number of the qualities possessed by the genus. That does not mean that we need be so limited in those we grow and the ways we grow them: quite undemanding enquiries will reveal a much broader choice than the few-score favourite hybrid teas, floribundas, climbers and popular shrub roses stocked by most garden centres.

## A CHOICE OF ROSES

The variety of roses available is bewilderingly rich. The following list, restricted for the sake of space to only fifty kinds, looks at some which can be used in gardens in company with ground-covering perennials and other shrubs. The choice – inevitably arbitrary – concentrates on those which have qualities in addition to the production of stunningly attractive flowers.

### 'Abraham Darby'

| | |
|---|---|
| Apricot-yellow 2.0 × 1.75m Modern shrub Fragrant | A well-set bushy rose with very healthy foliage and large double flowers. Continues to flower well for a long season. |

### 'Alba Semi-plena'

| | |
|---|---|
| White 2.5 × 1.5m Alba Fragrant | Semi-double pure white flowers in small trusses during midsummer, on tall, upright plants. Blue-grey leaves are disease-free and attractive. The plants will tolerate light shade and poor soils. |

### 'Andersonii'

| | |
|---|---|
| Rich rose-pink 2.0 × 2.5m Species hybrid Hips | This is a selected form of the wild dog rose, with larger, deeper-coloured, more abundant flowers. The foliage remains healthy and good crops of bright scarlet, oval hips are attractive from autumn onwards. |

### 'Apothecaries Rose'

| | |
|---|---|
| Light crimson 1.25 × 1.5m Gallica Fragrant | Masses of large single flowers during midsummer. Grows as a compact shrub, which should be encouraged to sucker and form a clump of stems. |

### 'Blanc Double de Coubert'

| | |
|---|---|
| White 2.0 × 1.75m Rugosa Fragrant | Large, fragile-looking double white flowers through the summer. Foliage is healthy, and the plants are tolerant of infertile soils and light shade. Good yellow autumn colours. |

## 'Bloomfield Abundance'

Pale pink
2.0 × 1.5m
Chinensis

A remarkably upright plant; tall stems carry huge trusses of tiny flowers. Particularly good in late summer. Tolerant of poor soils.

## 'Buff Beauty'

Apricot-yellow
1.5 × 2.0m
Hybrid musk
Fragrant

Produces arching branches with full trusses of double flowers throughout the second half of the summer. Can be fairly hard-pruned or left to grow with little attention. Needs fertile conditions.

## 'Celestial'

Pale pink
2.0 × 1.5m
Alba
Fragrant

Very attractive clusters of flowers in midsummer. The leaden green foliage is practically disease-free and the plants are tolerant of in-fertile soils and light shade. Per-sistent and long-lived.

## 'Cerise Bouquet'

Crimson-rose
3.5 × 4.0m
Modern shrub

This produces an enormous, arching bush, with large trusses of flowers in midsummer. The foliage is grey-green and healthy. Best planted so that it arches over smaller shrubs and plants.

## 'Complicata'

Rose-pink
3.0 × 2.0m
Gallica
Good foliage

Like a large, clear-coloured dog rose with a ring of yellow stamens. Very vigorous, almost a climber, with bright green, healthy foliage. Tolerant of poor conditions and infertile soils.

## 'Comte de Chambord'

Rosy pink
1.25 × 1.0m
Portland
Fragrant

A vigorous but small bush, with fully double flowers throughout the second half of the summer. In spite of its small stature it is a rose which is tolerant of poor, infertile conditions.

## 'Dapple Dawn'

Clear pink
1.5 × 1.75m
Modern shrub

Large single flowers carried in trusses in great quantity and over a very long period. Make broad, spreading, disease-free mounds of foliage. Can be pruned hard or left to grow freely.

## 'Dentelle de Malines'

Light pink
1.5 × 2.0m
Modern shrub

Clusters of small, almost pompom-like double flowers on wide-spreading, arching stems in mid-summer. The dense growth makes a fast-growing, weed-excluding ground-cover.

## 'Dortmund'

Red
2.5 × 2.0m
Hyb Pimpinelli-
folia .
Fragrant

Large clusters of bold, single flowers, each with a white eye. Exceptionally vigorous shrub rose or semi-climber, with deep green, notably healthy foliage, and repeat-flowering in the autumn.

## 'Empress Josephine'

Rose pink
1.25 × 1.0m
Gallica
Fragrant

Large, informally double flowers in midsummer. Compact growth with dense healthy foliage. Able to perform well under infertile conditions.

## 'Felicia'

Silvery pink
2.0 × 1.5m
Hybrid musk
Fragrant

Upright growth, and clusters of extremely pretty, medium-sized flowers throughout the second half of the summer. Healthy, disease-free foliage. Can be moderately pruned each year or left to grow.

## 'Fru Dagmar Hastrup'

Clear pink
1.0 × 1.5m
Rugosa
Hips

Broad, single flowers in clusters on spreading bushes, followed by large scarlet hips. Foliage rough, bright apple-green and healthy. Able to do well on sandy soils and in exposed positions.

## 'Fruhlingsduft'

Lemon-yellow
3.0 × 2.0m
Hyb Pimpinelli-
folia
Fine foliage

Double flowers, flushed with pink in midsummer. Makes strong, upright, arching bushes with plenty of space below for ground planting. Masses of deep green, healthy foliage.

## 'Fruhlingsmorgen'

Cerise-pink
2.0 × 1.5m
Hyb Pimpinelli-
folia

Large single flowers with pale yellow centres and a prominent ring of anthers. Broadly arching shrubs with midgreen foliage, and plenty of space below for ground planting.

## 'Golden Chersonese'

Golden yellow
2.5 × 1.75m
Species hybrid
Foliage

Fairly small flowers carried singly along arching branches on tall shrubs. Attractive fern-like foliage casts only a light shade, and combines well with ground planting.

## 'Graham Thomas'

Soft yellow
1.5 × 1.25m
Modern shrub
Fragrant

Fully double flowers carried in small clusters from June till October. Healthy, disease-free foliage on shrubs that cope well with poor soils.

## 'Greenmantle'

Rose-red
2.5 × 1.5m
Sweet briar
Fragrant foliage

Strong upright growth with clusters of single dog rose-like flowers in midsummer. Associates well with other shrubs, and is tolerant of light shade and infertile conditions.

## 'Lavender Lassy'

Lavender-pink
2.0 × 1.5m
Hybrid musk

A very upright, floriferous rose in flower from early July to October. Bright green, healthy foliage; plants will cope with second-rate soils.

## 'Lord Penzance'

Buff-yellow
2.5 × 2.0m
Sweet briar
Fragrant foliage

Single flowers on vigorous, densely-foliaged bushes. A good rose for an informal hedge and for partially shaded, infertile situations. Combines well with ground planting and other shrubs.

## 'Nathalie Nypels'

Rose-pink
1.0 × 1.0m
Polyantha
Fragrant

Low-growing, sideways-spreading rose with attractive semi-double flowers. Healthy and vigorous in spite of its small size, combining well with other small, compact shrubs.

## 'Nevada'

White
2.5 × 3.0m
Modern shrub

Very widely spreading shrub, with long arching branches covered with large single flowers during June. Usually repeat-flowers, but less profusely. Provides plenty of space for ground planting.

## 'Parkdirektor Riggers'

Crimson-red
3.0 × 2.5m
Modern
    climber

Clusters of large single flowers, amongst healthy bright green foliage. Like many of the more up-right climbing roses this can make a dramatic impact when partially supported by other tall shrubs.

## 'Prosperity'

Ivory white
2.0 × 1.75m
Hybrid musk
Fragrant

Large trusses of very double, medium-sized flowers on long stems from early July till autumn. Deep green healthy foliage. Can be pruned moderately hard or left to grow freely.

## *Rosa californica* 'Plena'

Lilac-pink
2.5 × 2.0m
Species

Semi-double flowers on large rounded bushes in midsummer. Fits well into natural planting; foliage remains attractively green and healthy-looking when the flowers are over.

## R. chinensis 'Mutabilis'

Buff/Rose-red
2.0 × 1.25m
China

Progressively changes colour as the flowers open, from pale creamy, buff-yellow to a rosy crimson. Single, often rather floppy flowers on open, very thorny bushes, with healthy deep green foliage.

## R. farreri persetosa

Lilac-pink
1.75 × 2.0m
Species
Hips/autumn
colour

Small single flowers are followed by bright orange-scarlet hips. Attractive fern-like foliage develops rich autumn colours. An excellent small shrub to combine with informal planting.

## R. fedtschenkoana

White
1.75 × 1.25m
Species
Hips

Single flowers produced over a long period through the summer. Grey-green, densely foliaged shrubs with bright red hips from autumn onwards. Able to cope well with poor conditions and infertile soils.

## R. glauca

Pale pink
2.5 × 2.0m
Species
Foliage/Hips

Flowers are attractive but small, single and sparse; they are followed by deep crimson hips. The plant is grown for its handsome plum-purple foliage. Can be hard-pruned occasionally for maximum effect.

## R. hugonis 'Cantabrigiensis'

Pale yellow
2.5 × 1.5m
Species hybrid
Foliage

Single flowers, produced very early on tall upright stems. Attractive fern-like foliage and hips in the autumn. Never a showy rose, but combines well with other planting and puts up with poor conditions.

## R. moyesii 'Geranium'

Deep red

Single dark red, glowing flowers

2.25 × 3.0m
Species
Hips

followed by masses of large, flask-shaped, orange-scarlet hips. Grows well in association with other plants and will tolerate infertile situations.

## R. nitida

Rose-pink
0.75 × 1.0m
Species
Autumn
colour

Small single flowers produced profusely on short, upright stems. Should be grown on its own roots and encouraged to produce suckers. An excellent compact rose with brilliant autumn colours.

## R. omeiensis pteracantha

Blush white
2.5 × 3.0m
Species
Thorns

Small flowers followed by red hips, with attractive, ferny foliage. The real reasons for growing this are the broad, winged thorns along the stems: when young these are translucent ruby-red.

## R. roxburghii

Pale pink
2.0 × 2.0m
Species
Hips

Unremarkable single flowers carried rather sparsely on bushy plants, with attractive fern-like leaves. Grown almost entirely for its remarkable burr-like hips – a matter of interest rather than of beauty.

## R. rugosa

Deep rose-pink
2.0 × 1.5m
Species
Hips

Large single flowers appear during a long period and are followed by very striking round, deep red hips. The white-flowered form, 'Alba', is equally worth growing. Both respond well to hard pruning.

## R. sweginzowii 'Macrocarpa'

Deep pink
3.5 × 3.0m
Species
Hips

A large rose grown mainly for its hips. Combines well with other shrubs, and vigorous groundcover, especially in informal – almost natural – settings. Will tolerate infertile conditions and shade.

## R. woodsii fendlerii

Lilac pink
1.5 × 1.5m
Species
Hips

Clusters of bright single flowers are followed by persistent waxy, red hips. Attractive, daintily formed foliage, and the ability to grow well in poor soils and light shade make this a useful shrub.

## 'Rose d'Amour'

Deep pink
2.5 × 2.0m
Species hybrid
Fragrant

Double flowers are carried for a long period in late June and July. Forms a large, rounded, natural-looking bush, which combines well with other planting and will tolerate light shade.

## 'Roseraie de l'Hay'

Crimson
2.0 × 1.75m
Rugosa
Fragrant

Large informal, double flowers over a very long period. The bush grows strongly upright, with healthy foliage that develops attractive autumn colours. Out-standingly fragrant.

## 'Schneezwerg'

White
1.75 × 1.25m
Rugosa
Hips

Medium-sized, semi-double flowers formed almost as neatly as camellias. Remains in flower through the second half of summer, and carries scarlet hips in autumn. Attractive disease-free foliage.

## 'Smarty'

Soft pink
1.0 × 2.0m
Modern shrub

Clusters of single flowers, re-sembling large dog roses, over a long period. Deep green, disease-free foliage on low spreading plants that are tolerant of poor conditions and light shade.

## 'Stanwell Perpetual'

Blush pink
1.75 × 1.75m
Hyb Pimpinelli-
folium
Fragrant

Very double, rather informal flowers produced from June till September. A lax, arching shrub that may take several years to form a bush. Tolerant of poor conditions and a good mixer.

## 'Vanity'

Rose-pink
2.0 × 2.5m
Hybrid musk
Fragrant

Sprays of bright, single flowers on arching stems are produced from July to October. A very attractive rose that fits well into semi-natural settings and grows easily amongst other shrubs and plants.

## 'White Pet'

White
1.75 × 2.0m
Polyantha

Large trusses of small pompom flowers from July to September. Healthy foliage; forms a low, spreading shrub that covers the ground well. Able to tolerate light shade.

## 'White Wings'

White
1.5 × 1.0m
Hybrid tea
Foliage

Large, single flowers with a striking ring of brown anthers. Compact, easily grown shrubs which combine well with other plants in sunlit, fertile situations. Can be hard-pruned or lightly cut back each year.

## 'William Lobb'

Crimson-purple
2.5 × 2.0m
Moss
Fragrant

Large, double flowers produced in midsummer on arching, often very lax branches that may need supporting. Grows well mixed with other shrubs and with a good cover of plants below.

## PLANTS FOR PLACES

Finding plants to fill the borders is easy and enjoyable. A quick, exhilarating tour of local garden centres, and a return home with a colourful assortment of everything in stock that caught the eye. Then an imaginative tour of the garden putting one down here, another there till each has been found a place; a few hours spent planting them, and by the evening it's time to sit back with a well-earned drink in hand, and admire the result.

The immediate result will appeal to all men of action, but for years to come there will be misgivings that somehow the garden is not quite right – if not outright despair about its obviously hopeless state. One of the most enjoyable and exciting pleasures of gardening is acquiring new plants. So exciting and so easy is it, that few resist the temptation to rush into purchasing before deciding what plants are wanted.

There are so many plants, and so many ways to use them, that they bemuse us and leave us overwhelmed by choice. They are the vocabulary of gardening, through which we describe what we think a garden should be. Like any other vocabulary, this one is most effective when we know what we want to say before we speak.

Planting is a time to sit back – not rush off to the garden centre, or seize hold of a catalogue – and call up those two genii which direct all our choices: analysis and evaluation.

1  What are the plants wanted for?
2  What are they expected to do?
3  What effects are they meant to create?
4  How much time can be spent looking after them?

Answers to questions like these were sought earlier for the garden round that rather plain house in the south Midlands. They led to decisions on the kind of garden that was needed, and the ways that different spaces in it would be used. Now it is time to carry the process a little further to find the plants that are wanted. This is done below. Once again, the process is based on straightforward observations or responses to questions. Some appear to be statements of the obvious, but the trick when planting a garden is to *make* the solutions to problems obvious, and this is more likely to happen by trying to be simple than by trying to be clever.

A starting point is to describe the place to be planted, the **Setting**, and its effects on plants that grow there. Then decide on its **Significance** in the

The field beyond is brought into the garden by framing the view. The frame is made with the canopy of the old apple tree, tall shrubs to either side and a simple step of railway sleepers. The garden hedge uses the same range of shrubs as the field hedges – hawthorn, blackthorn, holly, dogwood and guelder rose, further strengthening the link

garden as a whole. Some areas will play a starring role, others will act as links between different parts or be left as almost forgotten corners. Then look at how things are likely to develop in the future, and think about what is wanted – the **Promise**. A natural effect that fits in with the surroundings could be the aim, or it might be tempting to go for bright colours and a strong impression of the gardener's hand.

The aim is to pinpoint the qualities needed by the plants, if they are to do what is wanted. These qualities can cover everything that has anything to do with plants, and can be remarkably varied – even within quite a small garden. Sometimes hardiness will be important, at other times cheapness. A particular colour or range of colours may be needed for a theme. Perhaps the plants will have to be able to cope with dry shade, or drought or cold winds. Particular shapes, the ability to grow very quickly, or impenetrable thorns may be wanted for special situations.

Coppice poles can be used to make a temporary pergola. The ends are let into drainpipes concreted in below ground; the tops are lashed together with rope.
Annual and quick-growing perennial climbers – morning glory, cup-and-saucer plant, runner beans and passion flower – are used on this structure, which will have a short life. In warm, sheltered places, quick-growing sun lovers will do well in gravel paving. Artemisias, lavender, rosemaries and thymes in variety will rapidly make a newly-constructed feature look established

The first decision about the garden around the house was to divide it into three. Later on each area was found to be made up of parts with different needs and opportunites, which had to be thought about and planned separately, so further subdivisions were made. Separate lists of plants were prepared for each one, and the results for the three subdivisions made within Area One are shown below.

This garden looks quite attractive when the herbaceous plants are at their best – for about three months

A simple layout can help to link garden and view. Replacing the tall screen conifers with deciduous trees allows a much greater choice of planting, because more light and moisture now fall on the bed beneath

In winter the framework is revealed. The beds look very fussy, and distract the eye from the good view with its gentle lines and fine trees. The bed of winter heathers and prostrate conifers looks incongruous

A simple layout takes advantage of the garden's surroundings in winter. Deciduous trees and shrubs can make a richly textured garden during the five months that they are without leaves

AREA ONE

**A  Semi-dry shade, in corner beneath sycamore tree**

*Setting*

A corner dominated by a semi-mature sycamore tree, which shelters and screens the rest of the garden and is to be kept. It will grow for many years to come, and its shade and the demands of its roots will increase from year to year. Plants beneath it already show the effects of shade, drought and infertile soil.

*Significance*

An area with low priority for time, attention or expenditure. The plants should be easy to find and cheap to obtain, tolerant of difficult conditions and able to survive with little help.

*Promise*

The sycamore will develop into an attractive specimen tree, well placed to shelter the house and garden. Meanwhile the planting beneath it will be in a minor key, aiming for an agreeable appearance, with occasional splashes of colour.

*Qualities needed by the plants*

1  Tolerance of shade and poor, dry soil. All the plants used must be able to survive and look flourishing under these conditions.
2  Availability. Plants must be cheap, or easy to propagate rapidly.
3  Persistence. Soil will sometimes become extremely dry; plants must be long-lived and able to persist without need for replanting.
4  Dependence on maintenance. Minimal weeding, pruning or protection from pests and diseases are requirements.
5  Appearance. Plants must look as though they are thriving, and keep this part of the garden appearing presentable.

*Plants that would be suitable*

**Shrubs** *Aucuba japonica* 'Crotonifolia' and 'Longifolia'; *Buxus sempervirens* cvs; *Daphne mezereon* 'Alba'; *Euonymus fortunei*; *Hedera helix* 'Neilson'; *Hydrangea petiolaris*; *Hypericum androsaemum*; *H. calycinum*; *Kerria japonica*; *Ruscus hypoglossum*; *Sarcococca hookeriana* and *buxifolia*.

**Perennials** *Acanthus mollis*; *Anaphalis triplinervis*; *Campanula latiloba* 'Alba'; *Dicentra formosa*; *Duchesnea indica*; *Epimedium* spp and cvs; *Euphorbia amygdaloides robbiae*; *Fragaria vesca flore plena*; *Geranium macrorrhizum*; *Helleborus foetidus* 'Wester Flisk'; *Lunaria annua* cvs; *Lychnis coronaria*; *Polygonum affine* and *campanulatum*; *Pulmonaria angustifolia* cvs; *Ranunculus ficaria* cvs; *Saxifraga urbium*; *Symphytum grandiflorum*; *Vinca minor* cvs.

**Ferns** *Dryopteris filix-mas*; *Polypodium vulgare* cvs.

**Bulbs** *Convallaria majalis*; *Crocus* spp and cvs; *Cyclamen coum*; *Iris foetidissima* cvs; *Narcissus* 'Thalia'; *N*. 'Tête-à-Tête'; *Ornithogalum nutans*; *Scilla bifolia*.

**B  Area between the house and the old field hedge**

*Setting*

Wind-swept and exposed; partially sheltered by a neglected field hedge and two semi-mature trees, a sycamore and a copper beech. Existing lawn and some uninteresting garden shrubs and perennial plants have been neglected for years. The two trees, the lawn and the plants conflict with the profile for this part of the garden, and none will be kept. The hedge will be retained.

*Significance*

Kitchen and dining room windows look across this area to attractive views over the countryside. A visually important part of the garden, but not one where eye-catching effects should interfere with the rural setting. An area with low priority for maintenance, and an urgent need for something to be done to improve its appearance.

*Promise*

Hedge to be laid, then kept clipped to make a low boundary that fits the pattern of field hedges around. Planting to be natural and informal, including many native species. Trees to be in small groups providing shelter, and directing views across the countryside. No strong contrasts of colour, texture and scale, but an attractive appearance and colourful flowers are important – particularly for perennial plants at ground level.

*Qualities needed by the plants*

1  Complementing the countryside. Trees and shrubs should convey a country atmosphere; the choice should avoid those with brightly coloured foliage.

2 Persistence and hardiness. The plants must be long-lived and tough so that they seldom, if ever, need replacing.

3 Appearance. A high proportion of the plants used should be attractive for at least part of the year.

4 Rate of development. Rapid growth and an early effect are wanted from some of the plants; others should develop reasonably quickly.

### Plants that would be suitable

**Trees** *Acer campestre; Amelanchier canadensis; Corylus avellana; Crataegus crus-galli* and *laevigata* 'Plena'; *Ilex aquifolium* cvs; *Mespilus germanica; Prunus avium; P. padus; Sambucus nigra* cvs.

**Shrubs** *Buxus sempervirens* 'Handsworthensis'; *Clematis recta; Cornus mas; Euonymus europaeus* 'Red Cascade'; *Hippophae rhamnoides; Lonicera caprifolium* and *periclymenum; Philadelphus* 'Virginal'; *Rosa eglanteria; Viburnum betulifolium* and *opulus* 'Xanthocarpum'; *Vinca major; Vinca minor* cvs.

**Perennials** *Aconitum napellus; Ajuga reptans* cvs; *Anemone nemorosa* cvs; *Aquilegia vulgaris* cvs; *Aruncus dioicus; Aster tradescantii; Astrantia major; Campanula glomerata; C. persicifolia; Centranthus ruber; Digitalis grandiflora; D. purpurea; Eranthis hyemalis; Euphorbia amygdaloides rubra; Filipendula hexapetala* 'Flore Pleno'; *Geranium* 'Mrs Kendall Clark'; *Helleborus foetidus; Hesperis matronalis; Lamium maculatum* cvs; *Lathyrus grandiflorus; L. latifolius; Lysimachia punctata; Meconopsis cambrica; Polemonium coeruleum; Polygonum bistorta* 'Superbum'; *Primula veris; P. vulgaris; Pulmonaria officinalis* cvs.

**Ferns** *Dryopteris filix-mas; Polystichum setiferum* cvs.

**Grasses** *Carex pendula; Luzula nivea; Stipa gigantea.*

**Bulbs** *Allium neapolitanum; Arum italicum marmoratum; Camassia leitchlinii; Crocus* spp and cvs; *Cyclamen hederifolium; Erythronium denscanis; Fritillaria meleagris; Hyacinthoides nonscripta; Narcissus obvallaris; Polygonatum* x *hybridum.*

### C Sunlit corner by kitchen door
#### Setting

A small, sun-warmed, enclosed garden is to be made here for breakfast or elevenses. Although south-facing, it is exposed to the east, and must be sheltered from that direction.

### Significance

A place where the right atmosphere is essential. It must look inviting and feel warm, sheltered and welcoming whenever weather conditions allow. The area is small and plants or materials needing above average maintenance are acceptable in the interests of appearance.

### Promise

A screen of climbers on trellis, backed by shrubs, is urgently wanted – particularly on the east side. Part will form a shaded arbour. Level surfaces for chairs and a table will be provided by paving, with gravel-filled spaces for plants. Tubs and other containers will hold plants that are rotated to give a changing display.

### Qualities needed by the plants

1 Appearance. Many of the plants must look good for much of the year, and/or be bright and colourful for long periods.

2 Rate of development. Screening shrubs and climbers should grow rapidly but be easy to keep under control later on.

3 Response to sunlight and warmth. Plants should be naturally adapted to thrive and look their best under warm, sunny conditions.

4 Culinary/herbal qualities. A proportion of the plants should be kitchen herbs, or have aromatic foliage or fragrant flowers.

### Plants that would be suitable

**Shrubs/Climbers** *Buxus sempervirens* 'Handsworthensis'; *Cistus* 'Silver Pink'; *Clematis macropetala; Clematis viticella* 'Mdm Julia Correvon' and 'Huldine'; *Eccremocarpus scaber; Hedera colchica* 'Variegata'; *Jasminum nudiflorum; Laurus nobilis; Lavandula* cvs; *Lippia citriodora; Lonicera standishii; Nandina domestica; Phlomis italica;* Roses 'Emily Gray' and 'The New Dawn'; *Rosmarinus officinalis* 'Sissinghurst'; *Salvia officinalis* cvs; *Viburnum farreri; Viburnum tinus* 'Eve Price'; *Vitis vinifera* 'Apiifolia' and 'Purpurea'.

**Perennials** *Achillea argentea; Alyssum saxatile* cvs; *Anthemis cupaniana; Artemisia schmidtiana; Aubrieta* cvs; *Campanula garganica; Cerastium tomentosum columnae; Dianthus* 'Pike's Pink'; *Diascia* 'Ruby Field'; *Digitalis ferruginea* and *grandiflora; Erodium chrysanthum; Euphorbia martinii* and *myrsinites; Geranium cinereum* cvs;

*Hyssopus officinalis; Origanum laevigatum; O. vulgare* 'Aureum'; *Tanacetum densum amani; Thymus citriodorus* cvs; *T. serpyllum* cvs.

**Grasses** *Festuca glauca* cvs; *Helictotrichon sempervirens; Stipa gigantea.*

**Ferns** *Adiantum pedatum; Blechnum penna-marina.*

**Bulbs** *Agapanthus* cvs; *Brodiaea* 'Queen Fabiola'; *Crocus chrysanthus* cvs; *Iris histrioides major; Narcissus* 'Hawera'; *Nerine bowdenii; Scilla tubergeniana.*

These lists of plants are tools to jog the memory, and there is no need for careful consistency. A particular cultivar may be listed to make sure a favourite plant is not forgotten; elsewhere unspecified cultivars of a species may be sufficient. Sometimes a genus is enough. The intention is to shortlist possibilities quickly; later time can be spent looking up details and deciding exactly which plants are wanted.

## USING PLANTS: CREATING EFFECTS

Country gardens may be colourful, shapely, informal, or fruitful and severely practical. They may be endowed with atmosphere and character. But the three passwords for successful results are generosity, compatibility and repetition. The first is a word to which we warm; pride in a mean streak is unusual. The second has a friendly, sociable ring to it. But the third has more complex implications – some of which are uncomfortably close to dullness and boredom.

### PLANTING GENEROUSLY

Gardeners are inclined to be open-handed with plants, cuttings and seeds when friends visit their gardens, and this exchange is one of the pleasant things about gardening because our plants become reminders of our friends and their gardens.

But gardeners have a darker side, which makes it hard for them to use plants in their gardens in the same generous spirit that they give them away. This is not just reluctance to spend money. Anyone might hesitate before loading fifteen or twenty *Hosta sieboldiana* onto a trolley in a garden centre and parading them before the till, even though the reward would be a fine bold group in the garden – and, once tried, the practice might become a habit!

This is a deeper meanness of crabbed imagina-

tion and intention. A few plants of *Hosta sieboldiana*, and many other attractive perennials, can be multiplied by division to produce all that anyone could want, but this is too seldom attempted. There is a feeling that duty is done when plants are set out in threes and fives; that space given over to several of one kind is space wasted; that something better might turn up in the future. There is suspicion that plants allowed to make a notable group might be halfway to a take-over.

Generosity is a virtue but, when planting, it offers more than the smug satisfaction of being its own reward. It provides aesthetic and practical prizes. Large groups simplify planning – there are fewer different plants to think about – and form uncomplicated patterns which are likely to look good.

There is no need to go to extremes. Acres of bluebells look stunning in woods in spring, but ninety plants of London pride under shrub roses do the same thing on a tiny scale and transform opinions of this plant based on ragged lines along shaded, narrow paths that lead to dustbins. Twenty blue-leaved hostas threading a way between other perennial plants and shrubs bring unity to the design of a border, and make more impression than three plants lost in a complex jigsaw pattern of colour, leaf texture and form. Eleven silver birches closely and unevenly spaced in a corner make a screen and a little spinney, made memorable by the patterns of the slender, bright, ascending stems that no single tree can match.

### PLANTING PATTERNS

There is a standard way to do a planting plan for a flower bed. First it is measured, and then drawn on squared paper – because that makes it easy to divide it into a number of roughly square blobs, those in the front being rather smaller than those at the back. Each is given a number, and the names of the chosen plants are listed against the numbers written at the side of the plan. Sometimes one plant will grow large enough to fill a block, but two, three, four or even five specimens of smaller kinds will be needed.

Generosity is a virtue but, when planting, it offers more than the smug satisfaction of being its own reward. It provides aesthetic and practical prizes. Large groups simplify planning and form patterns which are likely to look good

This garden is fifteen months old. It was originally level pasture lying on a heavy alkaline clay. It is very exposed, being open to north, east, south and west in a landscape wrecked by Dutch elm disease. It is pointless planting subjects which need shelter in the early stages of making a garden in an exposed place. Here, a bold framework of tough trees and shrubs has been planted first. It is logical to use some of the trees and shrubs which grow happily in the surrounding countryside – these will form a reliable 'skeleton' which can be dressed with possibly less tough plants once the shelter has grown. The main trees used here are common oak, common cherry, ash, field maple and hawthorn. A variety of sizes were used from two-year-old seedlings to 2m standard trees. The main shrubs are dogwood, hazel, elder and guelder rose. Other trees are red oak, Norway maple, apples, pears and plums. Some shrubby willows and shrub roses are also included – *Salix eleagnos, S. pentandra, Rosa rugosa, Rosa glauca* and *R. moyesii*. These were field-grown plants put in in December. None of the beds have been dug. To convert grass to planting beds, the grass was sprayed with glyphosate herbicide once. The areas were then covered with a layer of wood shavings and bark about 10cm thick, and this mulch is topped up once a year. Digging was only necessary to make the planting holes – digging the complete beds would have been a very hard, and unnecessary, job. Planting holes do need to be carefully forked round – just cutting with a spade will often form a vertical pan in heavy clay, preventing plant roots from spreading sideways

The garden is now five years old. There are now sheltered areas within the garden, and trees and shrubs are beginning to divide the formerly open garden into a series of spaces – long sweeping walks; intimate, hidden paths under the canopy of trees; a formal, circular secret garden; spacious areas full of light; mysterious, secluded areas in dappled shade. This can be achieved quite rapidly by careful planning of bold planting, with an emphasis on plants which are known to enjoy the physical conditions of the site. Gradually some of the original quick 'space fillers' were coppiced or thinned out to create sheltered pockets for less tough favourites.

A tennis court looks totally alien in a rural garden. The desire to surround it with a fast growing evergreen hedge was strongly resisted – the outline of bold plantings of trees, shrubs and perennials will 'break up' the harsh lines of the play surface and fencing. Some plants have been used repeatedly, not just in groups but also in sweeps or swathes through the beds. This has helped to emphasise the shape of spaces in the garden and make it easy on the eye. Other plants have been used repeatedly to mark entrances to different spaces. These devices help to make the garden feel comfortable by creating continuity and a sense of logic

Filling in the squares produces a graceless, mechanical plant mosaic which has many disadvantages. Gertrude Jekyll described these firmly and lucidly before most of us were born, but plans for standard flower beds displayed in garden centres, and used as illustrations in catalogues and in many gardening books produced to guide amateurs, stick loyally to this formula. It provides little scope for imagination and reduces opportunities for effects from varied forms and shapes and sizes, leading to stiff, regimented patterns of planting. It minimises the interest that results from changing views of the border from different angles and positions, and has the practical disadvantage that gaps caused by differences in flowering time are conspicuous and cannot easily be avoided or concealed.

Another pattern substitutes drifts longer than they are wide for the squares. This encourages more

Spotted, dotted planting need not be and should not be unattractive – it is the way it was done in traditional cottage gardens, and is still typical of more recent, more sophisticated developments of the cottage garden style

flexibility when plants with different characteristics are grown close together, and adapts more readily to variations in the shape and topography of areas being planted. The patterns reward those who take the trouble to move around a garden by changing, depending on whether the planting is seen end-on or from directly in front. Long, narrow spaces are more easily filled unobtrusively by the plants on either side, so that variations in flowering time do not produce such noticeable gaps to spoil the display.

But there is no rule that ordains one pattern rather than another. Some plants, some compositions, do tend to squares in spite of their limitations, others to drifts; and combinations of the two can be very effective. This is a simple and natural way to combine shrubs and perennials, using the shrubs to form outcrops amongst swirling ground planting. When this is done there are plants which look well planted in ribbons forming boundaries or divisions or tracks that divide or bring the rest of the planting together, depending on how they are used.

Finally, and in spite of, a general stricture that

condemns 'spotty planting' so that the thought is stifled almost before it is expressed, planting can be made up of mixed groups. These create impressions that are quite different from the defined forms produced when blocks of a kind are planted side by side.

Spotted, dotted planting need not be and should not be unattractive – it is the way it was done in traditional cottage gardens, and is still characteristic of more recent, more sophisticated developments of the cottage garden style. It creates impressions that are informal and can be formless; their success depends on introducing some sense of structure and pattern by repetition and other means, to hint at some kind of intention and order. There are ample opportunities for imaginative and subtle use of plants and their effects, and the informality and unstudied charm of gardens planted in this way fit well into country settings.

### USING REPETITION

Anyone who lives by selling plants soon discovers that most customers take a dim view of repetition. A description of a plant that is wanted may suggest a mahonia, but the answer – immediate and definite – is 'No! We've already got a mahonia'.

*In gardens where control is understated, repetition becomes one of the most effective ways to create the visual logic which helps the brain to see what the eye is looking at*

Other plants are needed; suggestions are made and rejected because the garden already holds a berberis, a hosta, a buddleia, a geranium, even a fern! Sometimes a carefully phrased suggestion that there are many different kinds of berberis, geraniums or ferns reduces resistance and leads to an acceptance – on the understanding that the one proposed is nothing like the one already there.

Yet the couple who find the idea of buying two of a kind dull, repetitive, unimaginative or boring live in a house where every window is painted the same colour. They lay the table with matching plates, cutlery and glasses – they may not when on their own, but they will do when friends come to dinner; and the colours of the walls, the paintwork and upholstery of the rooms are thoughtfully coordinated, and most likely based on the repetitive use of a few hues or tones. They have chosen to restrict the colours, textures and designs of all these things – in spite of the temptations of an enormous

It need not take many years to make a 'woodland' garden. This planting is three-and-a-half years old and the atmosphere of a sheltered, well-textured garden is already developing. The garden started as an exposed, flat pasture on very heavy alkaline clay. In these conditions, to hesitate is to fail. The traditional method of leaving enough space around each shrub and tree for it to reach maturity untouched by its neighbours is not appropriate if you want to realise the picture you have in your mind. The beds originally were treated with glyphosate, then mulched with bark stable bedding. Most of the trees were chosen by recognising which species were thriving in adjacent hedges and copses and in neighbouring gardens. All the trees were 1.2m–1.5m tall when planted, bare-rooted, in early January. After three-and-a-half growing seasons the field maples are 4–5m tall and are very sturdy, bushy trees. Already they look substantial and make an impact on the garden. More slender than the maples, the ashes are also 4–5m high. The oaks grew almost 1m in their first season and are now 4–5m tall. This is not typical country for birches and rowans, but they thrive locally – the rowans are now 5–6m tall and the birches 6–7m. The birches are shallow-rooting and have not managed to establish a firm anchorage; some, unfortunately, are quite unstable and will probably have to be taken out. The failures are the whitebeams: often tricky to establish, they don't like this ground and thrive only in the driest spots.

The idea of a 'border' in this type of garden is a disaster – planting needs to create the walls of a series of spaces and to provide shelter. To do this it must be bold, and carried out in generous beds or areas, not prim, hemmed-in borders variety of exciting alternatives – because they know that repetition and co-ordination are the ways to make their home look agreeable, attractive, planned and stylish. But they have yet to discover that the same rules apply to their gardens!

Repetition introduces visual logic to a scene in simple, versatile ways and tells us that it is by intention and not happenchance. In gardens it can be used to:

Introduce points of reference that guide the eye.
Create patterns that contribute structure to compositions.
Unify separate features.

Plants whose distinctive appearance ensures that they attract attention convey clear and unmistakable impressions, and the repeated use of mahonias, columnar conifers, variegated aralias or clipped box peacocks emphasises the logic behind a design. Plants with more subtle qualities might be used – plants with white flowers, rounded forms, pinnate leaves, grey-green foliage – anything in fact which makes enough impact, and sometimes this need be only a very gentle impact, to convey a message.

Shunning the repetitive use of plants – and even of qualities like colour and shape – is consistent with the gardenesque nature of the suburban style. The evidence of deliberate activity is so obvious that onlookers need no subtle signals to reassure them that this is indeed a garden. The planting creates a series of incidents and repetition would be redundant. The single high-crowned bud of a hybrid tea rose, the massive spike of a delphinium, the crimson foliage of a smoke bush, the garden pool or the pergola, each is to be seen and admired individually, and their parts in the overall composition of the garden are incidental.

In other styles of gardening, especially those in which control is understated and the design is intended to relate the garden to its surroundings, or create an overall sense of place, repetition becomes one of the most effective ways to create the visual logic which helps the brain to see what the eye is looking at.

## REPETITION TO PROVIDE UNITY

Even in small gardens the pursuit of variety can lead to disjointed impressions that disturb the unity needed to convey a sense of place. This can be avoided – and very attractively too – by restricting the range of features and variety of materials used, limiting the plants to a few carefully chosen kinds, and concentrating on simplicity of effect and style.

However, the chief pleasure of many gardeners depends on the pursuit of plants, and themes based on very restricted ranges would never satisfy their magpie impulses. Dedicated plantspersons are inclined to disdain the arts of garden design, and splendid collections of plants are grown in settings which have little feeling of a garden. Like the showrooms of antique dealers where period furniture and fine pictures and porcelain create sumptuous impressions, they lack the homeliness and appeal of modestly furnished places where people spend their lives.

Anyone who sacrifices unity and the pleasure of making a garden for the pursuit of variety is shying at shadows. The plants may have to be infinitely variable but there are ways to unite them. The repeated use of a distinctive shape, a notable feature, or a particular plant of distinctive form or texture or colour; the patterns made by paths and the materials used to surface them; any of these would allow freedom to vary the planting within the setting, and provide the threads which weave the whole into a garden.

## REPETITION
## USED TO EMPHASISE ASYMMETRY

Almost as fundamental a division as that between males and females, and one where boundaries are more clearly drawn, can be found between those who insist on symmetry in a composition and those whose preferences are for asymmetry.

Asymmetry is a subtle instrument, of great value for its power to create interest and give pleasure, and one that is most satisfyingly used in the patterns of the plants that make the garden. It can be done by a deliberate imbalance of colours when glowing, sombre tones predominate in one part of a garden, and brighter, lighter colours in another. Or plants with slight and graceful foliage, including many with pinnate leaves, can make a dappled shade on one side of a walk, while across it darker, deeper, denser greens cast a heavy shade.

Two or three groups of a strikingly dominant plant, colour or form – bamboos, conifers, the blue bean tree, the golden robinia perhaps – placed predominantly towards one end of a border or in a corner change the balance of the garden, and their

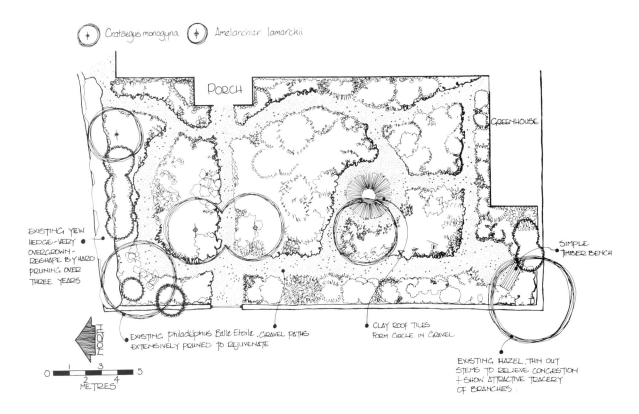

Crataegus monogyna    Amelanchier lamarckii

PORCH

GREENHOUSE

EXISTING YEW HEDGE - VERY OVERGROWN - RESHAPE BY HARD PRUNING OVER THREE YEARS

SIMPLE TIMBER BENCH

EXISTING Philadelphus Belle Etoile . GRAVEL PATHS EXTENSIVELY PRUNED TO REJUVENATE

CLAY ROOF TILES FORM CIRCLE IN GRAVEL

EXISTING HAZEL, THIN OUT STEMS TO RELIEVE CONGESTION + SHOW ATTRACTIVE TRACERY OF BRANCHES .

NORTH

0   1   2   3   4   5
METRES

repetition reinforces an effect which gives the whole area an atmosphere not to be found elsewhere.

Asymmetry can moderate formality. Strong structures, intimidatingly logical in some settings, can be softened by planting that creates its own more wayward compositions and gives the eye two alternative interpretations – the formal structure or the superimposed pattern. The latter can be a permanent feature – topiary forms for example, that are there throughout the year. It can be a major element in the planting – a pattern created by half a dozen shrubs with coloured foliage – that make their mark right through the summer. Or it can be graffiti written by transient groups of bright tulips, or gaily coloured annuals.

### REPETITION TO EMPHASISE SYMMETRY

Fan-trained plum trees lined along a wall behind a border, clumps of yuccas with spires of flowers and spiky leaves repeated along its length, measure off spaces, divide a garden into sections and establish a sense of order. Plants that make regular patterns like these bring a touch of symmetry where confusion would otherwise be the main impression.

This front garden to a village house used to be the usual lawn with a few shrubs. The back garden demanded a very simple style – the grass there is old, flower-rich meadow and there are some attractive old hazels and willows leading into meadows beyond. To garden it would destroy its appeal. The front is set in a village street, surrounded by stone houses, brick and stone walls and adjacent clipped thorn hedges. This setting can comfortably accommodate a colourful garden. Low shrubs, herbaceous perennials and bulbs are used to make a dense ground-smothering carpet

The superimposed pattern can be a permanent feature – topiary forms for example, that make their presence felt throughout the year

When borders are planned and gardens are planted, patterns can be created which impose symmetry on asymmetrical designs, or emphasise it in those which are already formal. Balances between symmetry and asymmetry, and formality and informality, are most sensitive tools for establishing atmosphere and relating a garden – or distancing it – from its surroundings.

A place where winding paths cross in a woodland garden could be left unmarked by anything that made the intersection significant. It could be made more notable if the four corners were filled with the same plant, and the place could be made striking by planting something deliberately emphatic – like four pyramids of clipped box, made the more significant for being unexpectedly formal in an informal setting. The impression could be more subdued for most of the year, enlivened by a season when it made a splash – for example by using the white-flowered Japanese azalea 'Palestrina'.

A few plants used to emphasise symmetry in formal layouts reduces the need for a careful balance in the rest of the planting, and gives greater overall freedom of choice. In a pattern of square beds intersected by paths, firmly defined shapes or characterful plants, symmetrically related one to another and to the regular layout of the beds, consolidate the sense of order of the design. The rest of the planting, however free and easy it may be, will fit into the strong framework, softening but not destroying the overall impression of harmony and control.

## CHAPTER EIGHT

Left to herself, one of the last items on a sheep's menu is rye grass. One of the first is hogweed, and when she pushes her way through the garden fence she dines enthusiastically on mock orange before returning to her field for a little after-dinner clover. The first things we are taught to do, when making pastures fit to be grazed, is plough out the hogweed, the knapweed, and every other weed and sow a mixture of scientifically selected rye grass and clover. Are sheep so stupid that they need us to make them eat up their greens, or does a sheep's-eye view reveal things we have forgotton to think about?

Rye grass and clover have ruled our pastures for over fifty years. During their reign meadows which used to be filled with wild flowers have been destroyed, and most of the common insects and other creatures which were in those meadows have gone with them. We can no longer walk through summer meadows bright with wild flowers and alive with the fiddling and whirring of grasshoppers. We can no longer see the spreading flower heads of hogweeds crowded with bluebottles and butterflies, wasps, bumble bees, soldier beetles, bishop bugs and crab spiders, and our steps no longer disturb dozens of butterflies and day-flying moths. Common blues and small coppers; meadow browns and ringlets; large, small and dingy skippers; the spotted burnet moths, humming bird and bee hawk moths.

It is not the rarities which are most missed – most of us seldom or never come across a red kite or a large blue butterfly – but the ordinary, everyday incidentals, still called common by botanists and zoologists, but now no longer the abundant, joyous accompaniment to every country walk that they were only a few decades ago.

Gardens, so some would tell us, could be places where the flowers that wild creatures need for food,

# The Garden Goes Wild

Garden-making, like gardening itself, concerns the relationship of the human being to his natural surroundings.

*Russell Page*

and the plants they use for shelter, could be grown to encourage their return. The impression given is that turning gardens, even little corners of gardens, into wildernesses is easily done. We are assured that this would enhance the quality of the biosphere and safeguard the heritage of planet earth. It is suggested that the ecological bonuses of creating habitats and favourable environments would be the survival of our native fauna and flora.

The jargon is well-meaning: the truth is that these wildernesses are not so easily made. Gardening has always been directed against the wilderness, and gardeners are uneasy, unskilled and unprepared when making day-to-day decisions about coping with plants that are growing in a state of nature. We cannot be confident that they would work. The reasons for the decline of so many common insects and other wild animals are not fully understood, and fondly trying to be helpful would not necessarily make life easier for them. The evidence is rather the other way. Meadows still exist which have never been ploughed, fertilised or sprayed and where nothing drastic seems to have happened to disrupt the lifestyles of the ancient inhabitants. Even in these places, insects which once were abundant are few and far between, and others which were regular visitors are occasional and notable rarities.

Going wild in the garden means changing the ways gardening is done. As one example: many bugs and insects spend some of their lives – it may be as eggs, pupae or hibernating adults – amongst old, dead stems of flowering plants and grasses, the kind of rubbish that tidy-minded gardeners cut down and consign to autumnal bonfires. These purges are lethal, and if the unkempt look of an untrimmed garden in winter is intolerable, the demands of a garden fit for wildlife may be intolerable too.

Going wild means leaving undone things that have always been done, and doing things that have never been done. It means abandoning chemical warfare against pests, and reducing the use of herbicides by finding other ways to fight weeds. It means thinking about plants for their value as food and refuges for birds and insects as well as for their appearance. It means learning to be more tolerant, more informed, and less fearful of creatures that are not familiar; and developing the confidence to rely on natural balances between prey and predators to protect the garden from disaster.

## CHEMICALS IN THE GARDEN

Many people have a fearful fascination for poisonous chemicals. They use them like talismans to banish pests and weeds,. moulds and mildews, and dare not believe they can keep their plants healthy without them. But they feel anxious about the effects of the chemicals on other animals, including their pets and their families.

Some of these feelings are justified. Many of the popular roses sold for gardens have little resistance to mildew or blackspot, and must be sprayed with chemicals to protect them from infection. Plants so dependent on artificial support cannot be said to be fit to grow in gardens, and should not be on sale for that purpose; anyone who has the misfortune to be sold one should take it back and claim a refund. Sources of resistance to these diseases exist – there are plenty of roses which thrive when left to themselves, and rose breeders could use them more assiduously than they do. The simplest way to reduce dependence on chemicals is to refuse to buy susceptible plant varieties – not just roses but others as well.

It is not alarmist to regard all poisonous sprays with suspicion. It is not cynical to take a large pinch of salt with assurances that such and such a one is '. . . quite safe, because . . .'! We are still repeatedly taken by surprise every time chemical use leads to results which had never been intended, in ways which had never been suspected. And it is prudent and sensible to do anything that can be done to make their use less necessary.

There are a great many alternatives to a trip to the nearest source of aerosols, solutions, powders and sprays every time a bug is found puncturing a bud, or a mould is noticed puckering a leaf. Amongst them are the following:

1 Substitute plants that are not seriously afflicted by pests and diseases for those that are.
2 Learn to live with low levels of injuries inflicted by pests, or symptoms of fungal infection. Many are transient and do the plants no lasting harm.
3 Encourage garden plants to form the self-supporting alliances which leave few spaces for weeds to invade.
4 Use natural or non-chemical methods to control pests, diseases and weeds. Caterpillars can be removed by hand; ducks are excellent slug-destroyers; cats are happy to help out against rabbits, rats and mice, even moles. Above all, remember that natural predators will do the work, if they are not destroyed by sprays; and that mulches and a cover of plants are the best defences against weeds.
5 Use chemicals as a last resort, with the feeling that their use represents a failure. Use them sparingly on precisely identified targets, and exactly according to the instructions; use only those for which there seem to be convincing reasons to believe that they will not be harmful to other plants, animals or people.

The single most effective way to avoid trouble from pests and diseases is to grow plants which don't suffer from them. Graduates of suburban garden styles brought up on roses, delphiniums, phloxes, cabbages, hollyhocks and gooseberries might recoil from a suggestion that seems to be aimed at everything that makes their garden beautiful. But most of our garden plants – particularly those not far removed from their wild ancestors – suffer little if at all from the attentions of slugs, caterpillars, greenfly, moulds or mildews.

These plants were separated from their natural pests when they were brought here, and do not provide attractive fodder for our native varieties. There are exceptions, and nobody who has tried to grow delphiniums, gypsophila or hostas can doubt the appeal of these foreign delicacies to slugs and snails. But a short walk round any garden listing plants that are scarcely bothered by pests and diseases will reveal dozens that are never eaten even by slugs. Writing down the names of all those that are not attacked soon becomes tedious, and it will not be long before the record is replaced by a much

Unsprayed roses look no less beautiful than the ones
next door which were dutifully and thoroughly sprayed
by a vigilant guardian

shorter list of those which are susceptible.

The next most effective action is to hold back
when the hand reaches for the poison bottle. Every
year there is a week in June when the buds of roses
seethe with greenfly, and the tills of garden centres
ring with the sales of aphid-death to gardeners
desperate to save their precious blooms. But anyone away from home that week returns to find the
greenfly gone. They also return to roses that look
no less beautiful than the ones next door, which
were dutifully and thoroughly sprayed by a vigilant
guardian.

So many other insects – and birds – eat aphids
that, in a garden that contains a mixture of plants,
their numbers seldom exceed the appetites of their
predators for long. The greater danger is that sprays
used to destroy the aphids will also kill so many of
the predators that next time the aphids multiply,
there will not be enough mouths to devour them.

Attempts to control unwanted creatures in
gardens using poisonous chemicals are fraught with
so many ifs and buts and conditional clauses that at
best they are hit and miss. Very often they do much
more harm than good.

## MAKING SPACE FOR WILD ANIMALS AND PLANTS

The belief that gardening and wildlife are mutually
incompatible has deep roots, and is linked to a
suspicion that gardens that are 'greener' are merely
gardens left to grow untidy and neglected.

These are very reasonable concerns and, for
gardeners who follow the suburban style, well-
founded. Meticulously maintained, closely mown
grass, trimly hoed flower beds, well-swept patios
and timber decking, carefully pruned rose bushes
and clipped conifer hedges are deserts for most wild
creatures. Their well-being depends on finding
more relaxed gardening alternatives, which make
places for native plants to grow, and leave more
dirt and disorder where wild animals can survive.

The point has been made that providing for
wildlife in gardens is a revolutionary idea. Now the
extent of that revolution is becoming more

obvious: alternative ways to garden, alternative priorities; a willingness to look on the wildlife – particularly the birds and insects – as an essential part of the excitement and interest of the garden. These add up to a new view of gardening which, once accepted, makes finding spaces for wild flowers and looking for ways to sustain and encourage birds and insects just as appropriate as skilfully pruned beds of roses in well-kept suburban gardens.

But how do we know what to look for, if this revolution means that plants are no longer chosen because they have large and beautiful flowers, or because we think they will make a bright display, or for the impression of orderliness and good gardening that they convey? The answers depend on understanding how wild creatures use and rely on plants, so that their needs become our reasons for choosing one plant rather than another.

All animals, ourselves included, depend for survival on:

Shelter, where they can reproduce successfully.
Food, for themselves and their offspring.
Cover, to protect them from enemies.

Gardens only become friendly places for wildlife when they supply these needs. This is done by choosing plants with the above needs in mind, and adopting methods of gardening which enable animals to benefit from the plants. Remember:

1 Many garden plants come from foreign lands and native animals, birds and insects make only limited use of them. However, they may produce widely used foods such as nectar or berries; and evergreens, in particular, provide cover.
2 Native plants serve the needs of native animals by providing specialised sources of food, and precisely the right conditions for birds to nest and insects to lay eggs. In gardens they do a great deal to encourage the arrival, and ensure the survival, of a variety of wildlife.
3 Grasses are some of the most useful plants for many kinds of insects, and the presence of a variety of native grasses is at least as important as the inclusion of attractive broad-leaved wild flowers.
4 Much of our native fauna is adapted to life in deciduous woodland, living amongst the trees, on the shrubs and climbers below them, or close

to ground level amongst perennial plants. Spinneys are easy to establish, need little attention, can be very decorative and provide food, shelter and cover for a wide variety of animals.
5 Pools and wetlands (or bogs) and the plants that grow in and around them provide food and shelter of a different kind, adding to the diversity of wildlife.
6 Dead and decaying remains of plants provide food and shelter for many small insects and other animals. These in turn are eaten by other insects, birds or mammals, and dead stems, twigs, small branches, piles of leaves etc are important resources which should not be wantonly destroyed.

The main obstacles to the acceptance of wildlife have more to do with finding space for it in our minds than in our gardens. Age-long divisions into friends and foes have to be very largely abandoned, and replaced by an awareness of the extraordinarily complex network of relationships between animals and plants, which makes it almost impossible to intervene to control any particular pest without affecting the lives and prospects of all sorts of other creatures.

Gardeners look warily at unidentified things they discover moving around their patches. Conspicuous, active animals are particularly likely to attract attention and be feared, but more often than not these will be predators on the hunt, whose activities are almost always beneficial rather than harmful. Even those we know we have cause to dislike – wasps for instance – are no exception! The grubs in their nests are not fed on plum jam and drops of sweet or alcoholic drinks robbed from picnickers, but on insects and grubs – including a great many that we don't care for, and should be glad to have destroyed. Wasps' nests sometimes hang so menacingly that it would be foolhardy to live as their neighbours, but they are often destroyed wantonly and without thought.

## HEDGES

A simple way to mark a boundary, prevent farm animals from straying, or keep wild animals out of a crop, is to plant a row of shrubs or trees and train them as a hedge. The earliest farmers planted hedges when they needed to enclose their fields and define the boundaries of their enclosures after clearing the forests. Now we have learnt that there are ways to tell how old a hedge is from the number of different shrubs within it, and discovered that some of these humdrum features of the countryside were planted long before the Romans came. Apart from ancient pathways, they are the oldest man-made objects still fulfilling their original purpose. Hedges are homes for numerous wild animals. Small mammals, birds and insects use them for food and shelter, nesting sites and places where young can be reared or left to grow by their own devices. But the value of hedges is usually disregarded when houses are built in country settings, and the garden feature most easily and beneficially able to complement the countryside and add to its assets is replaced by materials or plants which contribute nothing to either.

Neo-rustics moving into newly built executive homes, or completing the conversion of The Old Harness Shed or Ye Olde Smythie, talk disparagingly about farmers who destroy hedges to enlarge their fields, as they pile the remnants of old field hedges around their plots onto bonfires and plant screens of Castlewellan Gold in their place. Their feckless destruction of the old hedges ignores the ease with which they can be converted into vigorous, intruder-proof, easily cared-for garden surrounds. The automatic choice of the cypress takes no account of the dozens of other shrubs which make a good hedge, some nearly as quickly, most with far less trouble, and all with scope for imagination, individuality and variety, which the Leyland solution denies.

Amongst these shrubs are many native species, the components of the field hedges whose destruction has been so widely criticised. These species conform to country settings; they are the natural support and sustenance of many wild creatures and make easily maintained, cheap and effective hedges.

### NATIVE SHRUBS FOR HEDGES

**Barberry** (*Berberis vulgaris*): An upright spiny shrub, with hanging trusses of yellow flowers in May, followed by brilliant red berries.

**Beech** (*Fagus sylvatica*): Medium to tall; brown leaves hang on the shoots through the winter, young leaves in spring are particularly beautiful; can be a slow starter, especially in exposed positions.

**Blackthorn** (*Prunus spinosa*): Spiny stems make impenetrable, medium-sized hedges; establishes easily even on poor soils, and in exposed situations; masses of white flowers in early spring are followed by sloes.

**Bramble** (*Rubus* spp): Scrambling plants that use other shrubs for support; long prickly stems reinforce a hedge; pink/white flowers in midsummer, followed by clusters of blackberries.

**Buckthorn** (*Rhamnus cathartica*): An uncommon native shrub of broad leaves and twiggy growth; medium-sized; clusters of black berries in winter; leaves turn yellow in autumn.

**Bullace** (*Prunus insititia*): Twiggy stems, with some spines, make a dense medium-sized hedge; white flowers in early spring are followed by small, round, edible, usually purple fruits.

**Dog rose** (*Rosa canina*): An upright, scrambling plant that mixes well with other shrubs; strong, spiny stems deter intruders; beautiful pink flowers followed by scarlet hips.

**Dogwood** (*Cornus sanguinea*): Makes a compact medium-sized hedge, establishes quickly and easily under most conditions; flowers and berries not notable; fine smoky crimson/purple autumn colours.

**Elder** (*Sambucus nigra*): Gawky shrub, with shortcomings as a hedge plant; grows rapidly in most situations; trusses of fragrant white flowers in midsummer, followed by bunches of deep crimson berries.

**English elm** (*Ulmus procera*): One of a number of suckering elms much used in hedges; mature trees now mostly dead, but suckers and young trees are conspicuous in many hedgerows.

**Field maple** (*Acer campestre*): Small/medium tree that adapts well to hedgerow life, and establishes easily under most conditions; densely twiggy with small, lobed leaves and distinctive apricot autumn foliage; young shoots and leaves are bright crimson during the summer.

**Field rose** (*Rosa arvensis*): Scrambling shrub; tends to form dense hummocks of interwoven prickly stems; white flowers in midsummer, followed by hips in winter; tolerant of shade and wet soil.

**Gorse** (*Ulex europaeus*): An extremely prickly, impenetrable hedge plant that can be very useful on sandy soils, and in exposed positions where few other shrubs will thrive.

**Guelder rose** (*Viburnum opulus*): Medium-sized, branching shrub that will climb up through others; does well under wet conditions; fine

Holly forms a prickly, impenetrable, evergreen, shade-tolerant hedge, that will grow well even beneath large trees

white flowers in early summer, followed by clusters of glistening scarlet berries; striking crimson/scarlet/yellow autumn foliage.

**Honeysuckle** *(Lonicera periclymenum)*: Scrambling shrub that twines around others; comes into leaf very early; establishes easily amongst other shrubs; masses of fragrant, creamy yellow flowers.

**Hawthorn** *(Crataegus monogyna)*: The great standby of country hedges; densely twiggy, thorny stems make an impenetrable barrier; masses of clustered white flowers in early summer produce haws later.

**Hazel** *(Corylus avellana)*: Upright tall shrub or small tree; of moderate value as a hedge plant, but invaluable for the sake of its catkins in spring, and nuts and attractively coloured foliage in autumn.

**Holly** *(Ilex aquifolium)*: Forms a prickly, impenetrable, evergreen, shade-tolerant hedge; responds well to clipping; red berries can be an asset;

the remains of the prickly foliage are most unwelcome to anyone handweeding nearby.

**Hornbeam** *(Carpinus betulus)*: Medium to tall hedge; closely resembles beech but foliage hangs less durably in winter; easier to establish and develops much faster than beech in cold or exposed situations.

**Ivy** *(Hedera helix)*: Clinging evergreens that fill hedge bottoms and make deciduous hedges more attractive, and better screens in winter.

**Midland thorn** *(Crataegus laevigata)*: Very like the hawthorn and useful for much the same purposes and reasons.

**Privet** *(Ligustrum vulgare)*: Compact, medium-sized evergreen shrub that mixes well with others; trusses of scented white flowers followed by black berries; does well on thin soils above chalk and limestone.

**Spindle** *(Euonymus europaeus)*: Medium-sized bush, with twiggy growth; inconspicuous flowers are followed by pink and orange fruits; forms with outstanding autumn colours are available.

**Sweet briar** *(Rosa rubiginosa)*: Upright spiny stems make impenetrable hedges mixed with other shrubs; attractive rose-pink flowers and hips; the fragrant foliage is a major attraction.

**Wayfaring tree** (*Viburnum lantana*): Compact shrub with broad leaves, and flat heads of whitish flowers followed by black berries; establishes well on thin soils above chalk and limestone.

**Yew** (*Taxus baccata*): First-rate hedging plant; establishes well and grows steadily on all but waterlogged soils, to form dense, easily managed, formal shapes; can be poisonous to stock and should not be planted where farm animals could reach it.

Hawthorn, the foundation of so many field hedges, makes practical and economical garden hedges too, but its susceptibility to fireblight is a major problem. This bacterial disease is carried from its flowers by bees to the blossom of other woody plants in the rose family. Amongst those infected are several valuable berry-bearing small trees and shrubs, including rowans, pyracanthas and the broad-leaved cotoneasters. Hawthorn is so prevalent in hedges and so abundant wherever there are arable fields, that planting more would frequently add little or nothing to the risk of spreading fireblight. But where it is not already conspicuously present it would be sensible, for the garden's sake, not to introduce it.

A pleasantly informal way to make hedges is to plant a medley of different kinds of bush, which is most simply done by unrolling a 1m wide strip of black polythene along the course of the hedge and planting seedling transplants through it. The polythene mulch conserves water and deters weeds during the vital first few years of establishment and early growth, and avoids any need to use chemical weedkillers.

The shelter provided by hedges is less regarded on farms than it used to be, and an annual mechanised short-top-and-sides reduces many to token brushwood edgings to the fields. When kept similarly shorn in gardens with the shears or hedge-clippers, they develop a close-set, plump and rounded shapeliness. Their comfortable contours refuse to form sharp horizons across the view, but are trim enough to please fastidious newcomers from suburbia struggling to assimilate country idioms, and are almost impervious to the grasping tongues and forceful bodies of farm animals. But in this reduced state the variety of birds and insects,

The hedge is made of native plants – yew, hawthorn and holly. Its bobbly shape and the marbled effect of the foliage mixing together makes it look attractive throughout the year

including butterflies, that find them safe and congenial nesting sites or homes is quite small. When allowed to grow larger they offer perches and lodges for many more different kinds, and whenever possible the shears should be forsaken for less cramping methods of management.

Field hedges used to be kept in order by brashing or laying – the process of partly cutting through the stems of hedgerow shrubs and small trees, and inclining them one above another at an acute angle along the line of the hedge. This was done on a five to ten-year cycle, during which hedges went through a continuous process of reduction, growth and renewal. The result is particularly sympathetic to country settings and provides a great variety of opportunities for wildlife.

Now that farmwork is done from the seat of a tractor, hands are seldom available for this work and the craft has lapsed on most farms. Nevertheless, it is still a practical and satisfying way to look after hedges round country gardens, and those with the skill to do it are not so rare that searches for them are a waste of time.

## MEADOWS

More complex and much more difficult are meadows. First thoughts suggest that these would be the natural outcome of selling the mower and letting the lawn grow long. Sometimes that works.

This cottage cannot be reached by car, which is left in its lay-by two hundred metres away, so materials to make a patio have to be easy to carry. They also have to fit in with the woodland setting – a bark-covered patio and gravel paving suit very well. Large willow logs make good, fitting seats

There are ancient swards where years of casual treatment have impoverished the grass, and white clover, trefoils, plantains, field woodrush, buttercups, birdseyes and those indicators of thinness and starvation – hawkweeds, catsears, mouse-ear chickweed and yarrow – have moved in. Then leaving the mower in its shed can produce a sparse meadow where broad-leaved flowering plants hold their own with grasses.

Grasses left to themselves are more likely to grow thick and strong, producing a dense mass that would make champion silage but smothers any wild flowers. Gardens generally provide rich living for grasses, and some way has to be found to undermine their liveliness. In long-mown lawns, as in old flower-rich meadows, this happens as each year's growth is removed by mowing or haymaking. The fertility of the soil gradually decreases until the available nutrients, including those brought up by the deep-probing roots of herbs, support a modest annual replacement of leaves and flowers with nothing left over to encourage lush growth.

The removal of the cuttings after mowing is standard advice to those with garden meadows, and taking the mowings away, rather than leaving them to rot where they lie, is good practice. But using this technique to deplete a fertile soil is such a lengthy process that it is more likely to be wishful thinking than a practical solution.

A more effective method is to remove the old turf with 5 to 10cm of the top soil. This is usually suggested as a last resort, and one rather fearful to contemplate. But it is not difficult to do – with spade and wheelbarrow on small areas, and preferably with a mechanical digger when prairies are intended – and is very effective; far better than spending frustrating and toilsome years mowing and carting to reduce fertility founded on seemingly inexhaustible reserves.

Medieval Books of Hours picture gardens filled with people chatting, dancing or quietly strolling amongst grass spangled with wild flowers. Today's designer gardens are filled with plants and beautifully composed but, as the photographs in every glossy magazine and trendy book will witness, they are empty paradises. Their lawns are green – no daises, campions, stitchwort or wild strawberries there – and nobody plays on them, or chats or dances. Meadows in gardens should be flowery meads where children play and we go to sit on a rug with friends to relax or picnic.

The flowers are the essence of a meadow and are not random mixtures, but precise and complex communities of plants. They form matrices within which a particular mix of species lives in an alliance that provides each with space and makes entry by outsiders, whose habits or growth forms do not fit, very difficult. The trick is to match the conditions of the place with the band of plants that would find them congenial.

The main matrix-formers are grasses, and finding the right ones is a major step towards success. Perennial rye grass – that mainstay of seed mixtures for leys, playing fields, public parks and work-a-day lawns – is usually not a good start. It exists in many forms and some wild ones grow threadbare swards that are welcome in a garden meadow, but those we cultivate have been chosen because they yield or cover well and their aggressive habits make them swamping companions for broad-leaved herbs. Better choices are thinner, sparser grasses that are inclined to form more open swards.

## NATIVE SPECIES FOR MEADOWS

Many plants in this list have particular needs, and will only grow successfully when they are met; all grow best in sunlit situations, unless their tolerance of shade is mentioned. All are perennials.

### GRASSES

Meadow grasses are given pride of place as the most critical part of the sward, within which other components of the meadow survive. They are valuable food plants and refuges for the caterpillars and pupae of butterflies and moths, and a variety should be included in any meadow.

**Cock's foot** *(Dactylis glomerata)*: A coarse grass with multiple stems that can form dense hummocks; numerous strains enable it to grow in a variety of places; likely to be too vigorous to be welcome in most meadows.

**Common bent** *(Agrostis tenuis)*: A fine-leaved grass with light heads of flowers; does well on poor, acid, sandy soils, and in open woodland; forms a short, sparse sward and is an attractive and useful component of meadows.

**Crested dog's tail** *(Cynosurus cristatus)*: A compact, fine-leaved grass, able to form a short, open, drought-resistant sward; grows well on a wide range of soil types; a very useful all-purpose meadow grass.

**Crested hair grass** *(Koeleria cristata)*: Compact and fine leaved, with dense spike-like flower heads; very common on dry, calcareous and sandy pastures; makes dense tufts and spreads by wiry rhizomes.

**Creeping fescue** *(Festuca rubra)*: A fine-leaved medium-sized grass with creeping rhizomes; forms an open, short sward, grows in most situations and on most soils; makes a good all-round, general-purpose meadow grass.

**Meadow fescue:** *(Festuca pratensis)*: Tall, loosely-tufted, narrow-leaved grass; a valuable pasture on rich moist soils, very often found in water meadows.

**Meadow foxtail** *(Alopecurus pratensis)*: A tufted perennial with medium/narrow leaves and dense spikes of flowers; does best on rich, moist soils.

**Rough meadow grass** *(Poa trivialis)*: A medium-height, loosely tufted grass, forming an open sward; prefers rich, moist soils and tolerates light shade.

Meadows in gardens should be flowery meads where children play, and we go to sit on a rug with friends to chat or picnic

**Sheep's fescue** (*Festuca ovina*): Densely tufted fine-leaved grass; grows on poor, well-drained soils; drought-resistant and can be used to form short, open swards under infertile conditions.

**Small cat's-tail** (*Phleum bertolonii*): A typical grass of old meadows, short-grass downs and hillsides; does well on most types of soil; less vigorous than Timothy; spreads by rhizomes.

**Smooth meadow grass** (*Poa pratensis*): Forms a loose, open sward of very variable height; typical of old meadows; adaptable to most soils including poor, dry ones; makes a useful, general-purpose meadow component.

**Sweet vernal grass** (*Anthoxanthum odoratum*): An upright tufted perennial; variable height; able to grow in a wide variety of different soils and situations; one of the first grasses to come into flower.

**Timothy** (*Phleum pratense*): A major component of old hay fields and rich pastures; shallow-rooting grass that does best on fertile, moist soils, but will grow on most in sunlit conditions.

BROAD-LEAVED HERBS

These make the flowery mead, and meadows in gardens appeal in proportion to the medley of different sorts that can be persuaded to grow. Everything depends on balancing the tendency of grasses to take over, and of broad-leaved herbs to die out, by adjusting conditions and skilfully choosing plants.

**Autumn hawkbit** (*Leontodon autumnalis*): Rosette-forming perennial with deep yellow, red-streaked flowers on upright stems; widely distributed.

**Birdsfoot trefoil** (*Lotus corniculatus*): Spreading perennial with small heads of bright yellow, red-streaked flowers; in pastures on most soils.

**Bistort** (*Polygonum bistorta*): Erect, multi-stemmed perennial with short spikes of lilac flowers and a very long flowering season; average/moist meadows, often amongst long grass.

**Bulbous buttercup** (*Ranunculus bulbosus*): Early-flowering upright perennial with attractive leaves and glistening yellow flowers; calcareous/neutral soils on dry pastures and banks.

**Burnet saxifrage** (*Pimpinella saxifraga*): Erect, slender perennial with flat-topped heads of white flowers; calcareous/neutral soils, dry/medium dry.

**Catsear** (*Hypochoeris radicata*): Rosette-forming perennial with bright yellow flowers on erect stems; well-drained meadows amongst short, sparse grasses; will self-seed in the right conditions.

**Celandine** (*Ranunculus ficaria*): Very early, bright, glistening yellow flowers on low spreading plants; tolerant of most soils and conditions, including shade; liable to spread into the garden and become a weed.

**Chicory** (*Cichorium intybus*): An erect perennial with large bright blue flowers; for dry, sunlit calcareous pastures and banks, with sparse swards.

**Clustered bellflower** (*Campanula glomerata*): Erect perennial with clusters of deep purple flowers; calcareous soils amongst sparse grasses, will tolerate light shade; spreads insidiously by rhizomes.

**Columbine** (*Aquilegia vulgaris*): Flowers purple/pink/white on tall upright stems; attractive foliage; calcareous/neutral soils in damp meadows; will tolerate shade and establishes itself by self-seeding.

**Cow parsley** (*Anthriscus sylvestris*): Erect perennial, upright and branching, with flat heads of white flowers; rough meadows and hedgerows on most soils; shade tolerant; inclined to become overpredominant by self-seeding.

**Cowslip** (*Primula veris*): Low-growing perennial with clusters of yellow, sometimes rust-stained, flowers on short stems; does well amongst grass on dry/medium, neutral/calcareous soils.

**Cuckoo flower** (*Cardamine pratensis*): Pale lilac flowers on upright stems; damp meadows in sun/light shade; very variable occurrence from year to year; an attractive double form is worth looking out for.

**Daisy** (*Bellis perennis*): Mat-forming perennial with white daisy flowers on short stems; amongst short grasses in a wide range of conditions and soils; tolerates compacted, heavy soils with poor surface drainage.

**Devilsbit scabious** (*Succisa pratensis*): Erect perennial with rounded heads of dark purple/blue flowers; moist soils amongst rich grass swards.

**Dropwort** (*Filipendula vulgaris*): Upright perennial with flattened heads of white flowers; neutral/calcareous soils; a very long-lived plant on dry sparse pastures.

**Eryngo** (*Eryngium campestre*): Erect branched perennial with thistle-like heads of silver-blue flowers; dry, stony, thin soils with sparse grass cover on hot, sunlit banks.

**Field scabious** (*Knautia arvensis*): Erect branched perennial with lilac-blue flowers; well-drained pastures and banks on a wide range of soils.

**Germander speedwell** (*Veronica chamaedrys*): Short, sprawling perennial with brilliant sky-blue flowers; sparse grass in meadows, banks and amongst trees; tolerates light shade.

**Goatsbeard** (*Tragopogon pratensis*): Short-lived yellow flowers, and conspicuous spherical seed heads; amongst grasses in a variety of conditions and soils; best on hot, dry banks and sparse swards.

**Great burnet** (*Sanguisorba officinalis*): Upright perennial with bottle-brush heads of light crimson flowers; damp meadows on neutral, heavy soils.

**Greater knapweed** (*Centaurea scabiosa*): Erect, branching stems with heads of purple-red flowers; neutral/calcareous, usually well-drained soils; establishes easily and self-seeds.

**Hardheads** (*Centaurea nigra*): Perennial with woody rootstock and upright branched stems with purple/red flowers; wide range of soils and conditions.

**Harebell** (*Campanula rotundifolia*): Slender, upright perennial with open heads of blue, bell-shaped flowers; light, often shallow, well-drained soils on infertile ground or dry banks amongst sparse swards.

**Heartsease** (*Viola tricolor*): Wild pansies make bright, varied and attractive additions to meadows with sparse swards; on thin, sandy soils in pastures and on dry banks; short-lived but will self-seed freely.

**Hoary plantain** (*Plantago media*): Rosette-forming perennial with upright spikes of attractive green/white flowers; well-drained calcareous soils.

**Hogweed** (*Heracleum sphondylium*): Strong-growing, coarse biennial with large flat heads of white or pink flowers; wide range of soils and situations; maintains itself by self-seeding.

**Hop trefoil** (*Trifolium campestre*): Short-lived perennial/annual, small yellow flowers on upright stems; common amongst open swards of fine grasses in infertile situations; maintains itself by self-seeding.

**Horseshoe vetch** (*Hippocrepis comosa*): Low-growing perennial with clustered heads of yellow flowers; remarkable and characteristic horseshoe-shaped fruits; sparse swards on dry, calcareous soils and on banks.

**Jacob's ladder** (*Polemonium caeruleum*): Tall, erect perennial with bright blue or white flowers; grassy slopes and open meadows on calcareous/neutral soils; short-lived but will self-seed successfully.

**Kidney vetch** (*Anthyllis vulneraria*): Spreading, sometimes upright, long-lived perennial with bright yellow flowers in pairs; in sparse swards on dry, calcareous shallow soils.

**Lady's bedstraw** (*Galium verum*): Perennial herb, with creeping rootstock, forming extensive groups of upright stems with bright yellow flowers; wide range of soils and conditions.

**Lesser stitchwort** (*Stellaria graminea*): Small white flowers on ascending stems from a creeping stock; amongst thin swards on most soils, particularly light ones.

**Maiden pink** (*Dianthus deltoides*): Deep crimson flowers on sprawling stems; local on dry, sparsely grassy pastures and banks; able to maintain itself by self-seeding.

**Meadow buttercup** (*Ranunculus acris*): Yellow flowers on upright stems with attractive lobed leaves; can form large sheets of colour on calcareous and neutral soils of moderate fertility, and in damp meadows.

**Meadow clary** (*Salvia pratensis*): Short, upright perennial with spikes of striking, bright blue flowers; sparse grassland over thin, well-drained calcareous soils.

**Meadow cranesbill** (*Geranium pratense*): Long-lived perennial with heads of conspicuous, bright blue flowers; establishes well in most conditions, particularly on heavy calcareous soils.

**Meadow saxifrage** (*Saxifraga granulata*): Upright perennial with loose heads of white flowers; does best in undisturbed calcareous/neutral meadows on well-drained soils.

**Meadowsweet** (*Filipendula ulmaria*): Upright, very persistent perennial with tufted heads of white flowers; wet meadows and pastures; well able to hold its own amongst coarse grasses.

**Meadow vetchling** (*Lathyrus pratensis*): Scrambling perennial with attractive yellow flowers; rough grass and scrub on dry to medium soils, in sunlight or light shade.

**Mignonette** (*Reseda lutea*): Short-lived perennial with fragrant yellow-green flowers in conical heads; will maintain itself by self-seeding amongst thin swards on dry, stony, calcareous banks.

**Mouse-ear chickweed** (*Cerastium holosteoides*): Small white flowers on spreading, sprawling stems; amongst sparse swards on most soils in dry to medium-dry, well-drained situations.

**Mouse-ear hawkweed** (*Hieracium pilosella*): One of many hawkweeds; rosette-forming perennials with bright yellow flowers on upright stems and a long flowering season; in short, sparse swards.

**Musk mallow** (*Malva moschata*): Rose-pink or white flowers on clustered stems; neutral, fertile soils; establishes easily and competes well with grasses.

**Ox-eye daisy** (*Chrysanthemum leucanthemum*): Long-lived and persistent perennial; white flowers on upright stems from a creeping rootstock; will grow in a wide range of soils in sunlit positions.

**Pepper-saxifrage** (*Silaum silaus*): Erect, branching perennial with flat heads of yellowish white flowers; neutral meadows and on dry grassy banks.

**Primrose** (*Primula vulgaris*): Perennial with clusters of pale yellow flowers in spring; light shade in woodlands and hedgerows, but also in open grassy places; short-lived and depends on self-seeding to survive.

**Red clover** (*Trifolium pratense*): Upright perennial with large heads of crimson flowers; grows well amongst grasses in most soils and conditions.

**Purple milk-vetch** (*Astragalus danicus*): A small scrambling perennial with purple/blue flowers; sparse, short swards on dry calcareous soils.

**Ribwort plantain** (*Plantago lancéolatum*): Rosette-forming perennial with upright spikes of brown/green flowers; amongst grasses on calcareous/neutral soils, and in well-drained stony situations.

**Salad burnet** (*Poterium sanguisorba*): Perennial with rounded, spiky heads of green, purple-stained flowers; neutral or calcareous grassland, especially on dry, well-drained slopes with sparse swards.

**Selfheal** (*Prunella vulgaris*): Carpeting perennial with spreading stems and short spikes of violet, pink or white flowers; calcareous and neutral soils, in medium or damp situations; does well in light shade.

**Small scabious** (*Scabiosa columbaria*): Erect, branching perennial with pale blue flowers; in sparse grasses on well-drained neutral and calcareous soils.

**Sorrel** (*Rumex acetosa*): Perennial with upright stems and spikes of red flowers; found anywhere from dry banks to damp grassland, able to survive amongst long grass.

**Strawberry clover** (*Trifolium fragiferum*): Creeping perennial with strawberry-like heads of pink/white flowers; grass swards on heavy or saline soils.

**Toadflax** (*Linaria vulgaris*): Upright, with spikes of bright yellow flowers; thin grassland on well-drained, stony or calcareous pastures and on dry banks.

**Tufted vetch** (*Vicia cracca*): Scrambling perennial with short spikes of purple/blue flowers; competes well with grass in most soils and conditions.

**Yarrow** (*Achillea millefolium*): Mat-forming persistent perennial with flat heads of white, sometimes pink flowers; widely distributed on different soils; plants are tolerant of heat and drought.

**White campion** (*Silene alba*): Short-lived, tall, branching perennial with white flowers; thin swards on neutral/calcareous, dry and medium-dry soils usually on well-drained slopes and banks; maintains itself by self-seeding.

**Wild carrot** (*Daucus carota*): Erect biennial with flat heads of white flowers; stony pastures and rocky banks on light, dry calcareous soils; will self-seed amongst a thin cover of grasses.

**White clover** (*Trifolium repens*): Creeping perennial with heads of white flowers just above the leaves; neutral/clayey/loamy soils; competes well with grass, and can survive in moderately strong swards.

**Wild parsnip** (*Pastinaca sativa*): Erect biennial with flattened heads of yellow flowers; thin pastures and slopes on dry, stony, calcareous soils.

**Wild thyme** (*Thymus drucei*): Mat-forming herb covered with small purple flowers; open, sparse grassland on light soils, amongst stones and on ant-heaps in full sunlight.

**Wood cranesbill** (*Geranium sylvaticum*): Long-lived perennial with heads of violet-blue, white-centred flowers; damp meadows in sun or light shade, on neutral or slightly acid soils.

A major problem when meadowmaking is the feeling of sailing uncharted waters. Many problems depend for a solution more on understanding how plants survive under natural conditions, than on intervention by the gardener. Methods that work well in one place on a particular type of soil, or in a particular situation, may fail completely when tried out somewhere else. The challenge is to identify the needs of each situation; making the right preparations, choosing the right plants, and deciding on the most appropriate forms of management. The blunderbuss solution is to buy seeds of everything that is fancied, scatter them liberally amongst whatever plants are already there, and leave the rest to nature. But nature in the shape of the matrix effect will see to it that practically none germinate and survive long enough to become visible, let alone add to the picture.

A more subtle approach is needed. Remember that the chances of success when trying to establish a meadow in the garden, whether out of a lawn, flower beds and borders, or a pre-existing piece of rough grass, are improved if:

1 Any existing turf and top soil is removed and a seed mixture containing a carefully chosen assortment of grasses and herbs is sown on a seed bed prepared from the exposed surface; or

2 Seeds of the broad-leaved herbs are sown like the seeds of any garden plant, either in short drills or in containers, to produce small specimens which can later be planted out in the meadow. When this is done the grass around the places where the new plants are to go must first be removed or killed with a herbicide (eg Roundup/Tumbleweed); or

3 Strips of the existing sward are removed with a turf-lifter or spade, or killed by spraying with a herbicide, and the seeds are sown in shallow drills along these strips.

Mixtures of seeds with which to sow a meadow can now be bought, and can be broadcast over prepared seed beds as if sowing a lawn. Early results are often promising; sometimes because the chances of customer satisfaction have been improved by including seeds of cornfield weeds in the mixture. These germinate rapidly and well, and in the first year the grasses that come up are pleasantly and colourfully mingled with cornflowers, poppies, marigolds and corncockles. But these one-year

In the first year the grasses that come up from meadow seed mixtures are pleasantly and colourfully mingled with cornflowers, poppies, marigolds and corncockles. But these one-year wonders will not reappear

wonders will not reappear and the true test of the mixture comes in later years, when variety can be disappointingly limited.

Better results are likely when seeds of the desired species are sown in small containers and used to produce young plants, which can be set out individually to form the nucleus of the new communities. The seeds can be bought, or collected from wild plants growing on your own land, or with the permission of a local farmer or landowner. This is the simplest way to obtain the more common meadow plants and is not difficult. Seedlings are often easier to produce from freshly gathered seed than from older stuff in packets. Some, like ox-eye daisies, harebells and yarrow, germinate quickly and easily; others, especially the clovers and vetches and their relations, have seeds with hard, impermeable seed coats and, left to themselves, may not germinate within the life-span of the sower. However, if the casings are chipped or deeply scratched before the seeds are sown most of

these germinate rapidly and easily. Cowslips, mignonette and wild carrot can be sown in summer but will not germinate till the following spring. A few never comply with the captive conditions of garden plants and are very difficult to raise from seeds at all.

One way to cope with all these variations is to sow half the seed very soon after it is harvested and leave it outside through the autumn and winter. The rest of the seed should be kept and not sown till the following April. Seedlings should be pricked out or potted up during the spring and, as soon as they are big enough to fend for themselves, planted out in the area to be 'meadowed'. By the autumn they will have established themselves and the meadow mixture can be broadcast around them to initiate the matrix in which they will take their place.

Flower-spangled grass is the desirable face of meadows, but is followed by the less acceptable sight of ripening seed heads and tangled masses of declining foliage. Sooner or later meadows have to be mown. The times when this is done and the frequency, level and ways they are cut have great effects on how the sward develops, and which species play a part in it.

Terraces and paved or gravelled areas are useful spacemakers, which provide direct alternatives to a lawn

When redundant farm buildings are converted to dwellings, the spaces around and between them are often spoilt by the intrusion of tarmac drives and hammer heads. Woven panel fences and stiff conifer hedges are used to give rapid privacy. This farmhouse has a main view across the frontage of the newly converted barn and on, to a dramatic wooded valley backdrop. A concrete yard makes an ugly frontage and amounts to about a third of the outdoor space attached to the dwelling. The main aims of a new layout are:

♦ To make a welcoming frontage to the barn
♦ To create an impression of privacy from adjacent dwellings
♦ To make an attractive garden which is easy to look after and gives interest throughout the year
♦ To create a robust garden which young children can enjoy
♦ To retain the view from the farmhouse

A gravel path curves gently to the front door. Shrubs with a relaxed character are planted so that they appear to have found their own way into the garden. The same shrubs have been placed to form a partial screen from the other houses. Most neighbours don't peer through the shrubs so there is no need to make a dense barrier!

The view from the farmhouse has been considered and remains from some rooms. In the winter the view can be seen through the tracery of the deciduous trees

In favoured situations mowing is hardly needed. On dry sunny banks growth can be so sparse and open that a gentle clear-up sometime during the winter is sufficient. But the top growth of grasses that grow more densely must be removed, if broadleaved plants are to get enough light and space to survive.

The mowing moment most frequently proposed is about the middle of July – a little later than traditional haymaking – when the early flowers are over and, it is said, their seeds will be ripening. But very few seeds mature before the end of July, or even the middle of August, and tidying up the herbage before then has more to do with the urge to clear up what is seen as an unholy mess than with thoughtful management. In the interests of seed production, cutting should be delayed in occasional years at least, even though the compulsion to tidy up is too strong to resist in four years out of five.

The summer clearance is usually followed by a trim or two sometime during the autumn – to keep things tidy and make everything nice for the winter! If the meadow is intended to attract butterflies and other insects, these later mowings should be avoided. They destroy the cover that pupae and hibernating caterpillars depend on for their winter survival.

Until Mr Budding transformed a cloth-napping machine into a lawn-mower a hundred and sixty years ago, grass was universally cut with a curved blade on the end of a stick; a scythe for the skilled, a sickel for those in search of a bundle of greens for the rabbit. The mower soon replaced the scythe for lawns, but curved blades on sticks continued to be the easiest way to cut small, awkwardly shaped pieces of rough grass until quite recently. Now we enjoy the blessings of the strimmer, brought to us by a twentieth-century Budding and enthusiastically adopted by suburban man to accompany the lawn-mower in disturbances of the peace on Sunday mornings.

The whirring blades of these mechanical grasscutters are lethal to wild animals whose homes are in places where they are used; and small patches of rough, untrimmed grass are valuable resources and breeding grounds for all kinds of insects and other many-legged creatures and crawling things. Anyone with the slightest concern for wildlife in their garden should be reluctant to beg, borrow, hire or buy mechanical grasscutters merely to impose order on unruly grass.

This reluctance must be overruled by common sense when lawns have to be mown. No one would suggest a return to the scythe, when the grass is to be so closely and evenly shorn. But for patches of grass in corners or on verges and rough banks there is no need to reach for the strimmer whenever the herbage is a little less than neat and wild flowers begin to appear. A going-over with the shears or a sickle once or twice a year is all the maintenance they should need.

Larger areas of grass – the meadows of our gardens – present more of a challenge for those who abandon mechanisation. But a return to the scythe is not impractical, and as good for the health of its wielder as beneficial to the wildlife and the quality of the meadow. The knack of using a scythe adequately – if not expertly – is less difficult to acquire than ancient men beside bars in country pubs like to suggest, and it is a totally effective, economical, peaceful and very satisfying way to cope with a few hundred square metres of grass.

## POOLS AND PONDS

Once privacy has been assured by planting hedges or constructing fences, the next step in the occupation of the garden is making the lawn. For the lawn has a grip on neo-rustic imaginations that makes it an inevitable feature in any garden whose owner's apprenticeship was served in suburbia.

But lawns, which must be attended to week by week through eight months of the year, are burdens to those who have other things to do; an embarrassment to those whose presence is intermittent rather than constant; and an encumbrance to all who want to make the most of a small garden as a place to sit in, to stroll in or to garden in. For all that may be said in their favour – and there is much in their favour as features which flourish peculiarly well in Britain and can set off, and bring unity to, the flower beds, the house, the terrace, the pergola and other diverse features – lawns are neither inevitable nor necessary. They are options which we can choose to have or do without, like anything else in the garden.

The horizontal surfaces of lawns make spaces in gardens, and form compositions with the shapes and upright forms of the plants and trees and structures around them. Similarly useful spacemakers are drives, terraces and paved or gravelled areas, which provide direct alternatives to a lawn; and water in ponds and pools.

Even the smallest garden pool can give an impression of unplumbed depths, and feed notions of another world in the hidden voids beneath its surface. It is another world which should encourage imagination. The flexible liners now available put practically no limits on the shapes of pools, and the opportunities for introducing individuality and atmosphere that water offers in gardens.

The kidney-shaped pool, the squarish pool with wavy edges, and the gherkin-shaped pool make self-conscious entries into gardens whose designers shrink from the strength and graceful elegance of well-set rectilinear shapes or circles, but lack the imagination to be creative. Water in gardens makes such a strong impression – a direct visual impact, or a contribution to atmosphere – that it is essential to use it either to dominate its surroundings and be the focus of everything that goes on, or to fit it into the scenery so becomingly that it appears to be natural.

## WATER IN GARDENS

Ponds, pools, springs, streams, bogs, basins, torrents, cascades and falls, not to mention lakes and rivers, fountains, ditches and wells; water offers

A large pool could fill the greater part of the garden instead of the customary small corner

endless opportunities in gardens, and containing and using it are exciting challenges that deserve to be enjoyed to the full. Some of the alternatives are set out below.

The garden pond – seldom the garden ponds – reveals in a phrase the half-hearted, tentative approach to water that relegates it to a minor attraction. It is practically never the dominant, or even a major, garden motif. But water is most enjoyable as a series of pools and streams, springs, falls and cascades. A large pool could fill the greater part of the garden instead of the customary small corner, or a broad water-filled strip along a boundary could make a moat – secure against intruders, adding a feature to the landscape, and offering uninterrupted views of whatever lies beyond it.

Amongst the greatest pleasures of a pool are the animals, insects and birds that it attracts. Even the simplest fibreglass pool filled with water one summer's day, will have pond skaters and whirlygig beetles on its surface by the end of the week. Sometimes they arrive within an hour or two! And

## ARTIFICIAL

Artificial ponds, pools and streams etc can be made from a variety of materials and up to any size or depth, depending on the site and circumstances. They can be put wherever they are wanted, and grouped in any way that seems desirable. Usually they lend themselves to simple management and are highly controllable.

| Description | Merits | Limitations |
| --- | --- | --- |
| *Concrete pools* | Impose few limits on shape or form, easily fitted round curves and irregular shapes. Very long-lasting when well built. Concrete is well suited to the construction of formal pools. | Expensive to make; liable to crack due to ice or gravity, unless very well constructed. Hard to make look natural. Thorough surface-sealing must be done before filling with water. |
| *Puddled clay* | A natural material that can be used very flexibly to construct authentic-looking traditional ponds. Provides a good base for plantlife and pondlife in general. | Hard work to construct, and only a viable proposition where suitable material is readily available. Faults or problems at any stage likely to be difficult to correct. |
| *Lined pools* (butyl rubber or nylon-reinforced, heavy-gauge polyethylene) | Sheets of lining material can be prefabricated to almost any size or shape; cheap to install, and flexible and easy to use. Leaks can usually be located and repaired without much difficulty. | Must be carefully installed to avoid damage from roots and stones, or exposure to light, otherwise its life will be short. Not easy to conceal the material, particularly at the edges and on steeply sloping sides. |
| *Fibreglass pools and cascades* | Easy to buy in a variety of ready-made shapes and sizes. Tough, long-lasting material with very few installation problems. Can be used to fabricate on site, when it provides a versatile material readily adapted to different shapes. | Relatively expensive. Ready-made products often too small, too shallow, too complicated and too twee. Can be damaged by ice. Does not provide a naturally friendly surface for plants or other pondlife. |

the most formal rectangular pool, surrounded by stone flags, provides homes for a surprisingly varied medley of wildlife, which would not otherwise be there.

But when water is intended to be a place to shelter and provide a living for wild animals and plants, it should be designed to suit the tastes of as many different creatures as possible. There should be deeps and shallows, and places where barely covered mud is thick with the plants that grow around the edges of pools – bog beans, pickerel weed, flowering rush, sweet flag and others. There should be areas of clear water, others screened by the horizontal pads of lily leaves and water hawthorn, and hidden places where dense cover conceals creatures which like to live in secret.

### PLANTS AROUND THE EDGES

Plants on the edges of pools provide cover for creatures entering and leaving the water, and help to bind the banks against erosion. When liners are used it must be remembered that soil beyond the edge of the liner, however close to the water, will be no wetter than soil in other parts of the garden and some connection between water and soil should be arranged.

Adiantum
Alnus
*Asplenium
Astilbe
*Cardamine
*Carex
Chelone
Cimicifuga
Cornus
Darmera
Dierama
Dodocatheon
*Eupatorium
*Filipendula

*Gentiana
Gunnera
Hemerocallis
Houttuynia
Hosta
*Iris
Kalmia
*Leucojum
Lobelia
*Lysimachia
*Lythrum
Matteucia
*Mentha
Mimulus

*Myrica
Narcissus
*Osmunda
*Polygonum
Primula
Rheum
Rodgersia
*Salix
Schizostylis
*Scrophularia
Thalictrum
*Trollius
Veratrum

Acorus
*Alisma
*Butomus
Calla
*Caltha
*Carex
Glyceria
Houttuynia

*Iris
Ligularia
Lobelia
Lysichitum
Menyanthes
Mimulus
*Myosotis
Pontederia

Primula
*Ranunculus
*Sagittaria
Taxodium
*Trollius
*Typha
*Veronica
Zantedeschia

### PLANTS AT THE SHALLOW END

Stems, roots and leaves provide cover for small creatures, as well as food and places where their young can develop. Plants should be densely set in some parts and sparsely in others, to provide a mixture of cover and openness.

### PLANTS IN THE MUD

Plants in the mud at the margins of pools are useful visual links between the water and the surrounding planting, and as ecological links which help animals to move from one to the other.

*Callitriche
Egeria
Elodea
*Hottonia

*Nymphaea,
Orontium
Pontederia
*Ranunculus

*Sagittaria
Zantedeschia

---

## NATURAL

Natural sources of water are particularly valued in a garden, and may appear to offer plenty of scope for imaginative development. That may be so, but very often they are very difficult to use in any other way than that intended by nature; the levels of their flow, their tendency to flood, and their generally wayward behaviour can make them unpredictable and beyond the control of the gardener.

| Description | Merits | Limitations |
|---|---|---|
| Springs | Constant supply of moving water. Often make extremely attractive, semi-secret small features. | Water likely to be too cold to support much, if any, plant or pondlife. Liable to dry up periodically, even permanently, with no warning, or to break out elsewhere in the garden. |
| Streams and rivers | Provide very attractive features; likely to support a variety of wildlife, and bring a diverse range of plants and animals into the garden. | Likely to be very difficult to control; liable to flooding and changes in rate of flow. Seldom offer more than limited opportunities for planting up their banks, or other ploys. |
| Ponds | Likely to provide relatively stable bodies of water, which attract interesting birds and other wild animals; provide chances to introduce a variety of wild and garden water/marginal plants. | Silt up sooner or later, sooner if made in the bed of a stream, and must then be cleaned out. Some means of controlling the water-level should be provided. May become infested with dominant marginal or waterplants. |

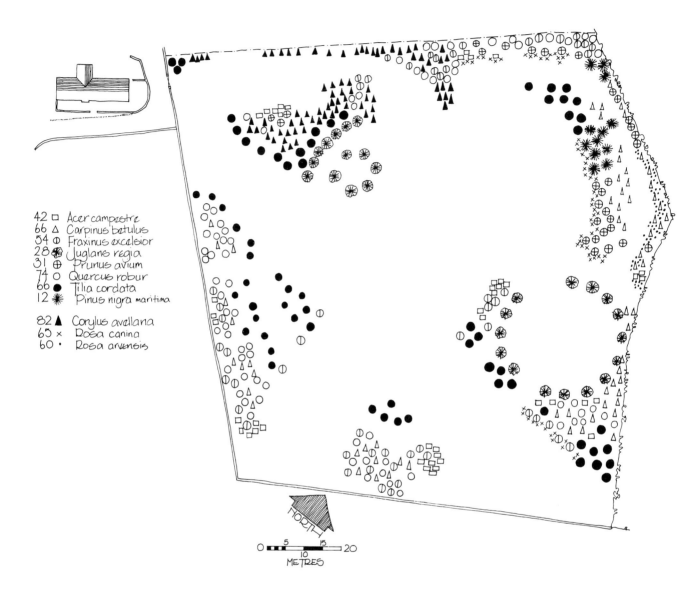

42 □ Acer campestre
66 △ Carpinus betulus
54 ⏀ Fraxinus excelsior
28 ✳ Juglans regia
31 ⊕ Prunus avium
74 ○ Quercus robur
66 ● Tilia cordata
12 ✲ Pinus nigra maritima

82 ▲ Corylus avellana
65 × Rosa canina
60 · Rosa arvensis

NORTH

0  5  15  20
    10
  METRES

Plantings in the countryside can often be seen across a wide area and can have a significant effect on the landscape – sympathetic planting is planned by first understanding the setting. This is a plan of a tree planting scheme on a 1.5-hectare paddock. The main aims of the planting are:

♦ To create sheltered areas in an open landscape
♦ To keep an uninterrupted open area for grazing
♦ To use species which look 'at home'
♦ To frame dramatic views of distant hills

The walnuts may seem an odd choice, but they like growing in this area and fit the scene very well

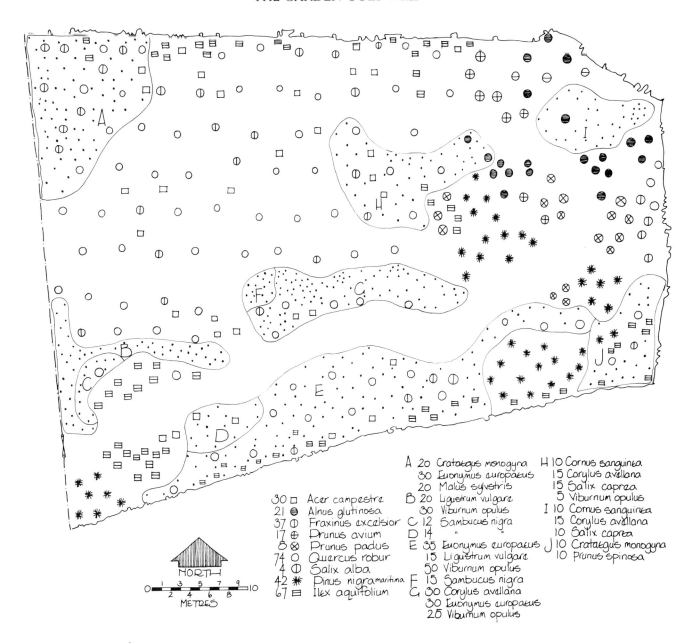

NORTH

0 1 3 5 7 9 10
  2 4 6 8
METRES

30 □ Acer campestre
21 ⊖ Alnus glutinosa
37 ⊕ Fraxinus excelsior
17 ⊕ Prunus avium
8 ⊗ Prunus padus
74 ○ Quercus robur
4 ⊕ Salix alba
42 ✳ Pinus nigra maritima
67 ⊟ Ilex aquifolium

A 20 Crataegus monogyna
   30 Euonymus europaeus
   20 Malus sylvestris
B 20 Ligustrum vulgare
   30 Viburnum opulus
C 12 Sambucus nigra
D 14     "
E 35 Euonymus europaeus
   15 Ligustrum vulgare
   50 Viburnum opulus
F 15 Sambucus nigra
G 30 Corylus avellana
   30 Euonymus europaeus
   25 Viburnum opulus

H 10 Cornus sanguinea
   15 Corylus avellana
   15 Salix caprea
   5 Viburnum opulus
I 10 Cornus sanguinea
   15 Corylus avellana
   10 Salix caprea
J 10 Crataegus monogyna
   10 Prunus spinosa

Amenity woodlands do not have to be set out in rigid grids. This is a plan for a 2-hectare paddock. The design is a direct response to the various growing conditions on the site: as the exposure and soil character change, so do the species planted. In this way an attractive wood will develop, full of interest and variety. All the plants used were field grown, except for the hollies which were pot grown. Only two- and three-year-old transplants and feathered trees were used – no standards. The oaks have been protected in tree shelters. The ground around the base of each plant is kept free of vegetation by spraying with glyphosate; this has a very significant effect on the growth rate of the plants and helps them to withstand long dry periods. The hollies did much better in the lea of the boundary hedge – cold winter winds damaged more exposed hollies very badly. The plants which were fastest to 'get away' were the field maples, goat willow, guelder rose and spindle

### PLANTS IN THE DEEP END

Some cover is needed even in the deepest parts of a pond, and lily leaves provide valuable shade and shelter close to the surface. The cover should not be dense and it is important to preserve a high proportion of clear, unobstructed waterways in these parts of ponds and pools.

*Aponogeton*
*\*Nuphar*
*\*Nymphaea*

### FREE-FLOATING PLANTS

Some of these, usually introduced as oxygenators, are rampant growers which compete remorselessly with other vegetation.

| | | |
|---|---|---|
| *Aponogeton* | *Stratiotes* | *\*Lemna* |
| *Hydrocharis* | *Trapa* | |

Genera marked * include native species; these are more likely to provide friendly conditions for wildlife than exotics.

## MAKING A WOOD

A wood need not be large, but there are few features which contribute so much to the surrounding countryside, can be created more easily, or make fewer demands on time and effort later on. There are few opportunities in gardening to do anything that seems more worthwhile, or provides such satisfaction in the doing. Making woods – particularly where their owners have other things to do than spend their lives endlessly gardening – has everything to commend it.

Trees are the sustenance, refuge and homes of animals and birds and insects, and the supporters and protectors of wild flowers and mysterious lichens, ferns and mosses. But different trees vary in value as providers and supporters of flora and fauna, and this value changes as trees mature, age and decay.

The oak's reputation, which puts it first amongst our trees, is well founded; not least for its contribution as a refuge and larder for wild creatures. Apart from willows and birches, which lag well behind it, no other tree supports a fraction of the variety of insects and other multi-legged small creatures that oaks do. Other common and characteristic trees like hawthorn, with half as many dependants; elm, with barely a quarter; and ash – the oak's main rival in many places – with barely a seventh, have a value for other wildlife which seems minor by comparison. Introduced trees, even those that have become long-established parts of the scenery like Norway maple, sycamore and sweet chestnut, have very few dependants indeed.

Birds are attracted by the varied and well-stocked larder that an oak provides, and those strange alliances between algae and fungi, the lichens, attach themselves and spread more profusely on its bark than on any other tree.

Trees are large, and mature trees are enormous – and thinking of an animal or bird or insect as living on an oak tree is a simplification that ignores the real needs of the creature, and conceals the ways in which trees support other wildlife.

A large tree, like a city, provides dozens of ways to make a living, and is divided into districts where different characteristics and opportunities support entirely different inhabitants. The older and larger the tree, the more numerous, complex and significant these districts become. Extreme examples are the master oaks – ancient specimens whose upper branches jut above the canopy of their juniors – whose rounded summits are the trysting places of purple emperor butterflies. These serve so many generations that they become part of the folklore of the population, and when the oak eventually falls, the population may collapse too, because its members are unable to agree on an alternative landmark where they can meet and mate.

A mature tree is such a complex organism, with so many niches where different animals make their living that it becomes irreplaceable. An acre of newly planted trees supports only a fraction of the wildlife of one mature oak, and when one is destroyed it takes decades, centuries even, before all the interactions and diversity can be restored. This emphasises the great importance of not destroying mature trees lightly, and justifies going to great lengths to preserve them. This might seem rather discouraging to those who plant in order to preserve and maintain wildlife. But, apart from the fact that little trees do eventually grow into big trees, immature woods are better than no woods at all. Many creatures and wild flowers thrive in them that would not exist otherwise. A familiar example is the richness of a coppiced wood, which is a wood maintained perpetually in immaturity.

# OAK CITY

An account of its districts and the nature of the inhabitants that live in them.

| DISTRICT | CHARACTERISTICS | INHABITANTS |
|---|---|---|
| *Roots* | Provide a year-round food supply and add to the dead and dying wood which supports fungi, which in turn supports many small insects and animals. | Gall wasps, larvae of weevils and fungus midges, springtails. |
| *Dead and rotting wood* | A major resource for many animals, which may feed on it or on the fungi which it supports. Many of the creatures will be widely distributed, and not restricted to oak trees alone. | Larvae of longhorn beetles; bark beetles; fungus-feeding bugs, beetle larvae; springtails, predatory bugs, mites, woodlice, millepedes, predatory centipedes and ground beetles. |
| *Trunk* | Deeply fissured bark provides shelter all through the year, but few insects feed on live bark. Lichens provide food for many species. Surfaces make resting places for moths, whose markings can make them almost invisible. | Gall wasps; caterpillars of moths; bark lice and beetle mites grazing on the lichens; a number of predatory insects and spiders; moths and, in winter, pupae of moths. |
| *Cavities and holes* | Provide nesting holes for birds, and add to the sum of decaying wood. May become more or less permanently filled with water. | Mites/fleas and other parasites of birds; beetles and fly larvae in droppings; springtails and woodlice, millepedes; aquatic larvae of mosquitoes and flies. |
| *Twigs* | Young twigs provide food for some species; and mature twigs, hiding places. Many animals overwinter on twigs as eggs, larvae or pupae and feed on the leaves as they open. | Larvae of sawfly and twig-cutting weevil, eggs of mirid bugs and flower bugs, eggs and larvae of overwintering moths, scale insects and aphids. |
| *Buds* | Buds are very nutritious, particularly flower buds, but they are protected for much of the year by scales; during bud-break in spring this protection is lost for a short time, and then the buds become a rich source of food. | Gall wasps, gall midges, weevil larvae, eggs and young larvae of purple hairstreak butterfly, young mirid bugs, aphids and capsids, eggs of moths during the winter and their larvae at bud-break in spring. |
| *Catkins* | The pollen of oak trees is not such an important food source as that of many other trees, notably willow; perhaps because it is dry and short-lived. | Gall midges; caterpillars of a very few moths; honey bees. |
| *Acorns* | Acorns are a major food source for birds and mammals but are much less important to insects. Decaying acorns support far more species than healthy ones. | Weevils, tortrix moths, gall midges and gall wasps. |

| DISTRICT | CHARACTERISTICS | INHABITANTS |
|---|---|---|
| *Leaves* | The major source of food for many small animals; a number hide themselves inside the leaves, or within galls. Other biting or sucking insects etc live on the surface of the leaves, which become progressively richer in tannins and less palatable as the summer proceeds. Honeydew secreted by aphids is a source of food to some other insects, either directly or through fungi which grow on it. | Gall wasps and midges, leaf-mining larvae of moths, beetles, flies and other insects; leaf-sucking bugs, eg bishop bugs, capsids, aphids, and leaf-hoppers; caterpillars of many moths, weevils and other beetles, and sawflies; adult weevils and other beetles; ants and adult purple emperor butterflies on honeydew; parasitic flies, mites and bugs; predators including the oak bush-cricket, ladybirds, lacewings, ground beetles, and flower bugs, ichneumon wasps and spiders. |

Planting a wood is an exciting aspect of gardening and a very rewarding thing to do. Not the least of its rewards is the fact that, in many circumstances, free expert advice and grants are available through which the government or local authorities will provide help and share the costs of planting and looking after the trees.

All trees are not equal. The pre-eminence of oaks as providers for insects and other animals has already been stressed; and the term oaks used in this connection does not include species from overseas. Some of these like the American scarlet oak, *Quercus rubra,* are more often planted in gardens and as ornamental specimen trees than native *Q. robur* or *Q. petraea.* Introduced trees, even those whose ancient roots almost convince us they are natives, are the homes of very few insects or animals; more recent, more exotic introductions have little or no value in this respect. Partly for that reason, and partly to avoid intrusive effects on the surrounding landscape, grants for tree planting are restricted only to native trees and a very select band of introductions.

Trees in the landscape inevitably grow into conspicuous features. Nothing else that we plant emphasises 'naturalness' so convincingly, or alternatively advertises exotic qualities so blatantly. There is no reason why anyone who plants a wood should restrict themselves to native species – unless wildlife is the only consideration – but respect for the countryside or the village where the planting is set should be a reason for taking care about the impression the planting will make.

## CHOOSING TREES FOR GARDENS IN THE COUNTRY

When choosing trees for a garden, or making a wood, time should be taken to think about their impact and they should be planted with some definite intention in mind. Possible intentions may be:

1 That they should blend with their surroundings and establish links with the countryside around them; or
2 That they should contrast with their surroundings and emphasise the individuality and separateness of their location; or
3 That they should fit into the countryside or village around them, yet maintain a feeling of a place apart from its surroundings.

In woodland and in large gardens – very often in small ones – there is space to play around with different effects. That converted barn now known as 'Casa Manuela' might suggest a brake of Chusan palms. Neo-rustics whose hearts are in Provence, but whose businesses are in Kent, might substitute a grove of oleasters for the olive trees they crave. Neither would do anything for the wildlife; neither would slip unobtrusively into a country setting; no grants would be given in their aid. But either could be a prelude – a light-hearted introduction – to a regular wood, filled with regular native trees, and a haven for all kinds of regular wildlife.

Evaluating trees for country settings depends on having a particular situation in mind, and a par-

That converted barn, now known as 'Casa Manuela', might suggest a brake of Chusan palms

Pyrus communis
Quercus robur
Salix caprea*
Salix pentandra*
Sorbus aucuparia
Tilia cordata
Ulmus carpinifolia
Ulmus procera.

Quercus petraea
Salix alba*
Salix daphnoides*
Sorbus aria*
Sorbus torminalis
Tilia platyphyllos
Ulmus glabra

ticular point of view about what should be done with it. It is seldom a dispassionate, impartial assessment of what is wanted; usually it is subjective, depending on an individual's viewpoint and prejudices, and that is its strength and its weakness. The object is to express the suitability, or otherwise, of possible choices for a particular purpose in such a way that you can grade the choices according to how closely they match some preconceived standard. The example which follows illustrates the author's view of how harmoniously a number of different deciduous trees fit into landscapes where native trees are a conspicuous feature.

*1 Native trees or long-established introductions, which harmonise closely with plants in the countryside*
Some, marked *, are trees which are very typical of particular soils or situations, and these are likely to look out of place in other surroundings.

Acer campestre
Acer pseudoplatanus
Betula pendula*
Crateagus monogyna
Fraxinus excelsior
Malus sylvestris
Populus canescens*
Prunus avium

Acer platanoides
Alnus glutinosa*
Carpinus betulus
Fagus sylvatica
Ilex aquifolium
Populus alba*
Populus nigra
Prunus padus

*2 Exotic trees which have close affinities with native species and combine harmoniously with them*
These are plants which can be used to broaden variety and add interest without introducing a markedly unnatural or alien character.

Acer saccharinum
Alnus cordata
Betula lutea
Carya cordiformis
Castanea sativa
Corylus colurna
Davidia involucrata
Fraxinus excel jaspidea
Ilex x altaclarensis
Juglans regia
Liriodendron tulipifera
Malus hupehensis
Nothofagus obliqua
Populus trichocarpa
Prunus sargentii
Pterocarya fraxinifolia
Quercus cerris
Quercus rubra
Sorbus cashmiriana
Sorbus 'Joseph Rock'
Tilia petiolaris
Zelkova carpinifolia.

Acer negundo
Alnus incana
Betula nigra
Carya ovata
Cercidiphyllum japonicum
Crataegus crus-galli
Fagus heterophylla
Fraxinus ornus
Juglans nigra
Liquidambar styraciflua
Magnolia salicifolia
Malus tschonowskii
Nothofagus procera
Prunus avium 'Plena'
Prunus x yedoensis
Quercus castaneifolia
Quercus coccinea
Robinia pseudoacacia
Sorbus domestica
Tilia euchlora
Tilia tomentosa

*3 Exotic trees, and forms of native species, which impart a garden character but do not contrast emphatically with the native flora*
The inclusion of a few of these in a woodland planting would convey an impression of ornamental, rather than natural, woodland, and the presence of a high proportion would set the planting apart from rural surroundings.

Acer davidii
Acer rubrum
Aesculus hippocastanum

Acer hersii
Aesculus flava
Ailanthus altissima

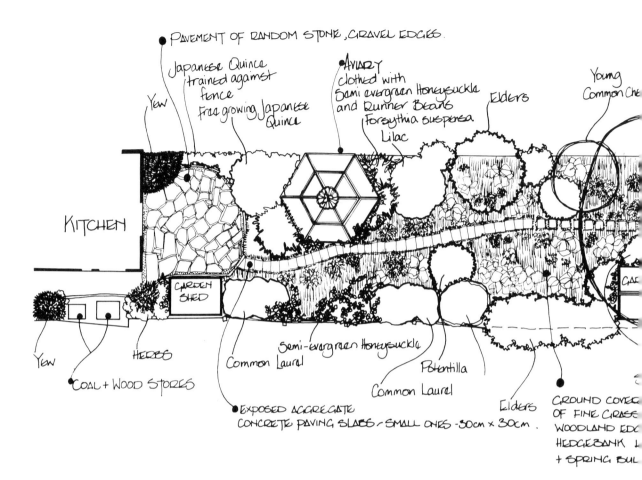

PAVEMENT OF RANDOM STONE, GRAVEL EDGES.

Japanese Quince trained against fence

Free growing Japanese Quince

Yew

AVIARY clothed with Semi evergreen Honeysuckle and Runner Beans Forsythia suspensa Lilac

Elders

Young Common Che

KITCHEN

GARDEN SHED

Yew

HERBS

COAL + WOOD STORES

Common Laurel

Semi-evergreen Honeysuckle

Common Laurel

Potentilla

Elders

GROUND COVER OF FINE GRASS WOODLAND EDG HEDGEBANK + SPRING BUL

EXPOSED AGGREGATE CONCRETE PAVING SLABS - SMALL ONES - 30cm x 30cm.

AVIARY

Simple, bold ideas usually work better than elaborate ones. Over-complicated planting designs can be difficult to manage and never really gel. This previously impenetrable garden has been very gently thinned out to give clarity to an inviting sequence of spaces and moods. All the work has been done by the lady who lives here. This has been possible because she has recognised the intrinsic character of the place and aimed to complement it, working *with* the site conditions rather than battling against them. New plants are chosen to be at home in the different areas of the garden: warm, sheltered and well drained; cool, dappled shade; dark constant shade; alkaline soil – no struggling to grow rhododendrons in this limy garden!

176

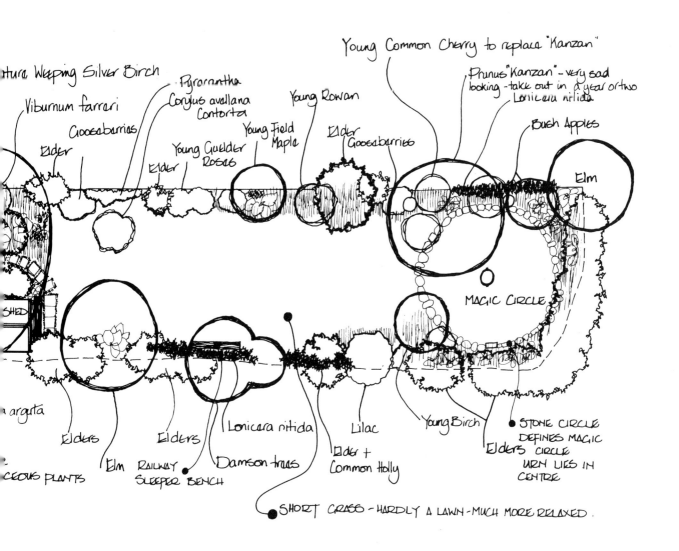

tura Weeping Silver Birch

Viburnum farreri

Gooseberries

Elder

Pyracantha

Corylus avellana
Contorta

Elder

Young Guelder
Roses

Young Field
Maple

Young Rowan

Elder

Gooseberries

Young Common Cherry to replace "Kanzan"

Prunus "Kanzan" - very sad
looking - take out in a year or two
Lonicera nitida

Bush Apples

Elm

MAGIC CIRCLE

a argita

Elders

Elm

RAILWAY
SLEEPER BENCH

Elders

Lonicera nitida

Damson trees

Lilac

Elder +
Common Holly

Young Birch

STONE CIRCLE
DEFINES MAGIC
CIRCLE
URN LIES IN
CENTRE

Elders

CEOUS PLANTS

SHORT GRASS - HARDLY A LAWN - MUCH MORE RELAXED.

GARDEN SHED

MAGIC CIRCLE

177

Betula papyrifera
Catalpa bignonioides
Crataegus azarolus
Evodia hupehensis
Koelreuteria paniculta
Ligustrum lucidum
Malus 'John Downie'
Nyssa sylvatica
Prunus serrulata
  'Tai-Haku'
Prunus subhirtella
Salix exigua
Sorbus hupehensis
Sorbus sargentiana.

Betula utilis
Cercis siliquastrum
Crataegus x lavallei
Ilex aquif 'Camellifolia'
Laurus nobilis
Magnolia campbellii
Malus 'Golden Hornet'
Prunus serrula
Prunus serrulata 'Yukon'

Pyrus nivalis
Salix hookerana
Sorbus intermedia

Nothofagus dombeyi
Platanus x acerifolia
Prunus padus
  'Colorata'
Pyrus salicifolia
Salix matsudana
  'Tortuosa'.

Paulownia tomentosa
Populus candicans 'Aurora'
Prunus serrulata
  'Shimidsu'
Quercus ilex

**4** *Trees which are distinctively unlike native species and make their mark as components of a garden*
The shapes, forms or foliage of the trees in this group are all emphatically exotic and the presence of even one or two specimens would create an impression of a planted rather than natural woodland.

Acer negundo 'Variegata'
Eucalyptus niphophila
Fagus 'Pendula'

Liriodendron tulipifera
  'Aureo-marginata'

Betula jacquemontii
Fagus 'Dawyck'
Ilex aquifolium
  'Golden King'
Malus x 'Purpurea'

**5** *Trees which introduce very strong contrasts into rural or village settings, and emphasise an alien character*
The following all have sufficient presence and impact to form dominant features which cannot be overlooked in any rural landscape. There are situations where these qualities would be desirable, but these trees should not be introduced into country settings inadvertently, haphazardly or without justification.

Acer platanoides
  'Crimson King'
Aesculus x carnea
Fagus sylvatica purpurea
Prunus serrulata
  'Amanogawa'
  and 'Kanzan'

Acer pseudoplatanus
  'Brilliantissima'
Eucalyptus gunnii
Populus nigra 'Italica'
Robinia pseudoacacia
  'Frisia'.

## CHAPTER NINE

Gardens surely are places where we should be free to do as we want and, provided we are satisfied, need we bother about what others think of our efforts? But gardens and the facades of houses are directly in the public eye: they *do* affect the appearance of their surroundings, they *do* attract attention, and when we look around at what others are up to we are not indifferent to what we see.

Neo-rustics launching into rural idylls move straight to the riddle in the centre of the maze of countryside problems. They find themselves trying to build new lifestyles, develop new expectations and impose new demands on foundations which supported a way of life that has gone for ever, but which are still a vital part of the quality of country life.

The neo-rustic intrusions have been largely passive – the search for a dream which may or may not be found. But already the effects of more active opinions are becoming apparent, which pay less attention to water that has passed under the bridge and more to expectations of what life in villages and the country has to offer. It will not be long before changes which today seem so significant, will be seen to be only the start of much more fundamental restyling.

What we do with our gardens matters, because it is there that we develop ideas about how we should like our surroundings to look. It is in our gardens that we form opinions which give us the confidence to pronounce on the good taste, or otherwise, of what we see going on around us. Once formed, these opinions extend to developments far beyond our domain, in widening circles which stretch out and eventually involve almost everything happening in the countryside today.

Our first encounters with the heritage effect are

# Rainbows and Shadows

We must combat everything that threatens the variety of interest needed for human fulfilment – the extermination of wildlife, over mechanisation, the boredom of mass production and conformity, the spoiling of natural beauty, the destruction of cultural traditions.

*Julian Huxley*

in our homes and gardens. We recognise the beauty of much of what remains from the past and the need to see that it is not destroyed or so changed that it becomes unrecognisable, but we also allow ourselves to become so marinaded in nostalgia, that we disdain today's artists and craftsmen and have little confidence in and less esteem for anything that is contemporary. We prefer pastiches of country tradition to original designs made from modern materials. Our children's children will find that their inheritance from the twentieth century consists of copies of lead watertanks bearing impressively ancient dates but made of fibre glass; simpering nymphs of resin; concrete slabs that mimic riven paving or cobbled stone; replicas of stone urns and heraldic beasts formed from moulded plastic, and aluminium filling the patterns once used to make cast-iron garden seats.

Fibre glass makes good water tanks: cheaper, easier to handle and not poisonous, like lead. Concrete is more practical for paving slabs than stone, and less slippery in wet weather. Aluminium seats can be carried about the garden by those whose backs cannot cope with cast iron. The materials are not at fault, nor the uses we put them to, but our failure to think creatively about how we use them. Instead of imprisoning a material as flexible and fluid as concrete in the less mobile forms of stone, we should look for ways to release its curves and swirls, patterns, shapes and textures. Concrete, plastics, fibreglass and aluminium have their own qualities, and our gardens are places where we can play with these materials and learn how to fit them to our needs. Instead, we are setting out to discover a new lifestyle by cobbling together sham settings from a world our grandparents  were glad to escape.

*These gardens remind me of a children's dressing up game – everything has been fetched out of the wardrobe and the make-up bag has been raided. It can be difficult to know where to start to plan a new garden. Here, the best approach would be to look closely at the village – its gardens, hedges, walls and trees – to determine what plants are used, which do well, and what is the local building style. These are important details which attract you to the village. Imposing the range of garden plants and features illustrated dilutes the character that originally attracted you*

Trips to the post-office or evening strolls through the village are enlivened by comments about gardens seen over fences or through gates. A harmless pastime – but one which gives form to our reactions to what we see, with results that can be penetrating when opinions surface as ribald remarks, or villages are entered for Best Kept competitions, and local pride adds barbs to the comments. For the attitudes that surface almost always favour androcentric gardening styles based on overt control, and a display of activity. Could there be a clearer example of this than the concept of a 'Best-Kept Village'?

Predictably, kept villages run the risk of becoming fallen villages. Their greens are manicured, their verges trimmed and their hedges clipped. Colour is splashed around to attract attention and a gaudy presence rather than cosmetic subtlety piles up the points. The pert and sensual silhouettes and the seductive foliage of conifers attract appreciative glances – less likely to be drawn by the spreading forms of broad-leaved trees and shrubs. Pools, neatly paved patios, rockeries and trim entrances adorn the village more beguilingly than

ancient, gappy orchards, meadows going to seed, cobbled yards with a frisson of green, and ponds, where a collapsed willow and a ragged frieze of plants around unordered margins shelter moorhens, frogs and grass snakes.

Casual comments about neighbours' gardens become Trojan horses that make suburbia the standard by which country settings are judged. More substantial than wooden horses are housing developments, often with little in common with the piecemeal growth and vernacular architecture of the past. Those whose hopes of protecting the countryside depend on fashioning it in a mould formed long ago condemn these additions as out of character with the needs and traditions of small villages – but the mould has been broken. Socially questing neo-rustics with fax machines and his and hers offices, an au pair and 1.9 children, and two cars and a golden retriever in the drive, do not fit into cottages where farm workers once brought up eight or nine children sleeping four to a bed. Terraces and cosy cotts once appealed to retired couples and families looking for second homes; their Arkadian charm made up for their short comings. Now they are too modest and too cramped, and their replacements are substantial, assertive houses grouped in closes.

Rather than follow the heritage effect's dictate that we must preserve the past by imitation, the challenge is to find agreeable ways to fit new buildings into old villages. That will not happen while houses grouped in humdrum, standardised formations arouse obnoxious reactions with their settings throughout the length and breadth of Britain. They do so because their developers, and then their occupiers, fail to see beyond the

boundaries of the estate, or even the individual houses. The developer concentrates on whatever equations of size and layout produce the greatest profit, and siting the houses and landscaping their surroundings to blend with the local character of villages do not improve these equations. Their owners see the gardens as retreats to be enclosed as quickly and opaquely as possible.

Trees can provide a bridge between the differences in scale of twentieth century developments and the longer, lower roof-lines of older village houses and cottages. But the token whitebeams, double red thorns or silver pears sited by developers on the lawns of open-plan front gardens serve little purpose. These trees are the doodles of architects, dabbed onto the plans with little rubber tree stamps long after all the decisions that matter have been made. It is too late to think about landscaping after the positions of the houses have been decided, the roads and entrances laid out and their materials ordered. It is too late to think about trees when the only spaces for them are those left over when every other feature on the site has had priority. Melding these houses into village settings depends on radical changes in our appreciation of landscaping, and acceptance of a more even balance between the number and value of the houses on a site, and the need to use space to make it part of the village.

New developments are not the only places where trees can be used more positively. In villages and country towns all over Britain, inadequate appreciation of their importance causes self-inflicted problems because the irreplaceable qualities of the forest trees have never been acknowledged. Their presence is taken for granted

*Gardens do not all have to look the same to fit into the village scene. These two designs show very different styles and tastes, but the theme that underlies them both is their reference to native plants, and plants which look comfortable in rural places. In addition, the layouts respond to their surroundings. In this scene the new properties start to blend with the adjacent houses, gardens and farm buildings. The way to achieve this harmony is learned and developed by really looking in detail at the surroundings*

and no priority given to making space for them, and to making sure that replacements are planted. One by one the large forest trees – the limes, the oaks, the ashes, beeches and willows – leave the stage. Their places are taken by trees that grow smaller and remain neater; trees with bright foliage or colourful flowers; trees that can be set out at calculated spacings in lines along roadsides, or planted symmetrically on plots of grass needed for nothing else.

The trees we plant in our gardens can show us their value as screens where screens are needed, and as links with surrounding features, and teach us methods of management which dispel our fear of them. Our gardens are the places where a broadly-based appreciation of trees can develop – and this is essential if those who press for a balance between trees and houses when planning approval is being sought for new developments are to receive the support they need.

The changing shape of life in the countryside has also stirred the interest of developers, industrial enterprises and entrepreneurs eager to meet our willingness to spend on leisure parks, pleasure worlds and activities of many kinds. Businessmen, more aware of the nature of the changes than romantics and traditionalists, see opportunities to make money by providing for the village's novel role as a part of the lifestyle of status-sensitive cottagers.

Amongst the attractions of these new enterprises are their rural settings, but these are places designed for people whose recent roots were in towns and suburbs, or who drive from the towns for a day out or a holiday in the country. Their country style is a romantic version designed to meet the expectations of their customers, that looks back to a highly selective past and makes no attempt to create new forms. Few of these enterprises attempt style or individuality when they landscape their surroundings, despite the fact that these provide every passer-by and visitor with first impressions of their existence. Executives committed to power dressing are blind to power planting, and are content when the entrances to their businesses and the surroundings of their offices are draped with hackneyed, off-the-peg planting schemes, so long as they are neat and trim and look well-pressed. Accountants and businessmen are not persuaded that money spent on designing and landscaping is money well spent, because they seldom think about it. Their own gardens are places where they might begin to explore alternatives to off-the-peg gardens, and discover the sense of individuality and place that landscaping would also contribute to the premises where they do business.

Arkadia is a dreamland which we all see dimly and incompletely in an endlessly moving and changing scene. It cannot be preserved because it doesn't exist, but visions of Arkadia can be the inspiration that points the way towards the changes we should like to see. We may deplore changes going on in the countryside, but protests will have little effect if they seem to come from an 'enlightened' minority telling neo-rustics what they should think. Gardens are places where we can all learn to leap fences, and find out for ourselves whether alternatives to suburban gardening offer the scope for imagination and individuality which could lead the way to our Arkadia.

The opinions we develop in our gardens acquire a very public face when they extend to village greens, commons, roadside verges and other open spaces vulnerable to individual or collective ideas about beautification and the improvement of the environment. The effects on village greens can be

Even in aggregate, gardens can play little part in prolonging the existence of rare plants or creatures – nobody expects to see swallowtail butterflies on their carrots as a result of abandoning poisonous sprays

dire. Humphry Repton enclosed part of the green beyond his fence and turned it into garden. Today such direct action is very rare, but everywhere the grassy centres of villages are being changed by well-meant, misplaced improvements. Their rough grass is tamed and mown. Their irregular boundaries, banks and ditches are cleaned up, kerbed and strimmed. Their ponds are dredged, sanitised and railed around, and their wet places drained. Scrub is cut down, cleaned out and replaced with shrubs. Tastefully chosen, carefully staked and guarded trees grace the edges in meticulously spaced arrangements. Once again cherries and conifers, silver birches and whitebeams appear as the hackneyed choices of those who have no sense of location or atmosphere.

The green as a left-over piece of rather unregulated country within a village; somewhere for ducks, geese or sheep to graze, or a pony to be tethered; a place to play or walk or sit quietly; a place where things happen, and plants grow somewhat haphazardly because no one feels obliged to trim or scrape; a place where boundaries, obscured perhaps by squatter-building in the past, become a little blurred; a space which provides the unity that links the houses, fields and gardens around its edges

– these all become items on an agenda attended to by tidy-minded committees, and are lost.

The gynocentric styles derived from Gertrude Jekyll would provide a more sympathetic approach to these changes. Her sensitivity to natural forces, and her recognition of the quality and value of native trees and forms, would bring gentler transformations than those we see today. But her followers are absorbed in their own gardens and are too busy with their mixed borders, too addicted to tumbled masses of mauve and pink amongst silver foliage, and too preoccupied with their potagers to make their opinions heard on committees set up by the green improvers. The needs of those who lived in the villages gave rise to the greens, and their appearance still reflects local opinion. If those who live around them have spared time and imagination to look out from their gardens to the countryside beyond, grappling with the problems of meadows, developing a feeling for wildlife and a recognition of it as a valued part of the scene, then the management of the green and other public spaces around the village will reflect those attitudes too.

Colossal, linear open spaces familiar to everyone are the verges of the motorways. The demands of the artic, the express coach and the motor car have created hundreds of miles of new countryside, and a perverse irony has placed responsibility for the most monumental and conspicuous landscaping of the century with the Department of Transport. These acres, with no purpose other than the separation of traffic from the real country on either side, challenged landscapers to create principles to guide their planting and management.

There must have been moments when these motorway verges seemed to offer a splendid opportunity to beautify the countryside; when factions pressed to have them planted with attractive ornamental trees to make our journeys bright and beautiful. Instead it was decided that the motorway verges should form a part of the landscape through which they passed, using native species of trees and shrubs adapted to local conditions and with an eye on those already growing round about. So, some would say, the opportunity to enliven our travels with a dazzling display of flower power was turned down in favour of a dull, unimaginative alternative; a decision, they might add, only to be expected of bureaucrats in a government ministry.

But that decision, made by a committee set up by the Department of Transport, provided the logic and purpose needed before any designer can begin to exercise imagination. It provided the key to the kinds of plants to be used, and ensured variety and diversity from one part of the network to another. It allowed imagination to focus on ways to group and combine trees and shrubs so that they responded to features in the countryside, and linked the planting with its surroundings. A problem in any country setting is the difficulty of introducing new forms and new plantings that add to, rather than detract from, what is already there. The firm guidelines for the motorways were the solution to this problem – and exactly the same applies when village greens, and open spaces of any sort in the countryside, are the objects under discussion.

An unexpected, but not unpredictable, consequence of the planting along the motorways has been the benefit derived from it by animals, birds and other forms of wildlife. There was a spell, only a generation ago, when roadside verges even along country lanes were routinely sprayed with herbicides, followed up by regularly repeated mowings. Public opinion approved rather than opposed this vandalism, and the arguments of the few who saw

The insects, birds and wild flowers that come into our gardens are the simplest and most direct introductions to wildlife we can have

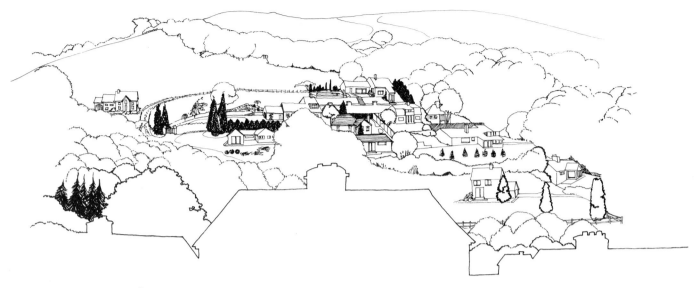

It is all too easy to destroy the very character which draws people to live in the country. Walkers' feet and overgrazing by sheep damages the hills – so does this sort of housing. The properties have been built to give a stunning view and a feeling of space to the people who live in them: they have the opposite effect on the valley they occupy. The conifer hedges and specimens, the shrubs chosen for strong colour effects, the preponderance of evergreens and the bright bedding schemes shout from the hillside. The neighbouring oak, ash and hazel woods provide lessons which are totally ignored.
There is no justification for this type of development, but improvements can be made to help lessen the impact

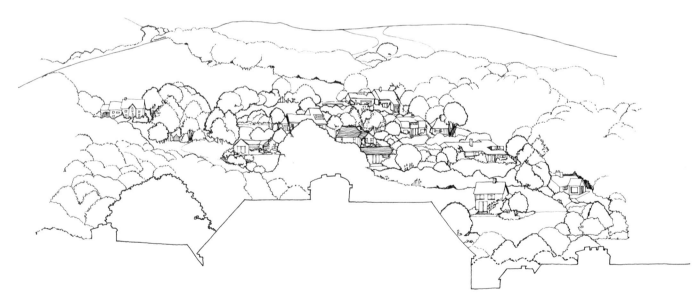

In this alternative, the alien shapes and colours have been replaced by predominantly deciduous trees which blend in with the neighbouring woods. 'Eyecatchers' nestle within the main planting, where they can be enjoyed inside the garden. The harsh lines of retaining walls, patios and roads, which cut across the contours, have been softened by planting the damage it was doing to wildlife, and tried to persuade councils to adopt less drastic methods, would have been more strongly resisted if they had not brought with them opportunities to make very welcome economies. It has now become fashionable to assume a hue of green and, after abusing nature for half a century, central and even local governments have become aware that seats can depend on not losing votes by being thought too uncaring. But the hint of green is very faint indeed, a mere film of verdigris, and will remain so while the majority of voters know little about the conditions which affect the survival of the flora and fauna around them.

Insects, birds and wild flowers in our gardens are the simplest and most direct introductions to wildlife we can have. They provide examples of the benefits of toleration by the extra interest they bring to any scene. It is in gardens that we can begin to learn that what appears to be rubbish may actually be essential resources for wildlife which should not wantonly be destroyed, and to discover ways in which an understanding of the needs of wildlife rewards us by increasing the richness and diversity of our daily lives.

Even in aggregate, gardens can do little to prolong the existence of rare plants or creatures – nobody expects to see swallowtail butterflies on their carrots as a result of abandoning poisonous sprays. But the green garden is a path to a broader understanding of the issues involved in conservation. Small beginnings, like giving up pesticides and discovering that disaster does not follow, lead to more sympathetic appreciation of the part played by wildlife. When protests need to be made, firm convictions based on this experience are much more effective than gut-tightening outbursts of frustrated emotion. Wildlife in gardens can change attitudes to wildlife in general, and in the long run contributes to the only foundation on which enduring conservation policies can be built.

Neo-rustics do not move only into old rectories, converted barns and clusters of executive houses in the centre of villages. Many have become thoroughly modern farmers, the owners of great estates and landowners of one kind or another on every scale. They move into a landscape which still owes much to the past: hedges, often no longer needed, are preserved by nostalgia and inertia rather than for practical or aesthetic reasons; the balance between woodland and farmland may reflect past opportunities rather than present needs; there may be places where pools or lakes would enhance the prospect and improve amenities. The landscape, like the villages, is being adapted to new roles for people with new priorities and expectations, and the results are inevitably conspicuous and have an all-embracing impact on the character of the countryside. If we can learn in our gardens to assess our needs and to relate what we do to what we want, we can extend the process to changes that have to be made on a larger scale. The fieldscape on an estate or farm can be analysed and evaluated in the same ways as the spaces round our houses that we plan to make into gardens.

The ideas and the means of expressing them first discovered and developed in our gardens expand until they define our feelings about how the countryside itself should look. New features can be introduced and old ones altered or destroyed, and now that machines have given us the power to change the countryside drastically, and circumstances the incentive to do so to accommodate new expectations and needs, this becomes a very potent force indeed.

Changes are underway, and during the next few decades will accelerate, altering the appearance of the countryside and the ways we live in it more than at any time since Saxon invaders transformed the landscape of post-Roman Britain. The tastes and prejudices which we first discovered in our gardens will be amongst the major influences directing this revolution and shaping tomorrow's countryside.

# SURVEYING A GARDEN: MAKING A PLAN

## PREPARING FOR THE SURVEY

Measurements made in metres and centimetres are much easier to use than feet and inches when deciding on scales and drawing plans. Those still unfamiliar with metric measurements will find it helpful to remember that:

1 A metre is nearly the same length as a yard.
2 30cm is practically equivalent to a foot.

20m tapes are a convenient length for all but the largest gardens, and can usually be hired from DIY shops.

The triangle is the classic foundation of all surveying. The method described here is based on it, and is simple and flexible. It can be used by one person, without help, to produce accurate and detailed plans. Everything depends on the fact that the lengths of its three sides define the size and shape of a triangle. Therefore all that is needed to draw a plan showing the relative positions of any three objects – three trees perhaps – are measurements of the distances between them.

Plans of gardens are bound to include more than three points of interest, and it may be necessary to find the positions of dozens of different features. Simple gardens – small ones perhaps, with one or two trees and regular boundaries – can be surveyed by measuring between all the features involved in order to link them by a network of triangles, which can be used to plot their positions. However, when this is attempted for more complex situations the process becomes confusingly involved.

The simplest way to avoid a muddled network of triangles is to set up a base line from which to take measurements to all the features which will appear on the plan.

### THE BASE LINE

The base line can go anywhere: choose whatever line is most convenient. More than one base line can be used when the shape or size of a garden makes that easier.

It must be a straight line marked by bamboo canes. The number of canes used, and the distances between them, depend only on circumstances and convenience.

Each point to be surveyed must be measurable, in a straight line, from two of the canes on the base line.

Three base lines, forming a triangle, are the best foundation for surveying a large garden.

The problem of finding a helper to hold one end of the tape can be avoided by slipping the ring at the end of the tape over the canes along the base line. *But* bamboo canes and eyes make a bad mix, and accidents happen when bending down to lift the tape off the cane. An empty bottle inverted over the tip of the cane avoids accidents and prevents the tape running up and off the top of the cane when pulled taut to take a measurement.

## DOING THE SURVEY

1 Draw a sketch plan of the site to be surveyed. This is done freehand and on the spot. It need not be accurate but must show the relative positions of all the features to be included in the plan, and record roughly where walls bend; where trees are, and how many there are; where paths enter and leave; the approximate positions of greenhouses, pergolas, summerhouses, dustbin shelters etc; and the relationship between house and garden.
2 Label the features to which measurements will be made with a letter of the alphabet.
3 Set out the base line, sticking canes into the ground to mark its course. Its course and the number of canes should be chosen so that measurements to all the points marked on the plan can be made with the fewest possible problems.
4 Mark the course of the base line on the sketch plan, numbering the approximate positions of the canes 1, 2, 3, 4 and so on.
5 Finally, draw up a survey table to record measurements as they are made. This will keep everything in order, and make sure that nothing is left out.

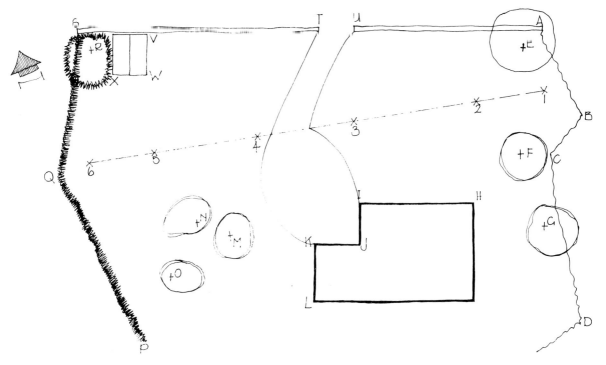

## SURVEY TABLE

|   | 1 | 2 | 3 | 4 | 5 | 6 |
|---|---|---|---|---|---|---|
| A | 3·1 | 4·2 | | | | |
| B | 2·2 | 5·0 | | | | |
| C | 3·5 | 4·4 | | | | |
| D | 10·9 | 11·1 | | | | |
| E | 2·3 | 3·1 | | | | |
| F | | 3·2 | 8·0 | | | |
| G | 6·1 | 6·5 | | | | |
| H | | 4·6 | 6·6 | | | |
| I | | | 3·6 | 5·5 | | |
| J | | | | 6·7 | 10·2 | |
| K | | | 5·9 | 5·6 | | |
| L | | | | 7·9 | 10·0 | |
| M | | | | 4·6 | 5·2 | |
| N | | | | | 3·9 | 5·9 |
| O | | | | | 5·5 | 6·4 |
| P | | | | | 8·3 | 8·2 |
| Q | | | | | 5·0 | 1·3 |
| R | | | | | 5·2 | 5·2 |
| S | | | | | 6·5 | 6·1 |
| T | | | 4·6 | 3·5 | | |
| U | | 6·6 | 4·3 | | | |
| V | | | 10·2 | 7·0 | | |
| W | | | | 5·9 | 3·5 | |
| X | | | | | 4·0 | 4·1 |

### DISTANCES ALONG BASE LINE:

| | |
|---|---|
| 1–2 | 3·1 |
| 2–3 | 5·8 |
| 3–4 | 4·4 |
| 4–5 | 4·9 |
| 5–6 | 3·2 |

Write down the letters which identify the features to which measurements will be made in the left-hand column of the table.

Write the numbers which identify the canes across the top of the table, spaced out so there is as much room as possible between each.

The distances from the canes to the features on the sketch plan will be recorded in the vertical columns, each headed by the number of a cane.

### TAKING THE MEASUREMENTS

Start at Cane No 1 and measure from it to any feature in convenient range, writing the measurements in the survey table as they are made. It is only necessary to be accurate to the nearest 10cm.

When the measurements from Cane No 1 have been done, move the tape to Cane No 2 and take measurements to features within easy reach, including those measured from the first cane.

Move on to Cane No 3, and so on down the line. It is not necessary to measure every point from every cane. Two records are needed for each of the features on the sketch plan, and once these two measurements have been taken no more should be done.

The table is complete when all the lines opposite the letters of the alphabet contain two entries.

Finally, measure the distances between the canes along the base line, and write them down on the sketch plan.

At the end of the survey make sure that the table is complete, and leave the canes along the base line while drawing the plan. They may be needed later to check inaccurate or doubtful records, or to add extra ones.

## DECIDING ON A SCALE

The figures recorded on the survey table will be used to draw the plan, but this can only be done after deciding what scale to use. The simplest solution is to draw a plan in which 1m outside is represented by 1cm on paper – that is, a scale of one to a hundred. Then the measurements recorded on the table in metres are simply read off as centimetres. This is very often a convenient scale to use for garden plans, being large enough to include most of the detail needed and small enough not to be drastically uneconomical with paper.

Other scales can be used: 1cm to 5m, perhaps, in a large garden, or 3cm to 1m to plot the details of an intricately planted border. In the first case all the measurements made during the survey would have to be divided by five, and in the second, multiplied by three. Mistakes are less likely when these sums are done before starting to draw the plan, and written out in a revised version of the survey table.

## DRAWING THE PLAN

The length of the base line can be found by adding together the distances between the canes. Once done, this will provide a rough idea of how large a sheet of paper will be needed for the plan. It helps if the plan fits neatly onto one sheet of paper, but it does not matter if part goes over the edge while it is being plotted. Just lay another sheet of paper alongside, and keep on with the plan – later a tracing can be made to bring it all together again.

The base line is drawn to scale on the paper, in what seems from the sketch plan to be an appropriate place, and the positions of the canes are marked on it.

The positions of the features to which measurements were made are plotted with a pair of compasses, starting with feature A. The survey table shows this is 3.1m from Cane No 1 and 4.2m from Cane No 2. The sketch plan shows that it is to the left of the base line.

If you have chosen a scale of one to a hundred, every point that lies 3.1m from Cane No 1 can be found by drawing a circle with a radius of 3.1cm centred on the position of the cane on the base line. In the same way, a circle with a radius of 4.2cm centred on Cane No 2 passes through every point which was 4.2m from the cane outdoors. The feature labelled A on the sketch plan can only be where the two circles intersect, but a complication arises from the disconcerting fact that the circles cross at two quite different places – one to the left and one to the right of the base line.

The sketch plan shows that the left-hand one is the one that is wanted, and usually it is only necessary to draw short arcs of the circles close to where they are expected to intersect.

The rest is repetition. The positions of the features to which measurements were made are plotted in turn on the paper, using the information on the survey table and the sketch plan. This should be done in pencil. When all is finished and checked and any problems have been sorted out, a tracing of this proto-plan can be used as a master from which photocopies can be made to provide working plans.

# Index